CAUSE OF DEATH

CAUSE OF DEATH

Cyril Wecht, M.D., J.D.,
with Mark Curriden
and Benjamin Wecht

A DUTTON BOOK

DUTTON
Published by the Penguin Group
Penguin Books USA Inc., 375 Hudson Street,
New York, New York 10014, U.S.A.
Penguin Books Ltd, 27 Wrights Lane,
London W8 5TZ, England
Penguin Books Australia Ltd, Ringwood,
Victoria, Australia
Penguin Books Canada Ltd, 10 Alcorn Avenue,
Toronto, Ontario, Canada M4V 3B2
Penguin Books (N.Z.) Ltd, 182–190 Wairau Road,
Auckland 10, New Zealand

Penguin Books Ltd, Registered Offices:
Harmondsworth, Middlesex, England

First published by Dutton, an imprint of Dutton Signet,
a division of Penguin Books USA Inc.
Distributed in Canada by McClelland & Stewart Inc.

First Printing, November, 1993
10 9 8 7 6 5 4 3 2 1

 REGISTERED TRADEMARK—MARCA REGISTRADA

LIBRARY OF CONGRESS CATALOGING IN PUBLICATION DATA:
Wecht, Cyril H., 1931–
    Cause of death / Cyril Wecht with Mark
Curriden and Benjamin Wecht.
        p.   cm.
    Includes index.
    ISBN 0-525-93661-0
    1. Forensic pathology—Case studies.   2. Death—Causes—Case
studies.   I. Curriden, Mark.   II. Wecht, Benjamin.   III. Title.
    RA1063.4.W43   1993
614′.1—dc20   93–13828
                                                           CIP

Printed in the United States of America
Set in New Baskerville
Designed by Leonard Telesca

This book is dedicated to Sigrid Wecht, Angela Curriden, and Flynne Wecht. Without their understanding and encouragement, this project would not have come to fruition.

Contents

Acknowledgments

There are so many people to thank for help-
ing us gather information for this project that we are certain to
unintentionally miss several. The assistance came from varied
sources—some helped us track down courtroom testimony, and
others actually spent hours of their time in personal interviews.

In the John F. Kennedy case, we are especially grateful to Larry
Howard, director of the JFK Assassination Information Center in
Dallas, Texas, and Attorney Jim Lesar, president of the Assassination Archives and Research Center in Washington, D.C. Over the
years, Mr. Howard and Mr. Lesar have been frequent and generous sources of information for us and other JFK researchers. Special thanks are also extended to Marina Oswald Porter and Tom
Wilson. Mrs. Porter certainly did not have to bare her soul to us
as she did. We deeply admire her courage and moral strength. No
person spent more time with us than Tom Wilson, educating us
on the intricacies of his unique computer system and sharing the
results he has come up with regarding the JFK assassination.

No person deserves more praise than my good friend and es-
teemed colleague Dr. Tom Noguchi, former chief medical exam-
iner-coroner of Los Angeles, for the excellent work he did in the
postmortem examination of Senator Robert F. Kennedy. Without

Dr. Noguchi, I would never have gotten involved in that fascinating investigation and puzzling case.

We are very appreciative of the generous cooperation we received from Dr. Charles Friedgood and Jean Harris in preparing their respective chapters. Both individuals met with us while they were incarcerated and spent numerous hours discussing their cases in a very candid and informative fashion. Mrs. Harris is now a free woman engaged in several significant endeavors, including the writing of another book.

The information given to me in the Jean Harris case by my good friend and frequent forensic scientific collaborator Professor Herbert MacDonell was invaluable. And a special thanks to Harvard University professor of law Alan Dershowitz, one of the premier attorneys in the United States, who helped us in compiling information for the Claus von Bulow and Jeffrey MacDonald cases.

We would like to express our deep gratitude to Karen and Michael Diehl, who have been kind enough to meet and correspond with us over the past few years, as well as to their former attorneys Thomas B. Shuttleworth and Paul E. Sutton, and to Tidewater Region deputy chief medical examiner Dr. Faruk Presswalla and deputy commonwealth attorney Kenneth A. Phillips for their time and courteous cooperation.

Syracuse lawyer Ralph J. Cognetti, private investigator Joseph Spadafore, and forensic consultant Bill Sullivan were extremely helpful in the Delbert Ward case. We appreciate the time Onondaga County assistant medical examiner Humphrey D. Germaniuk spent to share his side of the story. In Munnsville, Harry Thurston was very helpful. But no one deserves more thanks for assisting us in this poignant recitation than Delbert, Roscoe, and Lyman Ward.

We received a great deal of assistance in the Jack Davis case from Jack and Lisa Davis, Elaine Lynch, John and Marisa Lynch, Indiana County judge and former district attorney William Martin, Indiana Borough police chief Anthony Antolik, and investigative reporter Marlene Brennan. In the Art Jones case, we are very grateful for all the input we received from his daughter and son-in-law, Lisa and Mark Blohm. We also want to thank Washington County coroner S. Timothy Warco, and former deputy coroner George Hogan, for meeting and sharing investigative information with us.

And a special thank you goes to Dr. Bill Oliphant, who reviewed many of our case discussions and gave us much valuable assistance in organizing them in a professional manner. John Davis, an outstanding author, provided much professional advice and personal encouragement. We are indebted to him.

We are grateful to our agent, Elizabeth Kaplan of Sterling Lord Literistics, who encouraged and guided us from the outset of our relationship. Michaela Hamilton, our editor at Dutton Signet, has provided us with constant advice and encouragement. She is as gracious as she is knowledgeable. Maribeth Blettner has provided outstanding secretarial services from the beginning of this project. We are deeply appreciative of her assistance.

Foreword by
F. Lee Bailey

Cyril Wecht has been one of my close friends for more than twenty-five years. I have called upon him many times to lend his blazing brilliance as a medical detective to my efforts in the preparation of major cases. And although I have sometimes been disappointed when he was unable to tell me what my client and I wanted to hear, I have always found his integrity to be top-shelf, and his skills to be at the same level. When he comes to a conclusion after meticulously studying the available evidence, it is inevitably sound and well-supported. In court, he is one of the most effective witnesses alive today. Many a cross-examiner who has tangled with Cyril has come away with nothing but bloody knuckles. When I need the best, I always call him first.

I am both delighted and flattered to offer this Foreword for his book, for I feel that few lawyers have profited more from Cyril's acquaintance, and that very few—if any—know him better.

Many of the fascinating cases illumined in this book were my cases too in a sense, since I had serious, personal, and often confidential involvement. From that perspective I am able to flesh out some additional details (where that is possible without stepping on confidences). Some of these Cyril knew about; others he did not, until now.

The first and longest chapter in this book deals with the most controversial assassination of a world leader in all of history, the murder of John F. Kennedy in the fall of 1963. Because of the many mistakes and aberrations made in the aftermath of that murder, the odds are overwhelming that the truth will never be known. What is known is that the conclusions of the Warren Commission have completely lost the confidences of the forensic scientists of this world, the House of Representatives of the United States, a jury in Louisiana, and of the public at large. This is a shame, for in my mind Earl Warren was a great American, and I think his incalculable integrity was badly used by many whose goal in the investigation of JFK's assassination was to obfuscate the truth, rather than to reveal it.

My first personal encounter with the assassination of President Kennedy was bone-chilling. I was sitting in my office the night after JFK was killed when the phone rang. A man who said he was a U.S. marshal in Texas, and who refused to give his name, told me that he had heard firsthand that Lee Harvey Oswald was planning to demand that *I* be appointed to represent him, since he was indigent. Based on the publicity emanating from Dallas, I assumed that he had shot President Kennedy, and that he would be convicted and executed.

As a stripling of thirty, I had been winning murder cases for almost three years, and getting some substantial national ink (and very modest fees). The thought of being invited, or ordered, by a court to defend the most hated man in the world was frightening. I knew instinctively that Oswald needed and deserved outstanding counsel who was totally fearless. I also thought that whoever inherited such an assignment might well be shot himself, and would certainly be ruined for life. Edward Bennett Williams had explained to me two days after I took the Massachusetts Bar Examination how crassly America maligns those who defend its unpopular criminals, and he was right. I confess to voicing a sigh of relief when Jack Ruby obviated the need for America to come up with a criminal lawyer equal to the task of leading Oswald's defense.

I met and became friendly with Jim "Jolly Green Giant" Gar-

rison, recently lionized in Oliver Stone's movie *JFK*, in the mid-sixties. Prior to the trial of Clay Shaw, Jim approached me about taking an assignment as special prosecutor, and working with him on the case. On the one hand, it was an appealing idea. A chance to spotlight and punish *anyone* who had had a hand in the death of America's most charismatic president was a signal honor. On the other hand, Jim's ideas about broadsiding the CIA and the FBI as conspirators seemed to be based on very slender evidence. I told him that *if* I were to join him, and *if* the evidence came up short, I would be obliged to say so publicly. That was the last I heard about prosecuting.

But when Jim was indicted by the federal government—a vendetta, in my opinion, for embarrassing its minions—he turned to me, and I agreed to defend him. His trial was scheduled for the fall of 1973. In May of that year, just shy of my fortieth birthday, *I* was indicted in Orlando, Florida, on charges of mail fraud as an adjunct to charges brought against my then client, Glenn W. Turner. Jim was absolutely sure that it was a move intended to prevent me from defending him. Others thought it was a strategy designed to prevent me from defending Turner. A third school was sure it was revenge by the Postal Inspectors, whom I had thoroughly ridiculed for their "Keystone Kops" blunders in a bestselling book published late in 1971 called *The Defense Never Rests.* Whatever the reason, I defended both myself and to some degree Turner, and set a colleague from my firm, Fred Barnett, to defend Garrison. Jim was acquitted, Judge Gerald Bard Tjoflat severed me out of my case after seven months in the courtroom, and Turner's jury hung 9–3 for acquittal. When the government subsequently refused to go to trial against me alone, the case was dismissed. In retrospect, Garrison may have been right after all.

I could have helped Jim in his case against Clay Shaw had I not been shackled by the attorney-client privilege. Jim strongly suspected—and was anxious to prove—the involvement of Fidel Castro in the assassination of President Kennedy. What I knew from an involved client, and couldn't reveal until the facts became public in Senate hearings some years later, was that Jack and Bobby Kennedy, together with Dean Rusk, had approved the assassination of Castro, and had ordered a navy lieutenant commander to train a rifleman to accomplish the task. When the marksman arrived in Havana, Castro met him coming off the airplane and offered him a choice: join Castro, or be tried and executed. We think the marksman is still there. But however that information might have helped, Jim told me that one of the few good turns to come his way in the Shaw prosecution was his acquaintance with Dr. Cyril Wecht.

Despite the unfathomable pain that the Kennedy family has endured over the years from the batterings of tragedy after tragedy, I still believe that America and the world would be well-served if more truth could be known about this killing. Impossible though it may be at this date to discover who exactly pulled the many strings which so effectively buried the truth in the JFK assassination, the single most important spearhead of challenge has been Cyril Wecht. He has brought to the table not just rhetoric but cold, hard facts. Anyone with a basic comprehension of firearms, physics, and pathology easily understands why the "establishment" ostracized Cyril for "rocking the boat."

But his greatest contribution to the rightful doubt which casts a pall over the "official" version of the assassination may have been not his many expert opinions given from the witness stand, and not the excellent accounts in the first chapter in this book. In my view, the dramatic job which Kevin Costner did in *JFK* ridiculing the "single bullet theory"—under the careful tutelage of Cyril Wecht—brought home to more Americans the untrustworthiness of the Warren Commission Report than any other single event.

Cyril's involvement in the investigation of the firearms evidence in the murder in 1968 of Robert Kennedy is another example of the high quality everyone has come to expect of him. His disappointment that others did not follow up on his assertion that someone *other* than Sirhan must have fired the head shots which struck the senator is understandable. It also highlights a truth which most Americans do not readily comprehend: that our legal system is not in its essence a "search for truth" at all. The system is in reality a search for those truths which *at least one* of the lawyers want to bring to the fore, and not those truths which are too hot as "double-edged swords" for either of them to dare to handle. Such was the case here.

Few lawyers in my generation failed to revere Grant B. Cooper, a true giant of the defense bar. I was lucky enough to meet him in my first year of practice. He was not much happier to be stuck with the defense of Sirhan than I would have been to appear for Lee Harvey Oswald, but stuck he was. No defense lawyer worth his salt felt anything but sympathy and admiration for Grant. His only possible defense was insanity, since his client had been caught on the scene, weapon in hand. Grant knew that there was solid evidence that someone other than his client had fired the shots to the head, but it was information he could hardly use for two reasons: first, his client adamantly refused to name any co-conspirator; and second, proving the existence of a co-conspirator would completely negate the claim of a deranged mind. Conspiracies take planning and cunning, and do not pop out of the unchained conduct of crackpots.

The fact remains, however, that this damning evidence is unanswered, and Sirhan is alive and in custody, constantly whining that he should be paroled on his promise that he "won't do it again." If I were in charge of his possible release, I would ask him to submit to a searching polygraph examination as to just how the murder of RFK was plotted and executed, and would leave him in prison if he refused or lied.

The accident at Chappaquiddick Island, which led to the death of Mary Jo Kopechne, is one of the most unfortunate of all the heart-crunching calamities that have befallen the Kennedy clan. Cyril has correctly recounted the fact that I recommended his expertise to Ed Dinis, the beleaguered district attorney of Bristol and Barnstable counties in Massachusetts, who held jurisdiction in the Kopechne investigation. Ed consulted me early on in the case. He was a tough but sensible prosecutor who never shied away from tangling with giants, and was more than a little controversial as a result. He basked in that kind of controversy, and thought that beating big bad guys entitled him to a merit badge. The voters consistently agreed.

When the Kopechne drowning fell in his lap, Ed was not happy. He could see a mounting storm in the media, and correctly guessed that every option he had was a basket of snakes. He could not have been more right. His first stance was to support the work of police chief Dominick Arena, who had initiated the investigation in the case. The media promptly accused Dinis of being "in the bag" to the Kennedy family, his fellow Democrats, and of covering for the senator.

Ed bristled at the accusation. He called for an inquest into the cause of death of Mary Jo, which was duly scheduled. All of a sudden the faithless press doubled back on him, and berated him for "picking on our Teddy." Dinis was beside himself, and told me that he had been ill-used by the news media. I could not disagree.

Ed could not now cancel the inquest without being driven into a sea of public derision. He could see that he was being set up for an ultimate "lose-lose" situation. He asked me if I knew a medical investigator who was brilliant, tough, and totally objective, someone who would not bend to pressures of any kind or degree. He wanted to delegate charge of that phase of the case to someone to whom he could comfortably transfer a substantial responsibility. "That's easy," I said. "See if you can get Cyril Wecht." To his everlasting credit he did.

As a footnote, I must for the only time in my life disagree with my distinguished colleague, Dr. Wecht. As a scientist he is properly frustrated by the court ruling which prevented the exhumation of the victim, Ms. Kopechne. His desire to reach ground truth is commendable, and I am delighted to see that those fires within him which demand total access to the facts still burn brightly. But as a lawyer who has dealt with human tragedy for close to forty years, I agree with the stance of the Kopechne family. There was no compelling need to exacerbate the dread already suffered by the family at such a possibility. There is no nagging mystery left in this tragic drowning which merits the agony that would surely have resulted from the media blitz caused by digging at the gravesite. It was an accident, and nothing more. Had I been the judge in charge, I would have ruled the same way.

The last case in this book in which I was peripherally involved is one of the most bothersome, the conviction of Jeffrey MacDonald. In 1983 I was hosting a nationally syndicated television show called *Lie Detector*, in which the polygraph was used to check the believability of people who had stories to tell, most of them about an alleged involvement in criminal cases. A year or so earlier I had made the acquaintance of Ted Gunderson, a former SAC (Special Agent in Charge, FBI) of the Dallas and Los Angeles Offices. After his retirement, Ted was hired to reinvestigate the Mac-Donald case, and had come to fervently believe that MacDonald had been telling the truth when he described the invasion of the murderous hippies who had killed his family, and had nearly killed him. Ted wanted me to take Dr. MacDonald's case. I knew that he had been given a polygraph test early on in the case, and had not had a favorable result. I also knew, from years of experience, that failing to pass a polygraph examination does not mean guilt at all; it only means that the statement of the subject has been less than complete. I told Ted that I would consider MacDonald's case if, and only if, he would submit to a new polygraph test supervised by myself and my co-host in the show, Ed Gelb of Los Angeles, one of the best examiners alive. That offer was never accepted.

I agree with Cyril. The result in the MacDonald case is far from satisfactory, despite Joe McGinniss's condemnation of MacDonald in his book *Fatal Vision.* MacDonald was awarded a fair sum in damages as a result of that book, but its main theme was the same as the jury's conclusion: MacDonald's story as to how the murders happened was not credible, and if he lied, he must be guilty.

As a medical doctor, Jeffrey MacDonald understands full well how a polygraph works. He also knows that *anyone* can "pass" a polygraph test if they will only tell the complete and utter truth, no matter how painful it may be. In many cases, the complete and utter truth is legal guilt personified. In many other cases, that truth is something far less than guilt.

I believe that Cyril has detailed the medical evidence in Dr. MacDonald's case with precision. The only meaningful avenue of exploration remaining is the mind of Dr. MacDonald himself. I think there was an invasion of crazies that night, as does Cyril. I also think that given a couple days with the prisoner and the services of one of the dozen or so top-flight polygraph examiners in this country who are truly brilliant with their techniques, the missing pieces could be defined in a way which would answer Cyril's questions. Dr. MacDonald should try this route. All others have failed him, and he has little to lose.

My favorite chapter in this book—and I enjoyed them all—is the one about the trial of Delbert Ward. Here we see the inestimable Cyril Wecht at his best. A small and unheralded story to most, was the Ward case of interest only to the local community. That of an American of modest intellectual gifts being nailed to the wall by people who were quick to take advantage of the weak, and quick to claim credit for themselves; it was not a new or unique story, but a sad one. Delbert was a gone goose, until the relentless pathologist brought his formidable arsenal of knowledge to the fore. The eternal Wecht foe, incompetence, is targeted, and systematically dismantled. This is good theater. This is great investigation, scathing testimony, and justice served. This is the Cyril Wecht I know and admire.

When I was a young charger at the bar, full of vim, vinegar, and unlimited self-confidence, fans and detractors alike used to agree that I was "often wrong, but never in doubt." Cyril is like that in a way, with an important difference, for which I and many of my colleagues have cause to be grateful. He is almost never wrong, and very seldom in doubt; a somewhat healthier combination.

—F. Lee Bailey

Introduction

Call it mischievousness or simply boyhood, but
Cyril Wecht was never one to reject a dare. He once climbed down
a dangerously steep embankment, took his clothes off, then
jumped in and swam across the Monongahela River, which flows
through the center of Pittsburgh. Never mind the boats and
barges he navigated around, or the heavily polluted water from
the city's booming steel mills.

Then there was the challenge of sneaking into the city's
morgue. This is where all the dead bodies were on display for
relatives to come in and identify the deceased as their father or
daughter or neighbor. It also is the spot where the coroner performed the autopsies.

The morgue sat on the edge of town, about a half-mile from
the Wechts' house. Cyril and his buddies did not have to sneak
through some partially opened window or a back door. The front
entrance, a glass door, was almost always open, and there was
hardly ever anyone at the reception desk. When the coast was
clear, they would dart inside and through the foyer. Just ahead
was a second door, which they would crack open slightly to see if
anyone was inside. If not, on their tiptoes, they would walk in.

Before them, lying on pushcarts all around the room, were the
bodies of people who had died just hours earlier. Each body was

behind a slanted glass window, just like you see at a butcher shop. Many of them were awaiting autopsies, while others were already cut open. The room had a terrible, sickening smell.

Almost as if it were a teenage rite of passage, Cyril and his partners in crime would slowly step closer to each body. The faces looked pale. Other bodies still had blood streaming from the wounds that caused their death.

Just as the boys neared another body, it would make a moaning or belching sound, as gasses escaped from the lungs. Cyril and his buddies, envisioning scenes of *Frankenstein* and various late-night horror flicks, invariably ended their impromptu field trip by scrambling out of the morgue at record speeds.

Never did Cyril realize that, twenty years later, he would be running that morgue as Pittsburgh's chief forensic pathologist and later coroner. No, those early experiences developed no incredible attraction within him to the morgue or dead bodies. But he did have a love of mystery and suspense, and later medicine and the law.

Because he works hard and has an inquisitive mind, Dr. Wecht is among the world's most renowned forensic pathologists. With degrees in both law and medicine, he is the preferred expert witness on medical issues for lawyers like F. Lee Bailey, Alan Dershowitz, and Melvin Belli. His medicolegal expertise and his uncanny ability to uncover new evidence and spot evidence that has been overlooked have placed him in the middle of many of the nation's most controversial cases.

The investigative files in cases involving John F. Kennedy, Robert F. Kennedy, Mary Jo Kopechne, Jean Harris, Elvis Presley, Claus von Bulow, and Jeffrey MacDonald have all passed across Dr. Wecht's desk. His involvement in each case has been different. In many, he has testified as an expert witness. In some, he actually went to the crime scene and, using medicolegal skills, helped discover what really happened. Alan Dershowitz, a law professor at Harvard University who has defended boxer Mike Tyson, television evangelist Jim Bakker, and New York hotel queen Leona Helmsley, refers to Dr. Wecht as "the doctor to whom the dead speak."

Dr. Wecht's curriculum vitae is fifty pages long. He has lectured on forensic pathology across the United States and in dozens of foreign countries, including England, Israel, Italy, China, and

South Africa. Two of the most bizarre homicide cases he has ever been hired to investigate occurred in Taiwan. He has performed more than twelve thousand autopsies and reviewed another twenty-five thousand. He has served as president of both the American Academy of Forensic Sciences and the American College of Legal Medicine. He has been interviewed on hundreds of radio and television news programs, including ABC's *20/20* and *Nightline, The Larry King Show,* and numerous news specials with Dan Rather, Geraldo Rivera, Tom Snyder, and Maury Povich.

"I hire Cyril Wecht because he is the best medical expert witness in the country," says F. Lee Bailey. "When you retain Cyril, you know you are going to get the truth and you know you are going to get a great witness. The bigger and tougher the case to solve, the more you need Cyril Wecht."

At the top of his list of fascinating cases is the assassination of President John F. Kennedy. Few people, if any, have spent as much time examining the physical evidence in the Kennedy case as Dr. Wecht. Certainly, no person has a better grasp of the medical and forensic evidence than he. Appointed to serve on numerous governmental and independent panels researching the Kennedy assassination, Dr. Wecht has had access to nearly all of the physical and scientific evidence in the case. Using the government's own evidence, Dr. Wecht has been able to prove beyond a reasonable doubt that Lee Harvey Oswald did not act alone in killing President Kennedy.

"Once Cyril shows you the evidence and explains the laws of medicine and science, there can be no doubt that the Warren Commission's finding that there was only one gunman and only three bullets is completely absurd," says Mr. Bailey. "Cyril is no wild conspiracy theorist who dreams up scenarios of how President Kennedy was shot and by whom. Instead, he deals only with the medical and scientific evidence."

In his chapter on the Kennedy assassination, Dr. Wecht unveils new medical and forensic evidence that slams the door on the government's theory that one man gone mad acted alone that day in Dealey Plaza. He can prove that the "single bullet theory," the backbone of the Warren Commission report, is a lie. Dr. Wecht uses the chapter to introduce a colleague who has developed a new computer technique which has the potential to end all speculation about what happened that day in Dallas. Through the computer program—it's not computer imagery or colorization—the reader is taken back to Dallas in 1963. Using existing photographs and films taken that day, the computer picks out incredible pieces of evidence, including the face of the man who very likely fired the shot that killed the president. But it's not Lee Harvey Oswald and the shot did not come from the Texas School Book Depository building.

Dr. Wecht combines his knowledge of forensic sciences with his skills as a lawyer to explain very technical, perplexing medical issues in a clear, understandable manner. Because of his unparalleled ability, medical examiners, prosecutors, and defense attorneys across the country have hired him to assist in their homicide investigations.

"There are five ways that people die," Dr. Wecht says. "About 70 to 75 percent of all deaths are the result of natural causes— old age or some kind of sickness. About 15 to 20 percent of us die accidentally—a car crash or electrocution. Suicides and homicides account for about 5 percent of the nation's deaths, and the rest are undetermined. The suicide rate is actually much higher than reported. Many elected lay coroners, in an effort not to disturb the family, will rule a death an accident or undetermined when it is really a suicide."

Medicolegal investigations are nearly as old as man himself. The Code of Hammurabi, written in the 18th century B.C., is the first known law regarding medical malpractice. Ancient Egyptians and Chinese each developed their own methods of determining the cause of death.

"Ancient people used to pour water into stab wounds," Dr. Wecht says. "If the water went in deep, the people knew the wound was fatal.

"In Europe, a king would appoint a person to go to the scene of every suspicious death to determine if it was unnatural and who could have been responsible," Dr. Wecht says. "The people were known back then as crowners. Later, the name was changed to *coroners.*"

Using simple forensic science techniques, Dr. Wecht is able to prove that Sirhan Sirhan did not shoot the bullet that killed Robert Kennedy, that Elvis did not die of a heart attack, that Jean Harris, Jeffrey MacDonald, and Claus von Bulow were wrongly convicted.

Then there are the stories of Dr. Charles Friedgood, Delbert Ward, and the Diehls. All were charged with murdering people they loved. None made the national headlines, but their cases are quite possibly more fascinating than all the more famous ones.

But not all of Dr. Wecht's cases are homicides. In 1991, the *San Francisco Examiner* hired him as an expert to review medical records of people who had been killed in the October 1989 Loma Prieta earthquake. Based upon the autopsy reports and eyewitness testimony from the rescue workers who found the bodies, Dr. Wecht determined that at least four people who died when the Cypress Street Viaduct in Oakland collapsed on top of them probably would have survived if emergency crews had gotten to them more quickly. In each of these four cases, Dr. Wecht was able to determine that the individuals trapped in the rubble of the double-decked freeway were alive for a considerable period of time after rescuers stopped searching for survivors.

More recently, representatives of the Kuwaiti government contacted Dr. Wecht about exhuming the bodies of more than one hundred infants who were allegedly killed when Iraq invaded their country in 1990.

"There are allegations that the Iraqi soldiers committed a horrible atrocity by randomly disconnecting and seizing respirators and incubators which were keeping Kuwaiti babies alive," Dr. Wecht says. "The Kuwaitis were interested in my doing autopsies on each of the children to determine if the allegations were true."

"Cyril Wecht is the Sherlock Holmes of forensic sciences," says Alan Dershowitz. "Medical and forensic evidence is very complicated and very technical, but because he is a lawyer, he is able to break it down and make it understandable to the average person who sits in the jury box. In many cases, the medical and forensic evidence is the key evidence in a case. Unlike eyewitness testimony, the medical evidence never changes. For that reason, the testimony of Dr. Wecht and the evidence he presents will be or should be the deciding factor in a murder trial."

Unlike most forensic pathologists, Dr. Wecht does not limit his testimony to either prosecutors or defense attorneys. In fact, the percentage of cases in which he has testified for the state and the defendant are evenly split. In every case in which he testified for the prosecutors and police, the jury has always found the defendant guilty.

"I never testify unless I believe my conclusions are scientifically tenable and my opinions are sound," Dr. Wecht says. "My word, my credibility must remain above reproach. If you ever slip or fudge the truth as an expert witness, the lawyers will find out and your career is ended. There are many times every month in which some lawyer will call me and ask me to testify in his case about something. But after I read through the medical reports and review the evidence, I am professionally constrained to tell the lawyer that I cannot testify because the evidence does not support what he is wanting me to say."

Born to Jewish immigrants in 1931 in a small Pennsylvania coal-mining town near the West Virginia line, it was clear early in Cyril's life that he was exceptional. Straight A's were routine on his report cards. He always had the lead role in school plays, and he enjoyed sports. He lettered in basketball and football—though he had to hide his football playing from his father, who forbade his participation in such contact sports. "My father was afraid I would hurt my hands or my fingers and that would damage my violin playing," Dr. Wecht says. "So my mother helped me keep it a secret from my father by washing my uniform and covering for me when I was at football practice."

His father, Nathan Wecht, came to the United States in 1915 from Lithuania. He was eighteen. His mother, Fannie Rubenstein, was twenty when she moved here in 1927 from a suburb of Kiev in Russia. The couple met in Pittsburgh, and after two years of dating, they married. In 1931, they moved to Bobtown, where they ran a small country store and had their only child, Cyril.

For seven months, they tried to stick it out in Bobtown, but rural America did not recover quickly from the Depression, so the Wechts moved to Pittsburgh, where they opened a mom & pop grocery store, specializing in deli meats. The Wechts' store was located in the Hill District, and the family lived in a rented house near the store.

There can be no doubt how Dr. Wecht learned his work ethic. His parents' store opened at seven in the morning and closed around midnight seven days a week. Besides owning the store, his mother and father were the only workers as well. Every once in a while, Cyril would help out in the store—that is, when he was not swimming the river, sneaking into morgues, playing the violin, or playing pick-up baseball games on the street.

Violin was a major part of his younger life. His lessons began at age seven. At his father's direction, he practiced four, five, sometimes six hours a day, seven days a week. This continued through high school and into college.

Receiving a full academic scholarship, Cyril attended the University of Pittsburgh, graduating with honors, and was elected president of the student body and his fraternity. The medical school at the University of Buffalo in New York was his next stop, where he attended for two years. But he returned home and after completing his final two years at the University of Pittsburgh, he obtained his medical degree.

During his third year, he decided to explore the possibility of legal medicine as a career. Upon graduating, he decided to do his residency in pathology with an eye toward forensic pathology. While he was doing his residency, he also attended law school on a full-time basis.

"I also moonlighted in local hospitals about three or four nights a week, and most weekends, delivering babies and covering the emergency room," Dr. Wecht says. "Looking back, I'm amazed I did all that at once. I didn't feel deprived of social life, though. I would have dates over to the hospital and spend time with them between patients."

In 1959, Uncle Sam called and Dr. Wecht joined the air force as a captain. Because of his specialized training, he was assigned to Maxwell Air Force Base in Montgomery, Alabama, the major pathology center for the air force in the South. This proved to be a great experience for the young physician. During his stint with the air force, he met Sigrid Ronsdal. An immigrant from Norway, she had joined the air force and was serving in Montgomery under a government program that permitted newcomers to America to get their citizenship in three years instead of five if they joined the armed forces. She spoke eight languages—Swedish, Danish, Norwegian, German, Italian, Spanish, French, and English—and was hoping to go into translation work for the U.S. government. In October 1961, they married.

After two years in the service, Dr. Wecht became a research fellow in forensic pathology and associate pathologist at the medical examiner's office in Baltimore, Maryland, at the time one of the best medicolegal investigative offices in the nation. Being in Baltimore allowed him to attend night law school at the University of Maryland, from which he graduated in 1962.

"I was working full-time in the office, five days a week and every other weekend, which is when most of the murders occurred, and attending law school five nights a week from six until ten," he says. "I also worked as acting pathologist at a local hospital. I was basically just running back and forth and Sigrid was bringing me sandwiches to eat. It was pretty hairy sometimes, especially when I had exams."

Upon returning to Pittsburgh, Dr. Wecht accepted a position as pathologist and chief of laboratory science at the Leech Farm Veterans Administration Hospital. Months later, he took the Pennsylvania Bar examination and passed. Offered a position at a local law firm, he quickly accepted, working both jobs at once. As a lawyer, he concentrated on lawsuits involving medical malpractice, and within a year, he became a partner in the firm.

In 1963, a new district attorney was elected in Allegheny County in a huge upset. Even though Robert Duggan was a Republican and Dr. Wecht a lifelong Democrat, Duggan knew of Dr. Wecht's expertise in medicolegal issues and offered him a position as an assistant district attorney and medicolegal advisor. Dr. Wecht accepted and started his new job in January 1964, when Duggan took office.

Dr. Wecht spent the next eighteen months working with the prosecutors in the office, evaluating the medical evidence in homicides, rapes, and sexual assaults, and drug and alcohol offenses from the crime lab and the local coroner's office. He would then help the assistant district attorney prosecuting the case to prepare for trial. The Allegheny County coroner was Joseph Dobbs, a carpenter with no medical or forensic training. The coroner's office was run with such incredible incompetence that there were not even any microscopes, an instrument developed in 1597. There was no toxicology testing, no forensic scientific analysis, no trained personnel. It's amazing that the district attorney's office ever won a homicide conviction.

Attempting to bring the coroner's office into the twentieth century, the district attorney and Dr. Wecht publicly supported a local surgeon, Dr. William Hunt, a Republican, to run against the incumbent Democrat. After using the news media to point out the deficiencies in the coroner's office, Dr. Hunt was elected in November 1965 and named Dr. Wecht his chief forensic pathologist starting January 1966.

"This was certainly no political thing, because here I was, a

Democrat supporting a Republican," Dr. Wecht says. "My main mission was to upgrade the department. This office was literally in miserable condition. The first four months, in the dead of a bitter Pittsburgh winter, I had to perform autopsies in the morgue's basement while new autopsy tables were being installed upstairs. There was no heat; I wore an overcoat to keep from freezing."

Dr. Hunt also hired a full-time forensic toxicologist, Dr. Charles L. Winek, and improved the equipment and working conditions dramatically. In 1967, Dr. Hunt resigned at the urging of the GOP hierarchy to run for county commissioner, which office he won. An interim coroner was appointed to fill the remainder of his two-year term, and Dr. Wecht continued to serve in the office as chief forensic pathologist.

When the coroner's seat came up for election in 1969, Dr. Wecht approached the leadership of the Democratic party, expressing his interest in the job. He did run and won handily. In 1973 and 1977, he found re-election bids quite easy, despite opposition from the GOP.

The two times Dr. Wecht was re-elected coroner, he received more votes than any other public official, carrying all but one of Allegheny County's 161 political subdivisions, including some Republican strongholds that had not given a majority to a Democratic candidate in more than fifty years.

But in 1973, Dr. Wecht fell out of the good graces of the Republican party and his longtime friend Robert Duggan when he accused his former boss, the district attorney, of political corruption. Duggan promised revenge, but that summer, the very day that a federal grand jury handed down an indictment against Duggan, the prosecutor committed suicide. The Republicans were unable to scream political harassment because the U.S. attorney who oversaw the investigation and asked for the indictment was none other than Richard Thornburgh, who would later become the state's Republican governor and subsequently the U.S. attorney general.

A 1978 poll conducted for the Democratic party in Pittsburgh showed Dr. Wecht's approval rating higher than that of any other public official in either party. In 1979, he was elected as a county commissioner and had to resign his position as coroner. As one of three Allegheny County commissioners, Dr. Wecht set county policy, approved the county's budget, and controlled tax revenues.

In 1982, he accepted his party's nomination to run against incumbent U.S. senator John Heinz. Senator Heinz spent approximately $4 million in the campaign, compared to $250,000 for Dr. Wecht. As a result, Dr. Wecht was handed his first political defeat, by a 59 to 41 percent spread. That was the pathologist's last entry into the political world, though many called on him in 1992 to run against U.S. senator Arlen Specter.

"It's not that I would not truly have enjoyed running against Specter and kicking his butt," Dr. Wecht told a radio talk show host during an interview. "But I have decided against seeking political office again. I have too many other things going on in my life."

But the mere mention of Arlen Specter's name in Dr. Wecht's presence should cause innocent bystanders to duck and cover the ears of children. It was Specter who, as a junior counsel for the Warren Commission in 1964, dreamed up the "single bullet theory," the backbone of the government's contention that Lee Harvey Oswald acted alone in killing President John F. Kennedy.

"I often wonder how Specter came up with such a crazy notion as the 'single bullet theory,' " Dr. Wecht says. "Maybe he ate some bad baloney before he went to bed one night and dreamed the whole thing up."

No person has participated more in the examination and discussion of the medical, physical, and forensic evidence in the Kennedy assassination than Cyril Wecht. Six months after the Warren Commission issued its report in 1964, Dr. Wecht was asked by the American Academy of Forensic Sciences to study the report and present a critical discussion at the organization's annual meeting in 1965.

"At first, I believed the conclusions of the Warren Commission were probably correct—one gunman, three bullets, all from the Texas School Book Depository," he says. "But the more I studied the case, the more physical and medical evidence I examined, and the more witnesses I personally talked to, the more I became convinced that the Warren Commission had missed the boat. In fact, the medical evidence completely contradicts everything the Warren Commission and its supporters contend."

The next year, *Life* magazine asked him to examine a home film of the assassination taken by a Dallas businessman. The Zapruder film, named after the man who took the film, had never before been made public. It drastically changed the way Dr. Wecht thought about what happened at Dealey Plaza.

In 1968, Dr. Wecht was hired by New Orleans district attorney Jim Garrison to testify about the medical evidence in the case against businessman Clay Shaw, who Garrison believed was a member of the group that had organized the Kennedy assassination. In 1972, Wecht became the first nongovernmental forensic pathologist to examine the Kennedy assassination physical and medical evidence, which was stored at the National Archives in Washington, D.C. It was Dr. Wecht who revealed to the world in an article that ran on the front page of the *New York Times* in August 1972 that key medical evidence in the Kennedy case was missing, including the president's brain.

Dr. Wecht's official role in the investigation intensified in 1975 when he was interviewed extensively by lawyers for the Rockefeller Commission, which was allegedly searching for new evidence in the Kennedy case. Three years later, Dr. Wecht was appointed to a panel of nine forensic pathology experts which was asked to advise the House Select Committee on Assassinations. The HSCA was a committee created by Congress to investigate possible CIA or other governmental agency involvement in the Kennedy murder.

In 1991, movie director Oliver Stone hired Dr. Wecht to be a consultant on the medical evidence for the film *JFK*. A year later, when the movie came out on video, Dr. Wecht received a gift in the mail. It was a copy of *JFK* from Oliver Stone and there was some scribbling on the cover:

Dear Cyril,

I admire you enormously. You're a man that has ushered the important evidence that the official medical bodies have— much to their shame—wholly ignored.

My gratitude forever,
Oliver Stone

Because of his knowledge of the medical and physical evidence in the Kennedy case, he is asked to participate in dozens of radio and television interview shows every year and speak to an equal number of seminars and forums on the Kennedy assassination.

Along the way, Dr. Wecht has met and talked with dozens of people who have had personal involvement or concrete evidence on the Kennedy assassination. In chapter 1 of this book, he tells you about lengthy conversations with Lee Harvey Oswald's wife, Marina, and Jean Hill, the famous "lady in red," who was in Dealey Plaza that day in 1963 and saw it all.

Whenever Dr. Wecht speaks, Kennedy assassination buffs flock to him, inundating him with questions. He is frequently described as the "darling of the conspiracy buffs." The reason is clear—his credibility remains unquestioned. Every statement he makes, every position he takes, every theory he has is based upon the evidence he has personally examined. At a Kennedy assassination forum in Chicago in June 1992, Dr. Wecht received a thunderous standing ovation when he was introduced to the audience. A few minutes later, after Ed Asner had been introduced to a less enthusiastic applause, the actor responded, "I never thought I would see the day when a doctor received a bigger applause than an actor."

Similarly, Dr. Wecht is constantly asked about the 1968 assassination of Senator Robert Kennedy. Dr. Wecht's official involvement in the Bobby Kennedy investigation began even before the senator had died. The Los Angeles coroner, Dr. Thomas Noguchi, and Dr. Wecht were close friends, and Dr. Noguchi telephoned him in Pittsburgh seeking advice on how to deal with the Kennedy family, the government officials, and the news media.

"Besides being incredibly knowledgeable and an experienced forensic pathologist, Cyril Wecht was a friend whose advice I knew I could count on," says Dr. Noguchi. "And every single thing he suggested I found to be very helpful. His insight into complicated homicide investigations is unmatched. He's feisty and can sniff out a rat or a flaw in the investigation or evidence like nobody I have ever seen. I respect him tremendously."

Later that week in June 1968, Dr. Wecht flew to Los Angeles to review the forensic evidence and the autopsy and to assist Dr. Noguchi in reenacting the crime. "Solely from the forensic evidence, I can prove that Sirhan did not kill Robert Kennedy," Dr. Wecht says. But his involvement did not end there. A few months later, Sirhan's mother called Dr. Wecht at home and asked him to represent her son in court. For various reasons, Dr. Wecht reluctantly declined.

A year later, Dr. Wecht found himself testifying in a matter involving the third Kennedy brother, Senator Edward Kennedy. After attending a late-night party on Chappaquiddick Island, "Teddy," as he was known publicly, drove his car off a bridge and into the water. Senator Kennedy survived, but a passenger in the car, Mary Jo Kopechne, did not. She apparently drowned. The case aroused controversy after it became known that Senator Kennedy left the scene of the accident and did not report it for more than ten hours. Then, local authorities botched the investigation by not performing an autopsy. Dr. Wecht was called in to testify for the Massachusetts district attorney's office, who wanted to have the body exhumed and have Dr. Wecht perform an autopsy.

Throughout the 1970s and 1980s, Dr. Wecht handled dozens of fascinating homicide cases. Two of the more bizarre cases occurred in the Northeast. In 1975, Dr. Wecht was hired by lawyers defending Dr. Charles Friedgood, on trial for killing his wife by injecting her with a lethal dose of Demerol. The jury found him guilty and he is serving a long prison term. However, Dr. Wecht found interesting physical and medical evidence that suggests Dr. Friedgood may have been wrongly convicted.

In the early 1980s, Dr. Wecht spent a great deal of time working on cases in New York. He was first hired by lawyers representing Jean Harris, charged with killing her lover, Dr. Herman Tarnower, author of *The Complete Scarsdale Medical Diet.* Ms. Harris claimed the shooting was an accident. Using a simple roll of string and his knowledge of gunshot wounds, Dr. Wecht was able to demonstrate through the trajectory of the bullets that struck Dr. Tarnower's body and other items at the scene that the shooting most probably was an accident. The jury ignored the overwhelming medical evidence and found Mrs. Harris guilty. She spent more than eleven years at the Bedford Hills Women's Prison. Dr. Wecht wrote several letters of recommendation to New York governor Mario Cuomo, as did many other friends and supporters of Jean Harris. Mrs. Harris was finally granted clemency in December 1992 and released from prison.

As soon as he had finished his work in the Jean Harris case, Alan Dershowitz hired Dr. Wecht to examine medical evidence and testimony that had convicted his new client, Claus von Bulow.

"Cyril Wecht is not the traditional pathologist who follows the most obvious track of evidence," says Stanley Preiser, one of the most respected civil and criminal trial attorneys in America. "He, more than any other medical expert I have ever used, is willing to look beyond the obvious. He goes where the evidence takes him. He never allows attorneys to improperly influence what he thinks. I would say that in nine of every ten cases that Cyril Wecht testifies in, he is the star witness. He's simply that good of an expert."

A lot of people have differing opinions on Dr. Wecht. But from the standpoint of the professionals with whom he works as a medicolegal consultant, there is never any double-speak from this man. What you see is what you get. Twelve hours a day, six, sometimes seven days a week is not an uncommon work schedule for him. His reputation among other forensic scientists and trial lawyers across the country is widespread and occasionally controversial. However, even those who disagree with his opinions respect his interpretation of the facts and his ability to articulate his views and conclusions.

The following story demonstrates Dr. Wecht's prestige. In 1991 a plaintiff's lawyer involved in a wrongful death lawsuit stood before a federal judge in Philadelphia. The defense was asking that the case be dismissed, asserting that there was no evidence to prove that his client was responsible for the death.

JUDGE: What do you say about this?

PLAINTIFF LAWYER: Your honor, we have one of the nation's best forensic pathologists, who has examined the evidence and is prepared to testify that the defendant's actions most likely did cause the victim's death.

JUDGE: The best pathologist? Whom do you have, Cyril Wecht?

When the plaintiff's lawyer responded in the affirmative, the judge recommended to the defense that they settle the case out of court, which they did shortly thereafter.

—Mark Curriden
Benjamin Wecht

1

The Great American Murder Mystery:
The Assassination of President John F. Kennedy

Over the past three decades, hundreds of letters and telephone calls have come into my office at St. Francis Central Hospital in Pittsburgh from people claiming to have information on the assassination of President John F. Kennedy. Many of them have been helpful, even educational. Others related stories that would only be seen in a supermarket tabloid.

An elderly gentleman called one afternoon saying it was obvious who had shot the president. The man had reviewed a home movie of the incident and said it was clear as crystal: Lyndon Johnson, sitting in a car that followed President Kennedy in the motorcade in Dallas, jumped out of his car, ran up alongside the president's car, pulled a gun from his coat, and started shooting, then ran back to his own car—all completely undetected by those at the scene, and by the millions who have reviewed that same film in the years since the shooting.

Another favorite was the woman who telephoned with "top secret" details about the JFK slaying. "It was Marilyn Monroe dressed up as a Secret Service agent," she explained. No tips have come in yet blaming Elvis, Mother Teresa, or aliens from Mars, but I have many more years on this earth, and I am sure they will come.

I cannot count the number of times I have been interviewed,

written papers, or been asked to speak about the Kennedy assassination. It's a weekly occurrence. Very few people have spent as much time reviewing the physical evidence in this case as I have. Simply put, it is the world's greatest murder mystery, and the interest in it will not go away.

Much of my extracurricular time in legal medicine has been spent researching what happened in those few horrible seconds in Dallas. There are few events in history, other than when I was married or the days my children were born, when I can look back ten, twenty, or thirty years and tell you exactly where I was and what I was doing at that time. For me as for many Americans, the assassination of President Kennedy is one of those moments.

President Kennedy's death and the way it was investigated have been a source of constant intrigue throughout most of my adult life. As a young pathologist, I was not yet immersed in the world of politics, though, as a Democrat, I had voted for and supported Kennedy in the 1960 election. During his campaign trip to Pittsburgh, I was a face in the crowd listening to one of his many dynamic speeches. He talked of a need for reassessing our values.

"The time has come for Americans to look inward, to discover the greatness, the charity in each of us," then-senator John F. Kennedy told us that day. "Sure, we should strive to prosper. But we should also lend a helping hand to those who have tried but failed, to those who have not had the same opportunities and successes as we have found."

On November 22, 1963, I was in Los Angeles visiting a new friend and professional colleague, deputy coroner Thomas Noguchi, who would later become famous for his investigations into the deaths of Hollywood stars such as Natalie Wood, Marilyn Monroe, and John Belushi. We were standing in the middle of an autopsy room, corpses of all kinds around us as we discussed where we should go for lunch when his secretary, appearing distraught, came rushing into the room, and whispered into Dr. Noguchi's ear.

"The president's been shot," a stunned Dr. Noguchi said. Texas governor John Connally had also been hit as the president's motorcade drove through the streets of Dallas.

In the split second following Dr. Noguchi's shocking revelation, dozens of thoughts and questions raced through my mind. Why would someone do this? Has the person been caught? How bad are the injuries? Is the president dead?

As if he had read my mind, Dr. Noguchi spoke up: "They don't know how bad it is. He's been rushed to a local hospital."

After finding a restaurant with a television, we spent much of the next two hours absorbing every word that was broadcast on the shooting. Considering the initial reports that the president had been shot in the head and an eyewitness account that his head appeared to have exploded, Dr. Noguchi and I both concluded that the prognosis was not good.

As a medical examiner, I had dealt with death on a daily basis, but the fact that the president, a person very much in the prime of life, could be killed despite his wealth, power, and popularity —not to mention the dozens of Secret Service agents that protected his every breathing moment—gave me a sudden realization that no person is immortal.

In 1963, I was thirty-two, and my career in legal medicine was just beginning. Having earned postgraduate degrees in both medicine and law from the University of Pittsburgh, I was then serving as a director of laboratory sciences and pathology at Leech Farm Veterans Hospital in Pittsburgh and was a partner in one of the city's law firms.

As we sat and watched the news, I never imagined how closely involved I would later become in the investigation into the shooting of President Kennedy.

The president and his wife were touring Texas preparing for the upcoming election year. The morning of November 22, he had spoken to a Chamber of Commerce breakfast in Fort Worth. He arrived at the airport, Love Field, in Dallas at 11:40 A.M. Joined by Vice President Lyndon Johnson and Governor John Connally, President Kennedy rode through the streets of downtown Dallas in an open motorcade. Tens of thousands of people weathered the threat of rain, and by the time the presidential limousine was en route, the clouds had broken, allowing the convertible to travel without the "bubble top."

The motorcade departed Love Field at 11:50 A.M. The president and Mrs. Kennedy, who was holding roses she had been given upon arriving in Dallas, were in the limousine's backseat. Directly in front of them in the two jumpseats were Governor and Mrs. Connally. A Secret Service agent drove the car, with another Secret Service agent in the passenger seat. Following the president was an open limousine filled with eight Secret Service agents responsible for scanning the crowds, windows, and roofs for potential trouble. Third in the entourage was the vice president's car, carrying Mr. and Mrs. Johnson and U.S. senator Ralph W. Yarborough of Texas. Other cars and vans followed, carrying more Secret Service agents, dignitaries, and members of the press.

The procession was scheduled to conclude at the city's Trade Mart, where the president was to give a luncheon speech to business leaders. That evening, a Democratic fund-raiser requiring the president's attendance was planned in Austin.

The motorcade traveled down Main Street, a principal artery through the center of Dallas. As the entourage neared the city's western edge, the cars turned right onto Houston Street, went one block, and turned left onto Elm Street. At the corner of Houston and Elm was the Texas School Book Depository, a seven-story orange brick building. As the motorcade neared, a Secret Service agent noticed the clock on the building read 12:30 P.M., the time the president was scheduled to arrive at the Trade Mart. He radioed ahead, saying they would be there in five minutes.

At a speed of eleven miles per hour, President and Mrs. Kennedy waved at the thousands who lined the streets to get a glimpse of their leader. A great portion were schoolchildren on a once-in-a-lifetime class trip.

The last words John Kennedy most likely ever heard came from Mrs. Connally, when she briefly turned, pointed to the crowds that had gathered, and said, "Mr. President, you can't say Dallas doesn't love you."

Within seconds of making the turn onto Elm Street and passing the Texas School Book Depository, gunshots sounded. The president's hands lifted to his neck. He had been hit. No more than two seconds later, more shots were fired. Kennedy was struck in the head and Connally in the back. The First Lady was immediately sprayed with her husband's blood.

MRS. KENNEDY: My God, I've got his brains in my hands.

GOVERNOR CONNALLY: Oh my God, they're going to kill us all.

MRS. KENNEDY: They've killed my husband; they've killed my husband.

Agents, realizing the president had been shot, immediately sped away. Within five minutes of the shooting in Dallas, Secret

Service agents had taken the president to nearby Parkland Memorial Hospital, where doctors and surgeons, who had been contacted by radio, were waiting. There can be no criticism of the medical and surgical treatment administered by the hospital. All measures that needed to be undertaken were. The president's pupils were dilated and fixed. There was no obtainable pulse or blood pressure, and there was only a faint suggestion of a heartbeat.

As doctors scurried to save the leader of our nation, supply him with oxygen, and replace the blood he had lost, one amazing fact popped up: no one, not the Secret Service, not his aides, not even his wife knew what the president's blood type was. While it could have become a critical issue, it ended up being nothing more than an interesting footnote in history.

At approximately 1:00 P.M., twenty-five minutes after the president was admitted to Parkland, doctors pronounced John Fitzgerald Kennedy dead. It is clear that his life was beyond saving at the time he was wheeled into the hospital. No matter what therapeutic measures would have been attempted, he would not have survived. The wounds were simply too serious.

As Dr. Noguchi and I watched, a special news bulletin appeared. Dan Rather, then a cub reporter for CBS News, told anchorman Walter Cronkite that the president had died. At 1:38 P.M. on November 22, 1963, Lyndon Baines Johnson was sworn in as the thirty-sixth President of the United States aboard Air Force One.

Twenty minutes later, authorities announced live on television that they had arrested the assailant. He was twenty-four-year-old Lee Harvey Oswald of Dallas. Police said in his attempt to escape, Oswald had shot and killed a Dallas uniformed police officer, J. D. Tippit, a couple of miles from the spot where President Kennedy was slain. Eyewitnesses identified Oswald and told police they had seen him disappear into the nearby Texas Theatre. That's where police found and arrested Oswald. After several hours of questioning, police escorted their suspect before a sea of television and newspaper cameras to show the world who had killed the president.

"I didn't shoot nobody," Oswald told reporters shouting questions at him.

Around 1:30 A.M. on November 23, Texas authorities officially charged Oswald, an ex-marine, with the killing of President Kennedy. He was a crazed man who acted alone, police and federal agents told reporters. Oswald's history fascinated me. He allegedly was a Cuban sympathizer who had defected to Russia in 1959, where he was given full citizenship, a job, and an apartment in the Ukrainian city of Minsk. There he met and married Marina Prusakova, a Soviet citizen and niece of a KGB colonel. In June 1962, the couple returned to the United States with their baby girl and lived with Oswald's older brother in Fort Worth, Texas.

Federal agents announced that Oswald had purchased from a California mail order company the weapon with which he had shot the president—a bolt-operated 2766 Mannlicher-Carcano 6.5 mm rifle equipped with a cheap telescopic sight. The gun, made in 1940 in Italy, was found by federal agents behind some boxes on the sixth floor of the Texas School Book Depository building. Some spent shell casings were also discovered nearby. Despite mounting evidence, Oswald adamantly denied that he had shot and killed President Kennedy. He wanted to speak to a particular lawyer at the American Civil Liberties Union in New York. He was the only person Oswald said he would trust. However, the lawyer was out of town and could not be reached. Oswald would never get a chance to confide his story to that attorney or any other lawyer.

Two days later, as Oswald was being escorted by police from the Dallas city jail to a larger jail run by the Dallas County sheriff's department, he was shot and killed at nearly point-blank range by Jack Ruby, a local striptease club owner with known ties to the Mafia. Ruby told police he did it only to avenge the president's death.

In Los Angeles, as Dr. Noguchi and I watched the initial news reports the day President Kennedy was shot, there was definite confusion about what had happened. Televised interviews from the scene indicated that there might have been a second gunman firing from in front of the president's car as it passed through Dealey Plaza while Oswald, perched on the inside ledge of a sixth-floor window at the depository building, fired from behind. Dallas County district attorney Henry Wade was quoted as saying, "Preliminary reports indicate more than one person was involved."

But that theory was quickly quashed, and, as the day wore on, authorities made it clear that there was only one gunman. From what I initially read and heard about the shooting, the government's contention seemed to be acceptable. However, there were many who questioned the official version of what happened—so many, in fact, that President Johnson, in an effort to hush the voices of the critics, named a blue ribbon panel to probe the shooting.

To head the group, President Johnson appointed Earl Warren, chief justice of the U.S. Supreme Court, a man whose reputation for honesty was unquestioned. Six men, including four members of Congress and a former CIA director, also were named to the Commission on the Assassination of President Kennedy. In later years, it has been more frequently referred to as the Warren Commission. The main source of information and the sole investigative staff for the commission was the Federal Bureau of Investigation.

After ten months of interviews, the Warren Commission issued its findings in a nonindexed twenty-six-volume report:

The shots which killed President Kennedy and wounded Governor Connally were fired from the sixth floor window at the southeast corner of the Texas School Book Depository.

The weight of the evidence indicates that there were three shots fired.

The same bullet which pierced the President's throat also caused Governor Connally's wounds.

The shots which killed President Kennedy and wounded Governor Connally were fired by Lee Harvey Oswald.

The Commission has found no evidence that either Lee Harvey Oswald or Jack Ruby was part of any conspiracy, domestic or foreign, to assassinate President Kennedy.

In its entire investigation, the Commission has found no evidence of conspiracy, subversion or disloyalty to the U.S. Government by any federal, state or local official.

On the basis of the evidence before the Commission, it concludes that Oswald acted alone.

The bottom line: the panel concluded that three shots were fired. The first missile missed everyone and the car. The second bullet struck President Kennedy in the back, coursed through his upper back, and exited through the front of his neck at the level of the knot of his tie. The same bullet then hit Governor Connally in the back, went through the right side of his chest, smashed through his right wrist, and finally lodged in his left thigh. A third bullet hit President Kennedy in the head.

Before I continue, you must know my opinion of the Warren Commission report: it is absolute nonsense! Libraries should move the report to the fiction section. From a purely scientific standpoint, the finding that this one bullet passed through the president and then hit Governor Connally is an asinine, pseudoscientific sham at best, and, very possibly, a deliberate attempt to cover up the truth about what really happened. Putting aside the fact that this shooting involved the president of our country and the governor of a state, it was quite possibly one of the worst investigations of a homicide I have ever come across. Putting science aside and simply using reasonable common sense, much of the panel's rationalizations are downright silly.

Keep this thought in mind: I have always approached the assassination of President Kennedy no differently than I have approached the thousands of other homicide cases I have investigated during my three decades as a forensic pathologist—and that is from a purely scientific, objective, evidence-based perspective.

"Quincy" I am not! Nor are most murders solved in an hour. Nor do I go out looking for incredible, incriminating evidence that clears one person, implicates another, and ends with a suspect confessing. That is not how forensic pathology works.

As a forensic pathologist, I examine the physical evidence. What does the autopsy show? What are the angles, trajectories, and range of the bullet wounds? Do photographs of the crime scene show anything? Which bullet caused the fatal injuries? What was the sequence of the shots? What was the position of the assailant? The answers to all these questions are derived solely from the physical evidence.

When the Warren Commission report was released, I, like most Americans, accepted it as truth. We had no reason not to believe it, and I viewed many of those who challenged the government's theory and those who claimed Mafia, FBI, or CIA involvement as either political extremists looking for publicity or in dire need of psychiatric supervision.

About a year after President Kennedy's murder, the American Academy of Forensic Sciences (AAFS) asked me to review the Warren Commission report and deliver a paper on the subject to my colleagues at their annual meeting in Chicago in February 1965.

I had become an active member of the organization since returning to Pittsburgh. The AAFS is to medical examiners and coroners what the American Bar Association is to lawyers or what the American Medical Association is to physicians. I spent several days at the Carnegie Library in Pittsburgh reading the twenty-six-volume Warren Commission report. At this point, few books or articles had been published on the Kennedy case.

My first conclusion after reading the report—and this is what I told my fellow medical examiners—was that it was a botched autopsy, a terrible piece of medicolegal investigation. The people who did the autopsy were career military doctors who had no forensic pathology experience. It was incredibly orchestrated incompetence.

To begin with, the autopsy should have been done right there in Dallas by the city's medical examiner, Dr. Earl Rose. Murder was then and still is today a state crime, not a federal crime. Local and state authorities had absolute jurisdiction, not the federal authorities, even when the President of the United States was the victim. From law school I knew that the law does not change simply because the victim is the president. If Dr. Rose, a well-qualified and respected forensic pathologist, had been permitted to do that autopsy, we might know a lot more about the wounds than we do today.

When Dr. Rose announced he was planning on doing an autopsy, Secret Service agents, their hands gripping automatic weapons, announced with much authority and many vulgarities that they would not permit that to happen and used physical force to illegally remove John Kennedy's body from the hospital. Outside of laying their bodies on the ground and blocking all the doorways, what were Dr. Rose and the local authorities to do? After all, they were dealing with the FBI and Secret Service. Because all of this was happening so quickly, going to court to obtain a restraining order was out of the question. The vice president was on a plane waiting to be sworn in as president, and Lyndon Johnson refused to leave Dallas until Mrs. Kennedy and the casket were aboard Air Force One.

At Mrs. Kennedy's request, the body was flown to Bethesda Naval Medical Center, where at 8:00 P.M. the autopsy started. The president had served in the navy during World War II and had been treated at that facility during his years in the White House.

Had President Kennedy been a European head of state, his government would have appointed the most eminently qualified forensic pathologists in the land to conduct the autopsy. But in the Kennedy case, the men chosen for the task were inexperienced military pathologists who knew nothing of homicide investigations. This decision was made despite the fact that many of the nation's foremost forensic pathologists lived within one-hour flying or driving distance of Washington, D.C. By picking up a telephone, authorities could have gotten Dr. Russell Fisher in Baltimore, Dr. Joseph Spelman in Philadelphia, Dr. Geoffrey Mann in Virginia, or Dr. Milton Helpern in New York to participate in the autopsy. These men were among the best forensic pathologists in the country at that time. But because of the federal government's desire to control every action, they knew the safest place to turn was the military, even if that meant a far inferior examination.

The first autopsy flaw occurred before the examination of Kennedy's body began. The pathologists never talked to the doctors at Parkland Memorial Hospital before beginning their examination. It is a cardinal rule when performing an autopsy on a body which has been shot or stabbed to talk with the surgeon who treated the victim initially before examining the body.

Why? Because what happened in the Kennedy case can happen in any case. Because they had not communicated with the surgeons in Dallas, the autopsy pathologists were unaware that when Kennedy was wheeled into the hospital, the doctors noticed in the front of his neck a bullet hole that had perforated the windpipe. In an attempt to get oxygen into Kennedy's lungs and remove carbon dioxide as quickly as possible, the surgeons enlarged the wound in the trachea by performing a tracheotomy. In doing so, they almost completely obliterated the margins of the gunshot wound.

When the pathologists did their autopsy later that same day— November 22—they knew nothing of the bullet wound in the neck and thus made no mention of it when giving their oral report that evening to the FBI.

None of this is meant to be critical of the Parkland Memorial Hospital surgeons—they were simply taking whatever steps were necessary to keep the president alive. And while I do not think this one significant error represents any intentional coverup or conspiracy by the military pathologists at Bethesda, their failure to talk with the Parkland surgeons prior to the autopsy demonstrated nothing short of professional incompetence and inexperience. It was not until the next day, after the president's body was gone, that the autopsy pathologists talked with the Parkland doctors and learned of the bullet hole in the front of Kennedy's neck.

Because the autopsy was performed in a military institution and supervised by military brass, the pathologists had little control over their examination. For example, the pathologists were specifically told by federal agents and high-ranking military officials in the room not to dissect the bullet wound in President Kennedy's back. If they had dissected this wound, they would have been able to trace the bullet's path through the body. If that bullet had exited the neck, as the Warren Commission later claimed, the dissection would have proved it. Why were they told not to dissect the wound? No one has ever provided an answer. Who spoke such an order? According to those in the room, including Dr. Pierre Finck, an administrative forensic pathologist at the Armed Forces Institute of Pathology, it was Vice Admiral George G. Burkley, the White House physician.

Similarly, it was amazing that the pathologists never dissected President Kennedy's brain to examine the gunshot wounds. His brain was properly placed in a container of formalin for preservation. The brain is very soft tissue, like a soft-boiled egg. Formalin causes the brain matter to harden, much like a hard-boiled egg. So when you dissect the brain after it has been in formalin for two weeks, the bullet's path can be tracked through the head in a clear and definite fashion.

Two weeks later, the brain was examined, but only in a very superficial external fashion. The brain was not serially sectioned, which is the only proper way. No autopsy is complete without an exhaustive examination of the brain, especially when the cause of death is a gunshot wound to the head. The pathologists should have insisted on dissecting the brain in order to complete the medical study. This was an unforgivable and totally inexplicable decision.

The complete incompetence of the military doctors was magnified when navy commander James J. Humes, a military pathologist who did much of the physical examination of the president's body, announced months later that he had burned his original autopsy notes in the fireplace at his home on Sunday, November 24. This violates every rule of forensic pathology and official medical-legal investigation. If this case had ever gone to trial, those notes would have been subject to "discovery" under the rules of evidence, which means that the defense attorneys would have a right to see what was written down. By destroying those handwritten notes, Dr. Humes could have placed the entire case against Oswald or whoever else might have been a defendant in jeopardy. And what would the notes have shown? Dr. Humes has since said there was nothing in the notes that he did not put in his typed report. But then again, if there was nothing in those hand-scribbled notes, why did he take them home and destroy them in his fireplace?

If one of my assistants had done an autopsy like this on an average homicide victim, he or she would be severely chastised, possibly fired. The fact that this was the President of the United States made it that much more incredible to me. Was this simply benign bungling and professional negligence, or was something more sinister involved?

The basic investigation by the police was similarly shabby. Take, for example, the clothing worn by Governor Connally the day of the shooting. For reasons never explained, the governor's clothes were washed and cleaned prior to any examination by law enforcement. This, too, is incredible. It is quite possible that the governor's coat and shirt could have been examined to tell if the bullet that struck Connally had previously struck the president. But once it was cleaned, all accurate testing was impossible.

The crime scene investigation itself was another example of professional incompetence. Law enforcement officials did nothing to protect the evidence at the scene of the crime. The area should have been immediately roped off. The people who were there should have been detained and questioned. Names and addresses of every person should have been taken. Instead, people were allowed to roam all over the place. Witnesses left the scene. Elm Street was immediately opened to traffic. This crime scene investigation was nothing short of a tragedy.

Despite all of my criticisms, there was not enough evidence in 1965 for me to reject the Warren Commission's conclusions. And that is exactly what I relayed to my colleagues at the annual AAFS meeting at Chicago.

There was one moment at that conference that stands out in my memory. It is more significant to me today than it was in February 1965. Pierre Finck, the army forensic pathologist called as an afterthought, and who arrived after the autopsy had commenced, told me during a private breakfast meeting at the conference that he was extremely unhappy with the handling of the autopsy.

"You cannot believe what it was like," Dr. Finck told me. "It was horrible. Horrible! I only wish I could tell you about it."

With only a partial understanding of what Dr. Finck meant and with the delivery of my paper finished, I believed my brief inquiry into the Kennedy assassination to be over. I returned to Pittsburgh, expecting to put all this behind me.

Within days of my return to work, I received a call from Sylvia Meagher, who later authored *Accessories After the Fact.* Ms. Meagher was one of the first and most respected of the Warren Commission critics. When the commission printed its twenty-six volumes, there was no index. In an effort to make research of the report more expeditious and thorough, Ms. Meagher spent months developing the index herself. She had heard about my speech to the AAFS and wanted to talk with me about my thoughts on the assassination.

A year later, in 1966, Dr. Josiah Thompson, a professor at Haverford College in Pennsylvania, called to say he had heard about my paper and was impressed. Dr. Thompson said he was working on the Kennedy assassination as a consultant for *Life* magazine and asked if I had time to fly to New York to review an eight-millimeter film of the shooting taken by a Dallas clothing manufacturer named Abraham Zapruder. This gentleman, he explained, was standing along Elm Street filming the presidential motorcade as it went by and, quite fortunately, had captured the reactions of the president and Governor Connally as they were struck by the bullets. It was by far the best photographic documentation of those six momentous seconds. It had never been shown publicly.

A couple of days later, I was on a flight to New York. *Life* had enlarged each frame of the Zapruder film into eleven-by-fifteen-inch photographs. *Life,* which had bought the eight-millimeter film from Mr. Zapruder, and the FBI determined that the film moved through the camera at a speed of 18.3 frames per second, and they were able to enlarge each one. It was truly incredible.

We were able to examine the shooting in extreme detail. This analysis allowed us to see the facial reactions and body movements of President Kennedy and Governor Connally at a mind-boggling 1/18th of a second intervals.

The Zapruder film explicitly shows Kennedy and Connally being struck by bullets within approximately 1.5 seconds of each other. At first, federal authorities claimed that Oswald had shot Kennedy with the first bullet, then Connally with the second, and Kennedy again with the third bullet. Three shell cases were found by the sixth-floor window in the Texas School Book Depository building, where officials claimed Oswald had perched to shoot the president.

However, firearms experts using the Mannlicher-Carcano, a universally recognized inferior weapon, determined after testing that it would have taken at least 2.3 seconds for Oswald to have shot the gun, reloaded, and fired again. And that was without taking into consideration any additional time to reposition or re-aim at a moving target. That also assumed that the assassin was top quality. Oswald's shooting skills were less than impressive. In the marines, he failed his first marksmanship test, but eventually passed with only very mediocre results.

Realizing that Oswald could not have reloaded quickly enough to shoot both Kennedy and Connally, as federal agents had first supposed, but still refusing to admit the possibility of a second assassin, the Warren Commission developed its now infamous "single bullet theory," the contention that the second bullet struck both Kennedy and Connally.

But the Zapruder film also presents problems for those endorsing the "single bullet theory." If the same bullet struck both Kennedy and Connally, then why does the film show the president reacting to his injuries immediately upon impact, but the governor showing no reaction for approximately 1.5 seconds after he supposedly had been hit? If a person is shot in the upper right back by a bullet that pierces a lung, breaks a rib, shatters the wrist bone, severs a nerve, and lodges in the thigh, he or she would have an instantaneous reaction. Yet, Connally did not.

"We heard a shot," Governor Connally told reporters in December 1963 in his first public statement about what had happened. "I turned and looked into the backseat and the President was slumped. He had been hit."

Until his death in 1993, Governor Connally said, he, too, was hit. On many occasions he rejected the "single bullet theory."

Amazingly, he said he believes the basic conclusion of the Warren Commission—that Oswald was the lone gunman. However, it is impossible to accept the Warren Commission's findings if you do not accept the single bullet theory.

It was only after examining the Zapruder film and comparing the Warren Commission's findings with the autopsy report that I finally, in late 1966, came to realize that the so-called "single bullet theory" was scientifically absurd.

In order for this one bullet to have penetrated JFK's upper back and exit his neck, assuming it had been fired by Oswald from the sixth floor of the Depository, it would have had to be traveling from back to front, from right to left, and at a downward angle. For this same bullet then to have struck Governor Connally in the right part of his back behind his armpit, the bullet would have had to make a complete stop in midair after exiting Kennedy's neck, take an acute turn to the right for eighteen inches, stop again, and turn downward before entering Connally's back behind the right armpit. Without this impossible turn, the bullet would most probably have passed over the governor's left shoulder.

You do not have to be a forensic pathologist or a firearms expert to know that bullets travel in a straight line and do not make horizontal and vertical turns in midair like a roller coaster. Furthermore, in frame 230 of the Zapruder film, Governor Connally's right wrist and hand are clearly visible. Each finger is easily identifiable as he holds his large white Stetson hat. However, the Warren Commission's reconstruction of the events states that more than a second before this frame, the magic bullet had already shattered his wrist and severed the radial nerve. This is one of the nerves that enables the thumb and index finger to grasp objects. Yet in the film, he sits there with absolutely no evidence of pain on his face and his hand firmly gripping his hat, clearly visible to the spectators who lined the streets.

Several hours after the shooting, a Parkland Memorial Hospital employee presented a bullet to the FBI in Dallas that he found lying on a stretcher in the hospital's hallway. At first, authorities stated the slug had come from President Kennedy's back. Officials believed that the bullet had entered Kennedy's back, but had been forced out through the small hole in the skin when he was lying face up on the stretcher in the emergency room and the doctors applied pressure to the front of his chest during external cardiac massage.

The slug's mission changed the following day when the surgeons at Parkland Memorial Hospital informed the pathologists that there had been a bullet wound to the president's neck. With this new information, authorities decided that the missile, which traveled at a speed of twenty-one hundred feet per second, had entered President Kennedy's back and exited his neck just above the knot of the necktie. However, when the bullet struck the president's starched collar, it immediately stopped and fell onto the stretcher. That must have been some serious starch to stop a bullet traveling twenty-one hundred feet per second, I thought!

As the months passed and the Warren Commission searched for answers, this amazing bullet was given its final task: it was to eventually become the "magic bullet." In 1964, the Warren Commission unveiled the single bullet theory, the brainchild of now-Pennsylvania senator Arlen Specter. This magic bullet, which readily accommodated whatever purpose the federal authorities had for it, was now the projectile that entered President Kennedy's back, exited his throat, entered Governor Connally's back, exited his chest, went through his right wrist, and shattered his radius, before finally lodging in his left leg. While the governor lay on the stretcher, officials said, the bullet must have plopped out. Now, the stretcher bullet was from Connally's left thigh.

What absolute nonsense. The only time bullets plop out is when you have a big gaping hole. Governor Connally's leg wound was anything but large. It was also not a simple surface wound. The bullet went deep into the leg. When a bullet penetrates the skin and goes deeply into soft tissue, as happened with Governor Connally, it becomes immediately entrapped in the tissue because of the hemorrhaging and swelling. That fact, combined with the elasticity of the skin, would have made it impossible for the bullet to work its way back out, as the Warren Commission stated it had.

All this demonstrates how far the federal government would go to make the facts fit the scenario they had dreamed up. It was as if they had developed a murder scenario and were now trying to make all the pieces of evidence fit. Sometime in 1965, an official determination was made that all the physical evidence in the Kennedy assassination was the property of Jacqueline Kennedy. In October 1966, Mrs. Kennedy announced she was donating these materials as a gift to the National Archives. There were some preconditions, however. The materials would not be available for inspection by the general public until after the president's children had died. There was one exception: a recognized expert in the field of pathology could apply to examine the evidence after five years as long as his or her intentions involved a "serious historical purpose." Between the time of the assassination and the National Archives gaining control of the evidence, the autopsy materials had been in the possession of President Kennedy's personal physician, Vice Admiral George G. Burkley.

I found this outrageous. First off, evidence in a homicide investigation, especially autopsy reports and photographs, is never given to the family of the victim. That's completely unheard of and absolutely absurd. The part about not releasing it to the American public baffled me more than anything else.

As questions and criticism mounted, Attorney General Ramsey Clark gathered a group of four physicians—three pathologists and a radiologist—to review the Warren Commission's report and then to examine separately the evidence at the National Archives in February 1968. All of the individuals that Clark chose had close professional ties to the federal government, and all were sympathetic to the Warren Commission's findings. That gave me no confidence in the panel's final conclusions—one gunman, three bullets, and the single bullet theory to account for seven wounds to President Kennedy and Governor Connally.

However, the Clark panel did make one interesting observation: the bullet that struck President Kennedy in the head was not at the base of the head, as the Warren Commission reported, but actually four inches higher. The Clark group based their finding on the X rays they examined. The disparity led many to claim that the autopsy photographs and X rays had been altered to hide other wounds. Some others even talked of the feds switching bodies while Air Force One was on its way back from Dallas that day in 1963. While I believe the latter charge is ludicrous, I now believe there is little doubt that some of the autopsy reports, photographs, and X rays were manipulated, altered, or revised.

In the fall of 1968, an opportunity presented itself that I considered the perfect chance to review the physical evidence and the original autopsy report. I was in my office when I received a call from Jim Garrison, the district attorney of New Orleans. He said he had been investigating the death of President Kennedy. Mr. Garrison said he had uncovered evidence that linked various Louisiana organized crime figures with Jack Ruby, Lee Harvey Oswald, and the Kennedy assassination.

Mr. Garrison was a large man and was known for his distinctive stare and booming voice. He enjoyed controversy. He was one of the first politicians in the United States to use the power of television when he invited the press along to film his police raids on gambling and prostitution dens in the French Quarter.

He needed a forensic pathologist who could testify regarding the wounds and autopsy evidence in the shooting, and Mr. Garrison asked if I was available. But a roadblock stood in the way: the federal government. Garrison had been denied access to the original autopsy evidence.

"So why do you need me?"

"Simple," he responded. "I'm going to federal court in an effort to force them to turn the autopsy report over, and I need you to testify as to why this evidence is essential to my case."

I agreed. On January 17, 1969, three days before Mr. Garrison was set to start trying New Orleans businessman Clay Shaw for participating in the conspiracy, I took the witness stand before U.S. district judge Charles Halleck, Jr., in Washington, D.C. As the only medical witness who testified, I told the judge why the autopsy reports were a necessary part of any homicide investigation and in most cases are public record anyway.

By the end of the day, Judge Halleck agreed and immediately ordered that all the medical and physical evidence in the Kennedy assassination be made available for my review. Following the court's decision, however, attorneys for the federal government made it very clear they were not going to allow us to examine their evidence and would tie the case up in appeals for many years.

Every step of the investigation, Jim Garrison found the federal government blocking his way. He once told me they even offered him a federal judgeship if he would drop his probe. He was threatened with an IRS investigation. His office was bugged and his telephones were tapped. The U.S. attorney general, Ramsey Clark, even stated publicly that he might prosecute Jim Garrison—for what he did not elaborate. The news media made the New Orleans prosecutor out to be some kind of publicity seeker, yet the newsmen never pointed out that during the entire investigation and prosecution, Mr. Garrison had declined to talk to the press about the evidence or the case. As he told me later, he had run into powerful forces in this country. Because he was challenging their ideas and positions, they would do anything to discredit his case or destroy him.

Since Mr. Garrison had already lined up his witnesses against Clay Shaw, he could not wait three or four years to pursue the medical evidence through the appellate courts. Without the medical evidence, I was unable to testify. Mr. Shaw was acquitted by a New Orleans jury after less than two hours of deliberations. While Jim and I became good friends over the years, I must clearly emphasize that I have never been a believer in his multiple conspiracy theory—that the CIA, FBI, Secret Service, military-industrial complex, anti-Castro Cubans, right-wing extremists, and the Mafia all joined together in plotting and carrying out the president's assassination. But Jim did have a strong sense of justice and truth, and he was right when he stated neither was present in the Warren Commission report.

On October 22, 1992, Jim died at the age of seventy. Even after the Clay Shaw trial, he was re-elected district attorney and was later elected a judge on the Louisiana Court of Appeals, where he served for twelve years. The year before he died, Jim Garrison again became a household name when movie director Oliver Stone made a film about Jim's efforts in the Kennedy investigation.

Between 1969 and 1971, very little that was new surfaced about the Kennedy assassination. A few tabloid magazine articles came out proclaiming conspiracy, but there was nothing substantial to them.

As the summer of 1971 approached, and Americans watched on network television as our veterans returned home from Vietnam, I was acutely aware that the five-year moratorium regarding conditions under which experts could review the Kennedy evidence was to expire October 29. The provisions of Mrs. Kennedy's gift to the National Archives indicated that the executor of the agreement was the only person who could give permission. I contacted Burke Marshall, a former deputy attorney general under Bobby Kennedy and, in 1971, a professor at Yale Law School. Mr. Marshall was the executor of the agreement between the Kennedy family and the National Archives.

At that time, I was president of both the American Academy of

Forensic Sciences and the American College of Legal Medicine, as well as the coroner of Allegheny County. I also held four faculty positions at the University of Pittsburgh and Duquesne University in Pittsburgh. Various individuals from these and other organizations sent letters to Mr. Marshall asking that I be granted permission to review the evidence.

My quest to gain access was given nothing short of a deliberate runaround. For months, Mr. Marshall ignored my letters and did not return my phone calls. One day, when I somehow actually reached him on the phone, he told me I needed to get permission from the National Archives. The officials at the National Archives said that was ridiculous, that it was Mr. Marshall's decision alone to make. I immediately began trying to get in contact with Mr. Marshall again, but he continued to ignore my repeated phone calls and letters.

In late November 1971, an amazing thing happened. I have never been more happy to hear from a news reporter than when Fred Graham called me one afternoon at my office. Mr. Graham, then an investigative reporter for the *New York Times*, said he had heard through his many sources that I was trying to gain access to the Kennedy medical evidence. The *New York Times* always seems to know about things no one else does, and this was yet another example. To this day, I have no idea how Mr. Graham learned of my requests.

After telling Mr. Graham of my interest in the case and the problems I was having with Mr. Marshall, I still remember his reply: "Let me see what I can do."

It's amazing how a simple call from a *New York Times* reporter will get an otherwise indifferent or uncooperative person to become friendly and helpful. No more than a few days later, a letter arrived at my office from Mr. Marshall, saying he was going on Christmas vacation, but when he returned, he would contact me. It was obvious that Fred Graham had spoken to him.

However, January and February came and went without a word from Mr. Marshall. I sent a couple more letters pursuing my request, but received no response. In March 1972, Fred Graham again called me and asked if my permission had been granted. I explained to him what had transpired and told him that Mr. Marshall was still not being very responsive. Obviously puzzled by this information, he said he would certainly contact Mr. Marshall again.

Less than a week after I spoke with Mr. Graham, Mr. Marshall called, saying that, if I would meet with him at his New Haven office, we could work out the details of my visiting the National Archives. I believe he honestly thought I would not fly to Connecticut and that I would drop my request. He was mistaken. We met and he finally granted me permission after several weeks of deliberate procrastination.

And so, my efforts and perseverance finally paid off. I spent Thursday and Friday, August 24–25, 1972, at the National Archives in Washington, D.C., reviewing every single piece of physical evidence they told me was in their possession. I was placed in a rather large private room and was handed a list of all the items I was allowed to review. Marion Johnson, who supervised the Kennedy assassination materials at the National Archives, had an x-ray viewing machine in the room and a projector nearby so I could review the Zapruder and other films.

As I would request various pieces of evidence on the list, Mr. Johnson, who was very courteous and helpful, would bring them in from the storage room. The clothes worn by President Kennedy and Governor Connally were all neatly folded, separated by tissue paper. As I held President Kennedy's suitcoat in my hands, I was tempted to try it on. I decided against it.

Holding the jacket up, I examined the bullet hole through the back. It was exactly five and three-quarter inches down from the collar. That's exactly where the autopsy doctors stated the wound to Kennedy's back was. In fact, they went as far as to draw a diagram of the president's back placing the bullet wound about five and three-quarter inches down from the base of the neck. Six months later, when the Warren Commission told Dr. Humes that a bullet wound five and three-quarter inches from the base of the neck did not fit their single bullet theory, Dr. Humes volunteered that he and the other pathologists were wrong. Instead, Dr. Humes moved the bullet wound up four inches so it would match the trajectory of a bullet coming from the sixth-floor window. In other words, Dr. Humes was saying that his recollection of the bullet wound six months after the autopsy constituted better evidence than the diagram he and his colleagues made on the night of the autopsy. I found this to be ridiculous.

Everything at the archives was listed by exhibit number as it had been reviewed by the Warren Commission. It took eight hours each of the two days to go through everything.

I examined exhibit number 399—the magic bullet. It was housed in a small cardboard box with a cotton bedding. I opened the box and found a missile that was in near-pristine condition. It was barely flawed. The only true deformity I could see was a slight indentation at the base of the slug, which would have been caused by the explosion of the firing mechanism.

For this bullet to have done what the Warren Commission claimed it did and be in such near-perfect shape, it must indeed be magic! The Warren Commission said this bullet went through two people, fractured two bones, and left bullet fragments in four places—Kennedy's chest and Connally's chest, wrist, and thigh. Despite all this, the bullet I was looking at had lost only 1.5 percent of its original weight. This kind of bullet weighs 161 grains before it is fired. However, the bullet I had in my hand weighed just under 158.6 grains. According to doctors at Parkland Memorial Hospital, fragments from this bullet weighing more than two grains were removed from Connally's right wrist in surgery, and another piece remains in Governor Connally's leg to this day. This sole point single-handedly destroys the single bullet theory!

Among the evidence also were details of a test that the federal government had performed at the Edgewood Army Arsenal in Maryland to see if their theory proved true. Using the same kind of ammunition and a Mannlicher-Carcano rifle, the experts fired bullets into cotton wadding, goat carcasses, and human cadavers to simulate Governor Connally's rib and wrist fractures. What were the test results? All the slugs fired into the cadavers showed significant deformity. Even the slugs fired into the cotton wadding had more deformities than the "magic bullet." Keep in mind this was the government's own experiment, and it proved their theory wrong.

As I reviewed the X rays and autopsy photographs, I noticed a little flap of loose tissue visible just above the hairline on the back of President Kennedy's head. Amazingly enough, no one had previously reported this piece of tissue. Because I was dealing only with the autopsy photographs and X rays and not the actual body, I could not examine further what this material might be. Given the questions that have been raised regarding the authenticity of the autopsy reports and photographs, the significance of this discovery could be far-reaching.

From my examination of photographs of the scalp, the loose

flap very easily could be an exit wound, which would prove there was a second gunman shooting from the front. But even if it is an entrance wound from a bullet, it would destroy the Warren Commission's conclusion that only three bullets were fired. With the tight controls the military and Secret Service had on the pathologists doing the autopsy, it is possible they simply overlooked an additional wound. The only other explanation is, of course, a coverup. Without re-examining the body or the brain, it would be impossible to ever find out what exactly this flap of tissue is.

Since it was doubtful that President Kennedy's body would ever be exhumed, I looked down the list searching for the next best thing to examine: the brain. But I could not find the brain listed. When I asked to see the brain, Mr. Johnson informed me it was not there.

WECHT: Where is it? Who has it?

JOHNSON: I don't know where it is. It was not here when I took over and the inventory was done in 1966.

Extraordinary. The federal government had lost the brain of President Kennedy. It was gone. Disappeared. No trace of it anywhere. I immediately suspected foul play, but also thought that some other agency, such as the Department of Justice, could have it secretly stored away. The amazing thing about it was that despite the brain's six-year absence, no one had reported it missing. As I went down the list, other items also were missing, including microscopic tissue slides and various key photographs of the wounds in Kennedy's chest. Many individuals, including pathologists from the Ramsey Clark panel which examined the evidence in 1968, obviously had discovered that the brain and the other materials were missing, but none of them made their findings public. To me, this goes to show how people of the highest order have permitted themselves to be compromised by the federal government's influence and pressures.

As I looked over the scalp photographs one more time, something else appeared to be out of order. Where the doctors at Parkland Memorial Hospital had earlier said they saw a large hole—at the top back of Kennedy's skull—there was now hair. No gaping hole. But something else seemed strange. Because it is the top of the head, the hair in that spot should be long. But in the Kennedy scalp photograph, it was very short hair—less than an inch long. It was the kind of hair found at the base of the scalp. Was it possible that the scalp had been rearranged to cover up the wound that the Parkland emergency surgeons say they saw? Only those who were present at the autopsy when the photographs were taken can tell us for sure, but this certainly raises a question as to whether the body had been tampered with.

Everything that was there I carefully examined. I picked up the rifle the government claims Oswald used to kill the president. I can't explain the feeling I had as I held the rifle up to my shoulder and looked down the end of the barrel. I looked over all the photographs taken that day. It was an experience I will never forget.

Friday evening, as I departed the National Archives, Mr. Graham was waiting to ask me a few questions. I appreciated the role he had played in helping me gain access to the evidence, so I had no hesitation about sitting down and talking with him for a few hours. When he asked me what I saw that interested me the most, I responded that the most newsworthy finding was what I did not see. Later that evening, I boarded a plane at Washington's National Airport and headed home to Pittsburgh. No one else was aware I had even been to the National Archives.

That Sunday, as on every weekend, I went to the store to buy fresh bagels and the Sunday *New York Times*. There it was, splashed all over the front page of the world's largest and most influential newspaper: MYSTERY CLOAKS FATE OF BRAIN OF KENNEDY. The lengthy article detailed how I, Cyril Wecht, "a noted forensic pathologist," had discovered that the president's brain, supposedly preserved in a container of formalin, was gone.

According to the article, on April 26, 1965, Dr. Burkley, four days after receiving a letter from then-Senator Robert Kennedy, itemized all the Kennedy assassination materials, and the brain and other items were listed on his inventory. However, when all the materials were inventoried again for the logging in of Mrs. Kennedy's "private gift" to the National Archives on October 29, 1966, these items, including the brain, were not among those listed.

I told Mr. Graham that questions about President Kennedy's head wounds might never be answered as long as these objects were not available for thorough examination. In the years that followed, I requested of numerous federal agencies, including the Department of Justice, the FBI, and Bethesda Naval Hospital, that the location of these items be determined. However, officials at each agency said that they could not comment on the case or that they did not know the whereabouts of the missing items.

To further complicate matters, Mr. Marshall told the *New York Times* that neither the brain nor the slides were part of the autopsy materials given to him by the Kennedy family and that he had never possessed them. In 1966, then-Attorney General Ramsey Clark ordered that all the items relevant to the assassination should go to Mrs. Kennedy, who then gave everything to the National Archives.

The records of the Warren Commission show only that the brain was "removed and preserved for further study." After the autopsy, records show that the Secret Service and FBI delivered various medical items to the president's personal physician, Dr. Burkley. After Dr. Burkley did his inventory on April 26, he turned the items over to President Kennedy's personal secretary, Evelyn Lincoln, who was working on Kennedy memorabilia at the National Archives. Mrs. Lincoln acknowledges receiving the items, saying they came in a padlocked chest. However, she says she never opened the box and turned it all over to Angie Nevell, a personal secretary to Bobby Kennedy, who had been elected to the U.S. Senate from New York. After reviewing the items, Bobby Kennedy then put Mr. Marshall in charge of the materials and returned them to the National Archives.

Mr. Johnson was quoted in the *New York Times* article as saying the brain was among the items he gave to Evelyn Lincoln but that it was not returned when the evidence came back in 1966. That evening, as I sat and talked with Fred Graham, I believed the brain was still around somewhere.

"Who would have taken the responsibility to destroy the brain?" he quoted me as saying. (For a complete tracking of the missing brain and various autopsy materials and photographs, please see the appendix, "Where Is JFK's Brain?" It is the only time such a trace on these materials has ever been done.)

In the *New York Times* article interview, I described the pristine condition of the bullet and explained why it could not be the magic bullet the government claims it is. I pointed out that a bullet that goes through two men, breaking bones and leaving fragments in four places, would surely have lost more than 1.5 percent of its original weight and would have been severely deformed. I also informed Mr. Graham about the little flap of loose tissue I found on the back of President Kennedy's head.

Despite the *New York Times* article, there was little or no public outrage. People simply must no longer care, I thought. But as the years went on, I learned how wrong I was.

As the Watergate scandal calmed down in late 1974, the news media, looking for a fresh target to focus their newfound influence on, zeroed in for a time on reports that the CIA had been involved in the Kennedy assassination. All three television networks had obtained copies of the Zapruder film by this point and were showing the video as part of stories saying there might have been a second gunman.

Reacting to the controversy, President Gerald Ford, one of the Warren Commission's original members, empaneled a new body that was designed to investigate alleged CIA involvement in various domestic spying activities, among them the assassinations of President Kennedy and Martin Luther King, Jr. President Ford named his vice president, Nelson A. Rockefeller, to chair the commission. Ford then appointed David Belin, who had been an assistant legal counsel for the Warren Commission, to be the Rockefeller Commission's executive director. If President Ford's motive was to create a board that would have absolutely no objectivity or credibility, he could not have done a better job.

In April 1975, the news media had begun to criticize the Rockefeller Commission for interviewing only those experts who were sympathetic to the Warren Commission's conclusions. Soon after, I received a telephone call from Robert Olsen, senior counsel to the Rockefeller Commission, asking my opinions of all aspects of the Kennedy assassination. In a five-hour interview in Washington, D.C., I answered every question Mr. Olsen had. When he inquired about possible CIA involvement in the assassination, I responded that I had no great intelligence secrets to reveal. I was sincerely gratified that some governmental body was finally taking notice of my views.

While Mr. Belin denied my request to speak to the full commission, the deposition was very thorough, yet extremely confrontational. I later learned that a group of five experts had been appointed by the Rockefeller Commission to review the Kennedy autopsy reports and related medical evidence. Each of these men had ties to the Warren Commission; one had even been an employee of that panel. So it came as no surprise when these new experts returned with the conclusion they could find no disagreements with the Warren Commission's findings.

The Rockefeller Commission then took it a step further and said that I, Cyril Wecht, had told them that all of the shots could have come from the back of the motorcade and that I had no evidence whatsoever of any CIA participation. But then the Rockefeller report stated that this was all I had testified to. This was a vicious lie and a deliberate attempt to misrepresent my views. In my extensive interview with Mr. Olsen, I had repeatedly spelled out the significant problems with the Warren Commission's theories and conclusions, but not one word of this was mentioned.

It really angered me to have voluntarily given so much time explaining my position and then to have that position completely misrepresented. I asked to see a copy of my testimony as it was presented to the Rockefeller members, but my requests were repeatedly denied—supposedly because of national security. If releasing my testimony is a national security threat, it's a wonder we ever saw the Pentagon Papers.

Dissatisfied with the Rockefeller Commission, Congress created its own investigating body in 1977 to explore additional claims that the federal government's intelligence community had played key roles in the assassinations of President Kennedy and the Reverend Martin Luther King, Jr. At first, I feared this would be another puppet panel, catering to the establishment in an attempt to once and for all silence the critics by claiming to give them a forum, but in the end, disagreeing and putting their assertions aside as fiction.

It was termed the House Select Committee on Assassinations, and among its first actions was to gather a panel of nine forensic pathologists to again review the medical evidence in the Kennedy case and advise Congress of their expert conclusions. My good friend Philadelphia trial attorney and former chief deputy district attorney Richard Sprague was named by the committee to be its chief counsel.

Dick Sprague's record as a prosecutor was unsurpassed. He

wanted to approach the investigation as he had so many times in murder cases in Philadelphia—in a thorough, comprehensive manner. Mr. Sprague wanted trained, experienced homicide detectives and a staff of well-qualified lawyers working with him. He even contacted F. Lee Bailey, the famous Boston lawyer, for help. He also requested a substantial but reasonable sum of money that would permit him to conduct the investigation in a proper fashion. Mr. Sprague had worked many years in a large metropolitan governmental office that conducted homicide investigations. He knew what resources he needed.

He also had a big say in selecting those who would advise congressional members. Mr. Sprague wanted me to serve as a member of the pathology panel. I agreed even though many congressional staffers were leery of my participation because of the hostility I had shown earlier toward the Warren Commission. When they named several pathologists who were outspoken supporters of the Warren report, they must have felt obliged to get the other side's opinion because I was then invited to take part in the committee's work.

It soon became clear that Mr. Sprague was serious about his assignment and intended to conduct a full-scale, no-holds-barred, thorough investigation. He let everyone know he planned on ferreting out all information that the FBI had conveniently and deliberately ignored or covered up when that agency acted as the investigative arm of the Warren Commission. This brought much trepidation and concern to top governmental leaders, who ultimately forced Mr. Sprague out and brought in their own man, Notre Dame University law professor G. Robert Blakey.

I had never met Robert Blakey before. Our paths had never crossed and we had never been involved with each other directly or indirectly professionally, politically, or academically. Yet I was astounded by the palpable hostility manifested toward me by Mr. Blakey from day one. He was hostile to the point of being rude.

Blakey made it crystal clear from the beginning that he had no serious doubts about the medical and forensic evidence in this case, as set forth in the Warren Commission. It was apparent to me that he had no intention of really delving into the questions that loomed large over the Kennedy assassination. In fact, he did everything he could to guide, influence, and direct the Forensic Pathology Panel toward another whitewash conclusion.

After several long sessions at which we received the medical evidence and debated it among ourselves, I found myself alone in speaking out against the single bullet and sole assassin theories. At one point, I openly challenged the other eight pathologists on the panel regarding the weight and condition of this magic bullet:

"Go back to your respective cities and search through the thousands and thousands of bullets you have recovered from cadavers and show me one bullet that has done what you say this bullet has done and looks like this bullet looks."

I have repeated that challenge a hundred times publicly, but not one soul has ever come forward with a bullet as magical as this one. Isn't it amazing that there has never been another one like it in the entire world? I asked the House Pathology Panel to reconstruct or repeat the bullet firing test. When Mr. Blakey refused, saying such a test was too expensive, I offered to pay all the costs for such an experiment. He still refused. I could not believe it. Then my colleagues said a cadaver bone would be different than a bone in a live person. It was not like I was asking to have an Egyptian Pharaoh exhumed and used in the experiment!

Even my good friend and highly respected colleague, former New York City chief medical examiner Michael Baden, who served as chairman of our advisory panel, sided with the Warren Commission. A frequently asked question is if the Warren Commission missed the boat so badly, as I say it did, then why do so many of my colleagues disagree with my position. The other forensic pathologists who served on the committee's advisory panel were certainly competent and are unquestionably experts in this field. So my differences with them cannot be attributed to incompetence or lack of experience.

I believe it's more of a predetermined mindset that many of my colleagues have that a cover-up or conspiracy of this magnitude by the federal government is unthinkable, or at the very least, unlikely. Just as lawyers disagree over what a particular law or court ruling means, forensic pathologists frequently have differences of opinion. I have no reason whatsoever to doubt my colleagues' sincerity. However, it should be noted that many of these same people had a long-standing involvement with the federal government—many had received federal grants for research and appointments to various influential government boards. To be highly critical of a government action could end that friendly relationship with Uncle Sam. It was around this time that I began seeing doors once opened to me as a nationally recognized forensic pathologist starting to close. Several invitations to participate as a faculty member in seminars at the prestigious Armed Forces Institute of Pathology were no longer offered to me. There is no doubt that if I had kept my mouth shut and toed the government line in the Kennedy case, I would have been appointed to many more medicolegal positions directly or indirectly controlled by the U.S. government. I also have gotten the cold shoulder from several national pathology organizations since I became an outspoken critic of the Warren Commission.

For more than thirty months, the House Select Committee reviewed mounds of secret documents on the Kennedy assassination, and ultimately listened to experts such as me testify about our findings. Many eyewitnesses to the shooting were reinterviewed. Amazingly, eighteen witnesses who were standing in Dealey Plaza that morning had died mysterious deaths by 1966. The *London Sunday Times* estimated that the odds of that happening were 100,000 trillion to one.

One witness who was alive was Ed Hoffman, a deaf mute, who had been standing on a nearby overpass and had full view of the presidential motorcade and the grassy knoll area. Mr. Hoffman told the FBI then and has repeated it since that he saw a man wearing a badge behind the fence up on the grassy knoll. The FBI agents, he says, offered him cash if he would keep quiet about what he had seen.

However, very little of this incriminating evidence gathered by the researchers hired by the House Select Committee was ever brought forth publicly by Mr. Blakey. It was clear to me that Mr. Blakey and his handpicked sycophants would not tolerate an objective, fact-finding investigation into the death of President Kennedy.

As a minority report of one, I accepted an invitation to testify before the committee and carefully explained to them in the thirty minutes I had the scientific reasoning behind my opinions. One by one, I went over my problems with the Warren Commission's findings: the faulty autopsy, the pristine bullet, the physical impossibility of the single bullet theory, and so on. All nine pathologists agreed the autopsy was improperly and chaotically performed, but the other eight said they could find no flaws in the Warren panel's conclusions. Dr. Baden was the first to speak for the majority of advisors and then came my turn. While some of the representatives seemed skeptical of my views, several appeared to agree with many of the crucial points I made.

H.S.C.A. STAFF COUNSEL ANDREW PURDY: Is it your opinion that this bullet could not have caused all the wounds to President Kennedy and Governor Connally?

WECHT: Based upon the findings in this case, it is my opinion that no bullet could have caused all these wounds. For the past twelve or thirteen years, I have urged, beseeched, and implored my colleagues to come up with one bullet that has done what this bullet has. Just one bullet is all I asked for. At no time did any of my colleagues ever bring in one bullet that broke two bones and is in near-pristine condition.

PURDY: What is it about the normal paths of bullets which leads you to the conclusion that the bullet did not pass through both men?

WECHT: The inescapable fact that unless a bullet, especially one fired from a high-speed weapon, strikes something of firm substance, such as a bone, that bullet will travel in a straight line.

H.S.C.A. STAFF COUNSEL GARY CORNWELL: And if the single bullet theory is not correct, how many bullets, in your view, did strike the two occupants in the car?

WECHT: I believe the president was definitely struck twice, one bullet entering in the back and one bullet entering in the head. I believe Governor Connally was struck by one bullet, and I believe another bullet completely missed the car. I think most probably four shots were fired.

PENNSYLVANIA CONGRESSMAN ROBERT EDGAR: You say the brain, which you pointed out is missing, is a vital piece of evidence in determining the number of shots fired. How would you have us go about locating the brain?

WECHT: I would get the best-trained investigators and detectives and an attorney for proper legal advice and, under the auspices of this committee, track down the time and person to last have knowledge of the brain and the other materials.

Days before the House Select Committee was scheduled to wrap up its session, significant new evidence was unveiled by acoustics experts who had obtained an audio tape. The recording had been made from a Dallas police officer's radio microphone as the officer, who was riding his motorcycle with the presidential motorcade, talked with a dispatcher back at the police station. All radio transmissions between officers and the dispatchers are routinely recorded. The analysis of the tape recording, several independent nongovernment experts testified, made it clear—there were four gunshots fired at President Kennedy, three from the back and one from the right front, the area of the grassy knoll.

In its final report, the House Select Committee ruled that, with a high degree of probability, President Kennedy had indeed been the victim of a conspiracy and that there was little doubt a second gunman was involved. However, the committee added, the second gunman missed his target. The committee went on to say that certain members of the Mafia had the motive and means to kill our leader, but there was no direct evidence proving it beyond a reasonable doubt.

Now the ball is really rolling, I thought. Now we are going to see some serious action. The Kennedy case will be officially reopened, new evidence will be unveiled, and possibly additional suspects will be brought to justice. Here you had the Congress of the United States, the governmental body that most represents the general public, finally saying the Kennedy assassination did not happen the way we have been told. I thought that would certainly force the FBI or Department of Justice to take immediate action and find out once and for all what happened that day in Dallas.

I could not have been more wrong. Not only was there no intensive, massive investigation, but essentially nothing at all happened thereafter. The response by the FBI and Justice Department was zero. Each agency said they planned to examine the evidence the House Select Committee had uncovered. To its everlasting discredit, the committee did not press the FBI or the executive branch of government to do anything about their findings. They simply presented them as if it were an academic exercise. My frustration level by this point was at an all-time high.

As the years rolled by, it became evident that there was little interest by anyone with the authority to make things happen. Every once in a while, a newspaper article would pop up about some person making an accusation. Polls by magazines such as *Time* showed that three of every four Americans believed there was a coverup in the Kennedy assassination. Yet there were no renewed investigations and no real push by the all-powerful news media. The twenty-fifth anniversary of the event passed with very little interest, other than the occasional television program, or pictorial in a newsmagazine.

In the spring of 1987, I was introduced to Jean Hill, the famous "lady in red." Jean was the woman in the red dress who was standing along Elm Street directly opposite Abraham Zapruder as President Kennedy's motorcade went by. Sure, Jean wanted to see the president as he rode by, but she had a more specific reason for being in Dealey Plaza that morning—she was trying to get the attention of a cute police officer who was guarding Kennedy along the motorcade's route.

"I was staring directly at the grassy knoll area when the shots went off," Jean told me. Her contentions had never been truly publicized, but she said she was ready to tell her story and I encouraged her to do so.

"As soon as I heard the shots, I focused completely over that way because that's where I thought the shots came from," Jean said. "I saw two men holding guns. One was behind the picket fence. As soon as the shots were fired, the men began fleeing, and instinctively, I started following them."

That's when, she says, two men in trench coats grabbed her and forcibly took her to the Dallas County Records Building, where an interrogation began. Upon informing the "police agents" that she had heard four to six shots fired and had seen the men on the grassy knoll, they rebuked her and issued this stern warning: "You would be very wise to keep your mouth shut about this."

For years, very few people had heard about Jean's eyewitness account not so much because Jean wanted to keep it a secret, but because very few reporters or assassination researchers ever contacted her. In the years that have passed, Jean and I have become good friends. But even so, she will not tell me whether she ever landed the date with the police officer!

Despite an incredible number of different civic clubs, professional organizations, and dozens of radio and television talk shows inviting me to speak on the Kennedy case in 1988, the general news media remained remarkably silent. It was in 1988 that the FBI released a short statement saying it had reviewed the conclusions of the House Select Committee on Assassinations, particularly the acoustical tape, but found no persuasive evidence of the conspiracy.

As I stated earlier, I have received an incredible number of telephone calls and letters from people interested in the Kennedy assassination and from people who claim to have some knowledge or insight into the case. Two of the more intellectually fascinating contacts came in 1988 and 1989: one from Robert Russell, a convict turned mob informant serving time in the California penal system, and the other from Tom Wilson, a computer analyst in my own hometown, Pittsburgh.

Mr. Russell first wrote to me in 1988 saying he had seen me on television being interviewed by Dan Rather about the Kennedy assassination, and he commended me for my position. I responded by sending him a thank-you note.

Over the next two years, Mr. Russell, who readily admitted to me he was in jail for participating in a bad check writing and financial fraud scheme, continued to write, telling me he thought he might have some information that would be helpful. He never pretended to be anything other than a small-time crook.

But in February 1990, a package arrived at my office at the Central Medical Center in Pittsburgh containing some truly provocative documents. Mr. Russell had enclosed several court documents and signed affidavits that linked him to former Teamster president Jimmy Hoffa. One of the many conspiracy theories is that the assassination was a mob hit—a retaliation for the crackdown on organized crime by the president's brother, Attorney General Robert Kennedy.

Mr. Russell said he was a taxicab driver in New York City in 1958 when he met and became friends with Paul Monrow and Paul "Skinny" Damote, whom he described as Hoffa's lieutenants. Mr. Russell first met Hoffa at the 500 Club in Atlantic City. According to the court documents, Russell was "turned" in 1962 and became an informant for the Department of Justice. In the letter,

Mr. Russell stated he had access to certain evidence from the Kennedy assassination that would prove I was correct—that Lee Harvey Oswald was not the lone gunman. Mr. Russell asked if I would be willing to examine the evidence he had.

While all of this made good reading in bed while I watched reruns of the *Untouchables* on cable television at night, it offered no proof that Mr. Russell had any evidence or leads in the Kennedy assassination. In a letter to Mr. Russell, I said I would be willing to see what he had, but that I needed to be told in advance what I would be looking at so I could bring the necessary equipment with me.

Finally, in August 1990, I received the following letter from Mr. Russell's girlfriend, Donia Lacelle, who was writing at Mr. Russell's direction:

Dr. Wecht,

As per our conversation, I am promptly sending you the list.

1. Ten black & white negatives/prints.
2. Eight color negatives/prints.
3. Six autopsy photographs.
4. Six X rays.
5. Four photographs—interior cavity chest.
6. Four photographs—brain, head.
7. Three small wood boxes, 55 slides, blood smears.
8. Three small plastic boxes—microscopic wound slides— tissue—count 114.
9. A small steel container marked "Gross Material." The top is sealed. On top of memorandum, it states, "Material of P—— K——."

On the bottom of the memorandum, there is a small label taped over it—clear tape and on it reads: "Autopsy materials—physical specimens." Please be careful of everyone.

Lacelle

I had seen this list before. It was identical to the one I reviewed at the National Archives—the list that contained the missing or misplaced autopsy materials. These were the photographs and slides that no person had seen. And the "gross material," well, there's only one thing that could be—the president's brain.

Was it possible? Could this low-life scumbag actually have in his possession the medical evidence that could solve this case? And even if he did, had the materials been properly stored so that they could be examined almost thirty years later?

The brain, I believe, holds all the answers. If I could examine it today, I could tell you how many bullets were shot, from which directions they were fired, and at what angle. If Mr. Russell was speaking the truth, I thought, this could certainly be the biggest break in the investigation. While I had my suspicions that Mr. Russell could be a fraud, just the thought that he could be telling the truth kept me corresponding with him.

In the midst of the communications with Mr. Russell, I received a letter on June 14, 1989, from Tom Wilson, who claimed to have startling new evidence involving the assassination. He asked if I would call him and discuss his findings. According to the letter, Tom had worked in computer analysis and image processing for U.S. Steel in Pittsburgh for thirty years, but had retired as chief electrical engineer. I called Tom at the number he gave me in the letter.

In our brief telephone conversation, Tom said he worked extensively with computers and had developed a technique that could potentially prove there was a second gunman in the grassy knoll area. He piqued my interest, and we planned to get together at my office a week later.

On June 21, Tom came in, his briefcase jam-packed with materials. Now, I consider myself a reasonably intelligent person and a very quick learner, but the next few hours boggled my mind. One thing was clear—Tom had accidentally stumbled onto evidence that could blow the Warren Commission report out of the water.

At U.S. Steel, Tom had developed and used a computer program that examines metals for flaws by shining a light toward the metal. Take a can of soup, as an example. Tom's computer will monitor the can as a beam of light is sprayed at the can. The computer will then examine the light rays that return. If there are flaws, such as scratches or dents, the computer will pick them out because the reflection from them will not be the same as those from the unflawed parts of the can. If there are unwanted particles, the computer will be able to pick them out because their reflection of light is different.

Whereas the human eye can perceive only 30 shades of gray between black and white, Tom's computer program delineates 256 shades of gray. To find the exact flaw, many of which are so small they cannot be seen by the human eye, Tom programs his computer to remove shades of gray layer by layer until only the flaws stand out. Each time a shade of gray is removed, part of the photograph which is that shade of gray disappears and leaves the remainder of the photograph much clearer to the human eye.

"I have been working with this program for years, and I still don't know exactly how it works," Tom says. "But it's all basic computing and can be reproduced by anybody at any time."

In November 1988, for no particular reason, Tom videotaped a twenty-fifth anniversary special by Dan Rather of the Kennedy assassination. The television show had displayed a picture taken by Mary Moorman, a spectator in Dallas who had photographed the grassy knoll area at the very second the president was shot.

Because he was retired, Tom had some spare time, so he ran the video image of the grassy knoll through his computer program. Keep in mind that his program is designed to look for metals. The first time he fed the video through, the car in which President Kennedy was driving showed up, but so did a flash of sunlight from the grassy knoll area.

"Sun reflects very differently off metal than it does off other objects," he says. "So the computer program will distinctively pick up any sunlight that is being reflected back to the camera from metal."

For six weeks, Tom played with his new hobby. He would slowly eliminate layer after layer of shade, hoping to discover what the metal was that glittered from near the fence area of the grassy knoll. The computer also allowed Tom to enlarge and concentrate solely on a certain part of the photograph.

As each layer came off, different subjects in the photograph disappeared. The trees near the grassy knoll went early. Nearby foliage was eliminated a couple of layers later. Each time, the piece of metal became brighter until it was in full view—a badge. It was that of a police officer or security guard or police detective. On the top of the silver badge is an eagle's head. The badge rests on the man's left chest. An identification plate is over his right chest pocket. There is some engraving, but it is unreadable. The computer also highlighted the silver buttons on the man's coat.

"If I had the original photograph," Tom says, "who knows, I might be able to give you the name of the guy behind the fence from the ID plate!"

There's another sparkle the computer is also picking up. As the layers of gray continue to vanish, it appears that the fourth piece of metal is hidden behind smoke. The closer to the metal you examine, the denser the smoke is.

"It's like the headlights on your car," Tom says. "The further it goes out, the more dispersed it gets. That's the same thing here. The smoke is originating from this piece of metal."

Slice by slice, the outer smoke goes away. All at once, you are faced with an image of a man's head behind what appears to be a gun. It was hidden behind the smoke. The man has coarse hair parted on the left side. Another layer goes and the man's brown eyes appear. One more layer is eliminated, and you can see a small pockmark on his left cheek. But then, as the next layer of gray is removed, much of the picture also disappears and very little is left on the screen.

"One more thing to show you," Tom says, in an almost boyish, look-what-I-found voice. He calls up a file on his computer. I have watched Tom do his thing on the half-dozen computers he has in his home, and, to be honest, it looks very impressive, but I have no idea on earth what he or his computer is doing.

"I've taken frame 313 of the Zapruder film, where there is a pink cloud over the president's head, and transferred it over to my hard drive," he says. As he goes layer by layer, he is able to enlarge and focus on different parts of the photograph. At first, all you can see are particles flying in the air. Then, as he continues to eliminate a few layers of gray, it becomes clear what we are looking at—pieces of President Kennedy's scalp and head. This was the same second the bullet had struck the president.

As the computer scans the remainder of the photograph, Tom has it focus on the neck area. When he eliminates levels of gray, thereby removing shadows, he spots a hole in the neck area of Kennedy's coat.

"This is where the missile went in," he says. "Look, it clearly shows the coat's fibers going inward, meaning he was shot from the front."

This was some of the most amazing news I had ever heard, or certainly ever seen. If his technique can be duplicated by scientists at Massachusetts Institute of Technology or a similar educational facility and is not subject to inadvertent manipulation and variation, this technology could end the government's claim of a single gunman. The technique will tell us where the bullet holes were and whether they were entrance or exit wounds. It will not, of course, tell us who shot and killed President Kennedy or why it was done. But that is not for me to answer. I am interested in the physical evidence and what it shows or does not show. Many critics get hung up on the who and why. They start with motive and work backward, trying to make the physical evidence support their conclusions.

And while I do not fully understand Tom's method, I am a firm believer in him and his analytical technique. Let me tell you why. In 1990, I was involved in a products liability case in Michigan. A man was killed when a drunk driver came across the highway's yellow line and struck an oncoming car. The man was buried without an autopsy. In the weeks that followed, he was believed to have died of head injuries he suffered when the hood of the car in which he was riding sprang up at the moment of impact, smashing through the windshield and slamming the man in the face. Federal regulations require that car hoods not spring up from the base when impacted.

Lawyers for the family, still not clear if the head injuries were the main cause of death, were considering having the body exhumed and had asked me if I would perform the autopsy. Before a final decision was reached, I suggested giving a photograph of the body taken by a state trooper to Tom Wilson for analysis. Using his technique, Tom removed several layers of gray and shadows, and there it was, clear as day—the laceration on the forehead definitely appeared to have caused severe internal head injuries. The body was exhumed later that week, and we discovered exactly what Tom's computer program said we would. The internal head injuries were significant. There was severe damage to the brain. To me, this verified the scientific validity of Tom's method.

As of the writing of this book, I am trying to get Tom much

better photographs of the Kennedy assassination to review. He now tells me that there is evidence that several of the autopsy photographs of the president's body taken at Bethesda, which I have supplied to him, may have been doctored or altered. His computer program allows him to detect what various materials being photographed are made of. Tom says that there is "clear and convincing evidence" that some of the autopsy photographs we have been looking at for three decades show more than just Jack Kennedy's body—they also reveal some plastic surgery or wax images or sculpting. In other words, when Tom's computer sends light into a photograph of President Kennedy's body during or after the autopsy, it receives back two different reflections. One is that of his natural skin. However, the second is of a false substance made to look like skin. I'm sure we will hear more from Tom and his computer in the years ahead.

Throughout the years, my family, especially my wife, Sigrid, has probably wished I had never gotten involved in the Kennedy case. The time spent, the heartache endured, the criticism directed at me, and the late-night telephone calls from so-called tipsters who have somehow obtained my home number are all routine after so many years, but that does not make them any less disruptive. Sigrid and my children have been the one constant source of strength in that they have listened to me babble on and on about new evidence.

But even Sigrid could not believe it when she called me to the phone one evening in November 1991.

"It's Marina Oswald," she said excitedly. "She's calling from Dallas and wants to talk with you."

Marina had been asked to appear on a television show, but she didn't feel right about it and wanted to know if I would fill in for her. I agreed, but I also did not let the opportunity handed me slip by without discussing Lee Harvey Oswald.

"Lee is as much a mystery to me," she said. About three years after Oswald was gunned down by Jack Ruby, Marina married Ken Porter, who was in the construction business in Dallas.

"Lee was a lousy husband, a lousy father, a lousy person," she said. "He first told me he had no mother, that she had died. Then one day out of the blue, his mother showed up. I could never figure him out. I was not and am not the enigma. Lee was the enigma." Friends who know her well believe she is still in love with Lee Harvey Oswald.

Though she seldom speaks about Oswald publicly, Marina was completely open with me, telling me everything she knew about her first husband. I think she was so open with me for two reasons: First, there are very few people she trusts, so she has to hold back telling certain of her insights and opinions. This, I am sure, has been very frustrating. Second, she believed that her telling me various details would help my investigation.

Here is what Marina told me about Oswald. He was born in 1939 in New Orleans. His father died two months before his birth. His mother moved from New Orleans to Fort Worth to Dallas and back to New Orleans during his childhood. Each move was accompanied by a new marriage for her. At seventeen, Oswald joined the marines, where he was described as a loner who had few friends. Twice he was court-martialed. However, military brass regarded Oswald as a highly intelligent person who was well-versed in international affairs. Strong evidence exists that he was recruited as an undercover operative or informant for the military.

In 1959, Oswald defected to the Soviet Union, where he was given temporary citizenship status. The communist government provided him an apartment in Minsk, a job, and a government stipend. That year he met and married Marina.

"He spoke Russian well enough that I first thought he was from another republic," she told me. "I was shocked to find out he was an American. But the way he acted and spoke attracted me to him. We dated and we married."

In June 1962, the couple, now the parents of a beautiful baby daughter, returned to the United States and settled in Dallas. The federal government even paid their moving expenses. This was strange, I thought, especially since Oswald, who has been described by federal authorities as a procommunist supporter of Cuban leader Fidel Castro, had voluntarily defected to the Soviet Union, forsaking his native country.

"It was a really big thing for Russian citizens to be allowed to leave the Soviet Union for America," Marina told me. "I was really surprised when they granted my traveling request and said I could go. But it was all Lee's doing. He set it all up. He got all the papers. I don't know how he did it, but he did."

Marina spoke very little English when she moved to the United

States, and Lee did very little to encourage her to learn. "He would always talk to me in Russian, which made me feel like I never had to learn English," she said. "Because I spoke no English, I had no friends, and no way of making new friends."

Marina said their marriage was stormy. Oswald's near-violent rages became frequent. They were separated for several months while Oswald went to New Orleans to find work. But after he was fired from various part-time jobs, he returned to Dallas in October 1963, where Ruth Paine, a friend of Marina, helped him get a job at the Texas School Book Depository for $1.25 an hour.

During this time, Marina said she lived with Paine in Irving while Oswald rented a one-bedroom apartment in Dallas for $8 a week. The apartment was so small that only the bed, a dresser, and table would fit in it. On a recent trip to Dallas, I was amazed to discover that the same apartment was up for rent at $55 a week.

Witnesses later told the FBI that they had seen Oswald carrying a long thin object covered with paper to work with him the morning of November 22. He had told them it was curtain rods. Shortly before 12:30 P.M., agents say, Oswald went to the depository's sixth-floor window at the southeast corner, repositioned some boxes so he wouldn't be seen, and waited for the president's motorcade to come. When it did, he fired, hid the gun behind some other boxes, and ran down to the lunchroom. About ninety seconds after the shooting, Oswald, who was drinking a soft drink on the second floor, was confronted by a Dallas police officer. The officer later testified that Oswald appeared calm and was not out of breath. Not suspecting any involvement, the officer did not detain Oswald.

Oswald then left the depository and boarded a city bus headed toward his apartment. After a few blocks, he exited the bus and hailed a taxi, which took him to within a few blocks of his apartment. He changed coats, picked up a pistol, and immediately left. About a dozen blocks from Oswald's apartment, witnesses claim that Dallas policeman J. D. Tippit, driving a squad car, pulled up beside a man later said to be Oswald and asked to see some identification. The man kept walking, ignoring the officer. Finally, Officer Tippit stopped his car, got out, and began to approach the man. According to witnesses, the man pulled out the handgun and shot the officer twice in the chest and once in the head. The man then walked over to where Officer Tippit lay and, putting the barrel of the pistol against his head, fired again. From there, various witnesses watched as the man walked several blocks to the Texas Theatre, into which he slipped without paying. A shoe store owner spotted the man and called the police, who arrested him inside the movie house. A few hours later, Oswald would be named as the killer of both the police officer and President Kennedy.

When Marina, who was watching television, first saw that President Kennedy had been shot and killed, a terrible feeling came over her. For reasons she has never explained, she immediately had a feeling that her husband was involved. Within hours, police had arrived at Marina's house to take her in for questioning.

"Everybody, especially the Warren Commission and the FBI, thought I was a Russian spy or mole," she told me. "But I was not. I may be a wart, but I have never been a mole."

She was allowed to see and speak with Lee Harvey Oswald for a few minutes. They were separated by a glass window and spoke through a telephone.

"He said everything was okay, but he didn't want to talk about it very much," she said. "He looked really scared. He wanted to talk only about small, insignificant things, like my new shoes. He was nervous and I was afraid at that time that he had been involved."

That would be her last conversation with her husband. For years, she didn't know what to believe, not until 1979 when the House Select Committee on Assassinations conducted its hearings. It was then that she began to believe that it was quite possible that Lee Harvey Oswald was not the crazed lone gunman many made him out to be.

"I was scared to death to say publicly that my husband is not guilty of this crime," Marina said. "But I can finally say it now and believe it. I believe he was a patsy. He knew he was dealing with some pretty bad people, and I think he went back to the house to get the gun to protect himself.

"On one hand, Lee was a brilliant, manipulative person," she said in our conversation. "But at other times, he was as dumb an idiot as a person can be.

"The Lee I knew really loved JFK. I think he knew of the conspiracy, knew the people who did it, but I do not think he pulled the trigger. I think he realized too late that he was going to be the fall guy," she said.

In late 1991, Marina Oswald Porter was finally granted full citizenship in the United States. She told me she was planning a return to Russia. She had not been there in thirty years and much had changed. Then she added, "Even though I was not American, I was proud of President Kennedy. He was a great leader. When I got my passport, it read, 'This person is to be shown complete respect and dignity as a citizen of the United States.' " She began crying. "I just want my children and their children to know the truth about Lee. That's all I want."

I told Marina that I agreed with her, that Lee Oswald most likely was a patsy. In fact, I would venture to take that a step further and say there's a high likelihood he played no direct role in the actual shooting. But speculating and proving are two different things. The next time I was in Dallas, I promised Marina, I would call and we would get together for dinner.

In November 1992, I finally sat down and talked with Marina about Lee for several hours. She is an extremely bright woman, and stunningly beautiful. But she also is a very confused person, not sure whom to trust or what to believe. Many people have taken advantage of her—people who want to make a few easy dollars capitalizing on her situation. Marina goes along with these people because she frequently needs the money and because she hopes they will help reveal the truth about her late husband. But in the end, she discovers that most of these people are only looking to make a buck, not correct history's wrongs. Marina deserves much more than that.

No more than a few days after I had spoken with Marina, I was secretly supplied with a copy of the KGB's official report on Lee Harvey Oswald and the Kennedy assassination. The KGB was undergoing significant changes following the downfall of communism and the breakup of the Soviet Union, and through a source at the FBI, I was able to review a thirty-five-page file that the KGB had kept on Oswald. Mark Curriden, a reporter for the *Atlanta Constitution* with whom I am writing this book, had the KGB report authenticated by FBI agents he trusted. It was one of those agents, who was familiar with Russian, who interpreted the report.

According to notes in the file, the KGB believed that Oswald was a spy for the CIA or the U.S. military when he sought shelter in the Soviet Union in 1959. According to the translator, the more appropriate term was not *spy* but *snitch* or *informant.* The file said that Oswald was "under constant surveillance" during his stay in Russia. Among those it identifies as KGB operatives informing the government of Oswald's activities were a neighbor in his apartment building, three co-workers at his factory, and two women with whom he had sexual relations. The file refers only briefly to Marina, and then only as a companion to Oswald. According to the typed notes, Oswald worked alone, or at least the KGB was unable to ascertain any contacts he made with known American agents living and working in the Soviet Union. The notes describe Oswald as "anxious," sometimes quick to anger, and with a weakness for liquor and women.

Many of the documents are nothing more than descriptions of Oswald and his typical workday and those he associated with after work. There is background on his family and his brief career in the military. One document states that Oswald was taught Russian by the military intelligence division. However, it gives no data to support the statement. A completely separate document covers Oswald's decision to return to the United States. While much of it details his and Marina's request to the U.S. government, there was one very interesting statement. The note states that Oswald will assuredly be allowed to return if the American intelligence community believes he has fulfilled his purpose here or if they have another task for him domestically.

One document inserted into the Oswald file discusses the Kennedy assassination, but it gives very few details. The document is more of a summary closing Oswald's file. It states that KGB agents and operatives did not believe the U.S. government's position that Oswald acted alone. In fact, the summary states that, according to intelligence reports in a separate KGB file on the Kennedy assassination, there is evidence that factions within the American intelligence community, be it CIA, FBI, or military, played a role in the assassination. However, the report states that there is no indication that it was a government-orchestrated coup.

To me, this meant that the agencies themselves were probably not involved in Kennedy's death, but that various agents or officials within those branches supplied information or assisted in the coverup. The report acknowledges the claims that the Castro government played a role, but it also dismisses such a position as "capitalistic propaganda."

The bottom line, according to the KGB summary: Lee Harvey Oswald was not capable of plotting and carrying out the assassination of President Kennedy on his own.

The KGB file listed friends that Oswald associated with in Russia and upon his return to the United States. However, the file did not contain any names of Soviet agents who watched over or investigated Oswald. I found it quite ironic that the KGB was willing to open its files regarding the Kennedy assassination, but our own government refuses to do the same.

Just when this fiery issue seemed to be completely extinguished, it roared back hotter and heavier than it ever was. And it was no investigative reporting, scientific discovery, or political push that revived the interest, but a movie. It says something about the society in which we live when a film can dictate news events, and that's exactly what Oliver Stone's *JFK* did.

In the summer of 1991, Mr. Stone called, asking if he could hire me as a technical consultant for the movie. Realizing the opportunity, I quickly agreed and flew to New Orleans, where much of the film was being shot. I helped develop several of the picture's key scenes. One is the courtroom scene in which Kevin Costner, playing New Orleans district attorney Jim Garrison, demonstrates to the jury hearing the evidence against businessman Clay Shaw just how silly and incomprehensible the single bullet theory is.

Costner uses a chart and two assistants, one sitting in front of the other just as Kennedy and Connally were that day in Dallas, to show the acute angular turns and gyrations the bullet would have had to make in midair. It was my suggestion that led to the film's portrayal of this dramatic highlight. The chart he used was very similar to the one I had first displayed twenty years earlier on the ABC television news show, *20/20*, which was doing a program on the Kennedy assassination and invited me to be a guest.

None of this is to say that I fully agree with the scenario that Oliver Stone laid out. As I pointed out earlier, I do not believe in Garrison's multiple conspiracy theory, but I do believe *JFK* was a wonderfully written and produced movie with outstanding acting and technical direction.

The most amazing response to the movie did not come from the general public, nor from movie critics, but from the all-powerful news media establishment. The movie critics praised the film, nominating it for several Oscars, including best picture. Siskel and Ebert, the Chicago movie critics, gave it the all-important "two thumbs up." Roger Ebert went so far as to call *JFK* the best movie of the year.

However, the reaction from the news divisions was astonishing. Instead of reporting that more than three-fourths of all Americans do not believe the Warren Commission, and instead of using their investigative skills to dig up what really happened on November 22, 1963, in Dallas, the great newspapers, like the *New York Times* and the *Washington Post,* slammed Oliver Stone for allegedly exaggerating the truth or misstating history. Not once did any of the major newspapers ever challenge the FBI or CIA to find out what happened to President Kennedy's brain and autopsy materials.

The news media bought the lone assassin theory early on. It was, quite probably, an innocent acceptance. Remember, this was pre-Watergate and pre-Vietnam, so investigative reporting was not in vogue. Today, every journalist is an "investigative reporter." But I truly do not understand why today's newspapers and television newsrooms have not delved into this case. Maybe the news media feels backed into a corner. To stand up now and admit they were wrong would be terribly humiliating and extremely embarrassing.

Sometimes, it appears that the major news media has assumed the role of defending the Warren Commission and its findings. A perfect example of this came in May 1992 when the *Journal of the American Medical Association* (JAMA) printed an interview with Drs. Humes and Boswell and editorially endorsed them as telling God's truth. The article basically quoted the two pathologists as saying they stick by their initial autopsy report. The media reprinted the interviews and hailed them as "new evidence." Several newspapers, including the *New York Times* and the *Atlanta Journal,* published articles about the interviews on the front pages.

That night, I was called by the producers of *The Larry King Show,* which airs on the Cable News Network, and asked to participate in a roundtable discussion with the editor of JAMA. I agreed. The first question I was asked was really the only one I needed to answer.

"Does this new evidence or testimony change your mind about the way President Kennedy was assassinated?"

"First, there is nothing new in this JAMA report," I responded. "You can take these two guys [Humes and Boswell], freeze their bodies, unthaw them in a thousand years, listen to their story and it will still be garbage. These are the very same two people who wrote this fairy tale and for them to now come out of hiding and repeat it does not make it nonfiction."

While the news media tore into Oliver Stone for possible inaccuracies in his movie, the same reporters did not critique the JAMA article. They did not point out that the JAMA article and its editor, Dr. George Lundberg, relied solely on the testimony of Drs. Humes and Boswell. It was a completely one-sided article. It's like Pat Buchanan saying that after interviewing G. Gordon Liddy and Howard Hunt, he has determined that everything was all right with the Watergate break-in and that Nixon committed no crimes!

The journalists did not point out that all the forensic pathologists on the House Select Committee panel, including Dr. Baden, have been openly critical of the autopsy performed by Drs. Humes and Boswell. I also found it remarkable that Dr. Lundberg said he decided not to address the single bullet theory in his article because it was not relevant. To say the single bullet theory is not relevant to the Kennedy assassination investigation is like saying the Nazis were not influential in World War II.

Four months later, in early October 1992, JAMA came out with yet another article on the Kennedy autopsy, this time featuring an interview with Dr. Pierre Finck, the army pathologist at the autopsy. While the other article quoting Drs. Humes and Boswell made me angry, the second article left me frustrated.

"I have nothing to hide," Dr. Finck is quoted as saying. "I am not part of a conspiracy. There was no military interference. The direction of the fatal wound traveled from back to front."

This statement completely confused me. This is not what Dr. Finck had told me fifteen months after he performed the autopsy. The morning after I had given my critique of the Warren Commission report at the 1965 annual meeting of the American Academy of Forensic Sciences, Dr. Finck came up to me and told me how right I was about the investigation and autopsy being botched. Very explicitly, he told me he was not pleased with the way the autopsy was conducted. Then there was his sworn testimony in 1969 in the Clay Shaw case which appeared to completely contradict what he was now saying. Feeling a need to vent the frustration, I immediately fired off a letter to JAMA.

Dear JAMA:
    Dr. Finck now states in his interview with you that there was no interference with the autopsy by an Army General. In 1969, testifying under oath in the Clay Shaw trial in New

Orleans, Dr. Finck stated that he and his colleagues were ordered by a General (whose name he was unable to remember) not to dissect out the bullet wounds of JFK's back and neck. Which statement do you think is more likely to be true—the one made six years after the autopsy under oath, or one made twenty-nine years later in an unsworn, self-serving interview?

Dr. Finck now states in his interview that the postmortem examination on JFK was a "complete autopsy." However, in his written report to the commanding officer at the Armed Forces Institute of Pathology in 1963, just days after the autopsy was completed, Dr. Finck stated that the autopsy was "incomplete."

Cyril Wecht

There can be no question that Oliver Stone's film and the attention it drew to the Kennedy assassination have led to many significant developments in the case. At the very least, the film refocused widespread public attention on the crime. As I wrote this book, there was a growing momentum among members of Congress to open the files of the House Select Committee on Assassinations, which are supposed to remain closed until 2029, as well as all records of the CIA and FBI.

In fact, a special five-member commission was established by the JFK Records Collection Act of 1992 to review all government documents related to the assassination to see if there is any reason those documents should not be made public. The review board will have great powers to require all government agencies, including the CIA, to provide them with every file the agency has. Once the records have been reviewed by the board, they will be made public at the National Archives within thirty days.

Unfortunately, the law excludes the autopsy records donated by the Kennedy family to the archives.

Under the law, which was passed in October 1992 and signed by President Bush, organizations like the American Bar Association, the American Historical Society, the Society of American Archivists, and the Organization of American Historians submitted names of nominees to the president to appoint to the review panel. However, President Clinton was not limited to just those names, but was only required to consider them. As of this writing, the president had not yet selected any of the five members to serve on the commission.

Generally, I think this legislation is a good thing. However, we should expect no bombshells or smoking guns. There will be no minutes of the Board of Directors of the CIA stating that at a particular meeting in early 1963, the board voted to have Jack Kennedy assassinated.

Thinking otherwise would fit a skit on *Saturday Night Live.* Just imagine. The press spokesman for the Central Intelligence Agency hands out a 350-page, newly released document detailing evidence from the Kennedy assassination. "There's really nothing new in this," the CIA press guy begins, "except on pages 176 and 177—there is something we have overlooked for years. It appears there was evidence that Oswald was assisted by two CIA agents and a couple of Dallas police officers after all. Our mistake. We're sorry. Hope all's forgiven and forgotten."

This is never going to happen. But I do believe the opening of all the files is a positive move, and while it will not produce a smoking gun, it may give us names and evidence that will point us in the right direction. And it certainly will send the rats protecting the myth of the Kennedy assassination scurrying for cover.

Among those saying the secret documents should be made public is Representative Louis Stokes, a Democrat from Ohio, who chaired the committee. In a brief telephone conversation, Representative Stokes told me the public would be most interested in secretly recorded, never-before-released tapes of undercover FBI agents talking with Carlos Marcello, a well-known Mafia crime figure who lived in New Orleans.

Representative Stokes told me that the secret conversations occurred in the late 1970s when Mr. Marcello was under investigation for bribery involving Louisiana state insurance contracts. The House Committee found in 1979 that Mr. Marcello "had the motive, means and opportunity to have President Kennedy assassinated, though it was unable to establish direct evidence of Marcello's complicity." The committee also noted links between Oswald, Jack Ruby, and Mafia figures, specifically Mr. Marcello and Jimmy Hoffa. In the end, the House Committee found that Kennedy "was probably assassinated as a result of a conspiracy."

In January 1992, I spoke by telephone with Tampa, Florida, trial lawyer Frank Ragano about detailed allegations he had made that Hoffa had ordered President Kennedy killed. Mr. Ragano had represented several major organized crime figures in the 1960s and 1970s. He said he was told by Hoffa in early 1963 to carry a message to Florida mob boss Santo Trafficante and Mr. Marcello. Mr. Ragano claimed that Hoffa selected him to relay the message because he was attorney for all of them and therefore was covered by the attorney-client privilege. That privilege, he said, bound him ethically from revealing the message to authorities.

"Jimmy told me to tell Marcello and Trafficante they had to kill the president," Ragano said. "Hoffa said to me, 'This has to be done.' "

When Ragano met the two mobsters later that week and transmitted Hoffa's message, he expected the two to laugh as if it were a joke. "But they didn't," he said. "They glanced at each other in a very serious vein."

Within minutes of Kennedy's assassination being announced on television, Ragano says that Hoffa called him to ask if he had heard the "good news." Later that night, Ragano says he joined Trafficante in a hotel bar to share a drink "celebrating Kennedy's death."

Adding support to the theory that the mob was responsible for Kennedy's murder was a revelation in 1967 by a high-ranking Miami police official who said he had obtained direct information just days before the president was killed that there would be an assassination attempt. Until days before he actually journeyed to Texas, President Kennedy's itinerary originally called for him to visit South Florida first, then go to Dallas and Fort Worth. About a week before the trip, Miami Intelligence Division lieutenant Everett Kay heard from a confidential informant that rumors abounded in "right-wing circles" that Kennedy would be shot and killed on his visit to Dade County.

Lieutenant Kay had the informant wear a wire to record any such conversations. As the movie *JFK* prepared to open amid controversy, Lieutenant Kay played a twenty-eight-year-old tape of the informant to members of the news media. On the tape, a wealthy Georgia man named Joseph Milteer, a known white supremacist, is heard telling the police informant that "Kennedy is a marked man." The informant is told that Kennedy would be killed "from an office building with a high-powered rifle."

"Oh yes, it's in the working," Milteer is heard saying. The informant is told that the gun would easily be broken down into pieces. Milteer also dismissed the informant's concern that the assassination of the president would cause a major furor.

"Hell, they'll pick up somebody within hours after, if anything like that would happen, just to throw the public off," Milteer says.

Lieutenant Kay said he immediately informed the FBI and Secret Service of the report, and the Miami motorcade, which was planned to be open just like in Dallas, was canceled. The detective says he turned a copy of the tape over to the FBI after the assassination, but there was never any followup by the federal agency.

Just as many tips have helped point me in the right direction in this case, many more only muddy the water. Take the Robert Russell claim as an example. Much of what I was hearing from other people seemed to give what he was saying credibility. In fact, when I spoke with Frank Ragano, he said he did remember an associate of Jimmy Hoffa's by the name of Robert Russell. However, Mr. Ragano said he could not recall what their association was.

Mr. Russell explained to me that in 1967, he met a woman named Cindy, who had been an employee of Jack Ruby's in New Orleans. The pair had become close, though he did not elaborate on their relationship other than to say they lived together for a period. Cindy claimed that on the day Kennedy was killed, she had driven an associate of Ruby's named Ralph Raul to the parking lot behind the grassy knoll. The man, she said, carried a violin case. A few minutes later, the man returned to the car and she drove him back to her apartment, where he met a Secret Service agent and Jack Ruby.

A couple of hours later, the men departed, but they left behind the violin case. Cindy said she looked inside and found a rifle, ten bullets, a map of the president's motorcade route, and a check for one hundred thousand dollars payable to Jack Ruby. Cindy told Mr. Russell she stashed the items in a container and drove to New Orleans. It was there that Mr. Russell met her.

While staying at Cindy's apartment, Mr. Russell said he noticed pasteboard missing from under the kitchen sink in her apartment. After pulling away the plywood, he discovered a small room, nothing more than a crawl space, with no windows or doors. There he

found the items Cindy had described and took them to his bedroom. He then replastered the hole.

Mr. Russell said that it was Bobby Kennedy who took the president's brain and had it safely hidden for further examination.
This made sense. Who else would have had access to the autopsy
materials other than Bobby Kennedy? After Russell came in possession of the rifle and the other materials from Cindy, he said
he contacted Bobby Kennedy, who told him to keep the evidence
in a safe place and let no one know he had them.

Russell also stated that Bobby Kennedy had taken the autopsy
evidence, including the brain, to a priest at a small church in rural
upstate New York and told him to keep the items in case something ever happened to him. By this time, Bobby Kennedy had
begun his bid for the U.S. Senate seat from New York. According
to Russell, Kennedy told the priest that if he were killed, the priest
should contact Robert Russell and release the evidence only to
him. And when the senator was killed in 1968 in California, Russell
claimed he came in possession of the autopsy materials, including
the brain.

Much of Russell's story was difficult to believe, but one point
in particular I believed to be fantasy. Of all the powerful and influential friends Bobby Kennedy had, why would he confide all
this to a low-life snitch? All my strong doubts were further compounded by the fact that, despite my repeated statements that I
would be willing to examine the evidence Russell had at my laboratory in Pittsburgh, he constantly delayed any such proceeding.
As he went in and out of jail on God only knows what charges,
Mr. Russell kept delaying things. I was beginning to doubt such
an examination would ever take place and realized that Mr. Russell fit into one of the two categories I have previously mentioned:
he was a world-class scammer or a nut.

As the days, weeks, and months passed, it became clear to me
that Mr. Russell wanted something besides the truth—he wanted
money. This man whom I had never met wrote to me one day
asking me for a loan. I have a long-standing philosophy that I only
lend money to people I believe and trust. After Mr. Russell denied
my demand to examine the evidence he had, I told him I would
cease my correspondence with him.

He made one last attempt to convince me. He sent me a VHS
home movie he had made. The movie, filmed in a swamplike area,

possibly the Everglades, shows Russell, a man about forty-five years old, five feet, six inches tall, weighing about 150 pounds with graying brown hair, digging up some items, including the rifle allegedly used in the Kennedy homicide.

I was unconvinced and terminated our correspondence.

In the meantime, Mr. Russell had contacted several other people also researching the assassination of JFK. One who took a particular interest—by that I mean he bit hook, line, and sinker—was Peter Lemkin. Mr. Lemkin, who came to my office twice to discuss Mr. Russell's information, was quite convinced of Mr. Russell's claim to have missing evidence. He was so persuaded that he confided in me that he had already paid Mr. Russell one hundred thousand dollars for two of the guns Mr. Russell said were used in the assassination.

Mr. Lemkin said he understood my doubt, but asked if he did get his hands on these materials, could he convince me to take the time to examine them. I agreed, realizing I was investing no money or time and had nothing to lose.

But then, on December 30, 1991, I received a letter from Mr. Lemkin that I had long predicted would come.

Cyril,

I don't quite know what to say. This is one of the most mortifying moments of my life. It now appears that Russell and Lacelle were pulling a world-class confidence scam—a total fraud.

I fell for it and so did several other researchers. I apologize profusely and plan to crawl into a hole for a long time.

I will be bringing suit for fraud and a variety of other things against Russell. I have lost a fortune and much more in spirit and hope for a break in the case. I will probably never recover the $100,000.

Begging your forgiveness,

Peter Lemkin

By now, I had become extremely fascinated with Robert Russell, so I personally contacted and interviewed Russell's parole officer in California, Chris Brown. He told me that what he had learned about Russell was "enough to write a book." The parole officer said he had viewed a videotape confiscated at Mr. Russell's house in which a brain, or what looks like a brain, is contained in something resembling a pail or a bucket. The brain, he said, has missing chunks. He said there is some information to believe that Mr. Russell had ties to the Mafia in the 1960s, but nothing to the extent to which he boasted.

"The whole thing is a farce, a scam, and Robert Russell is nothing more than a professional con man," Mr. Brown told me. What if it had been true? I thought. It might have solved this case once and for all.

Mr. Brown said that Mr. Russell had confessed to him that the whole thing was a fraud. "This guy is very good at this," he said. "He had several exclusive contracts with people all over the country, individual JFK researchers, tabloid magazines, and television shows, all which have paid him significant amounts of money but have never gotten a drop of true evidence about the Kennedy assassination."

Mr. Russell's parole had been revoked, and he was sent back to San Quentin prison. The Santa Clara district attorney's office also was considering prosecuting Mr. Russell on fraud charges. Besides lying about the brain, he had also lied to Lemkin about the guns, which he said were used to kill Kennedy. "We traced the guns and found out he bought them from a pawnshop just last year and then claimed they were the Kennedy murder weapons," Mr. Brown said.

"The Secret Service and the FBI came down here to interview him about what information he really had about Kennedy, and he tried to get them to pay him money," the parole officer said. "In the end, he admitted to them he really had zero evidence."

Incidents like this and people like Robert Russell are the reasons the Kennedy assassination may never be solved. For every legitimate researcher, there are five people like Mr. Russell who muddy the waters for the rest of us. They are true wackos who are not interested in truth or justice, but are greedy con men preying on those who are afraid not to pursue every alleyway, every pawnshop or strip bar, read every document just to see if there are any clues there.

It seems like there's a new solution or twist to the Kennedy assassination every couple of months. This also hurts the real investigation. Take, for example, the researchers who claimed to be able to prove that the president was indeed shot by a second gunman—a Secret Service agent—but that his gun went off accidentally. To me, this is completely absurd and without any supporting evidence. If the case is going to be solved, it must be with physical evidence. That is the only way it will satisfy the American public.

So what do I believe happened that day in Dallas? Based on the physical evidence I have personally reviewed, I know what did not happen—Lee Harvey Oswald did not shoot and kill President John F. Kennedy by himself. Most probably he was not a shooter at all that day. In any event, there had to be a second gunman shooting from the grassy knoll area. The physical and medical evidence demands it. And so does the testimony of dozens of witnesses.

Take my good friend Dr. Charles Crenshaw, who was a surgical resident at Parkland Memorial Hospital the day the president was carried in to the emergency room. He looked at Jack Kennedy's body that day. He saw the gunshot wound to the front of the neck, and he says unequivocally it was an entrance wound. His testimony today matches what two other surgeons who worked on President Kennedy told a press conference just an hour after they declared the president dead—that the bullet wound in the neck was an entrance wound.

I do have my own thoughts about what could have happened that day in Dallas, but they are all based on speculation after talking with dozens of people who were witnesses and people who have investigated this crime for thirty years. I believe there probably was a small group of maverick or rogue agents within the CIA who, for many possible reasons—they disliked Kennedy's stance regarding Cuba and Castro; they were not pleased with his talk about thawing the "cold war" between the U.S. and the Soviet Union; they were concerned about his announced plans to withdraw all military and intelligence help from Vietnam—independently decided that President Kennedy was a threat to their American way of life. When I say small, I mean three, four, possibly six people maximum.

To the people who say that, if there was such a conspiracy within the CIA, someone would have spilled the beans by now, I say, hogwash. These were professional, career agents—and I'm not talking about the director of the CIA in Washington—who were well entrenched in the business of domestic and foreign intelligence. Their informants and sources were widespread, from high in the Kremlin to the Washington political establishment to organized crime. These guys were in the business of keeping secrets. That's what they did for a living—plot and orchestrate in a clandestine fashion. These are agents who would not tell their wives or children or best friends about the secrets they harbored. This was their religion; to violate it would be to violate the most coveted trust of their religion.

We know that the CIA had a working relationship with the Mafia. It was top crime kingpins the intelligence community turned to in obtaining information about invading Sicily and Italy in World War II. So the contacts and relationships were already in place, and the channels of communication already developed. The CIA used Mafia figures in several attempts to kill Fidel Castro in Cuba.

I believe the CIA agents' role in the Kennedy assassination was this: they presented members of organized crime, who had a major bone to pick with the Kennedy administration, with the opportunity and plan; all the Mafia had to do was carry it out. And that's exactly what happened. There was a secondary coverup of an extensive nature that involved J. Edgar Hoover and the FBI, but it had nothing to do with the killing of President Kennedy. The secondary coverup dealt solely with the investigation that followed.

Were President Johnson or FBI director J. Edgar Hoover involved in the assassination? I simply cannot believe that. That's not to say that either man shed many tears about what happened that day in Dallas. There was probably joy in their hearts. In fact, President Johnson stated publicly and to many of his staffers years later that he never believed the Warren Commission report. But that he or Hoover was involved or even had some kind of advanced notice is something I doubt very seriously.

Now, I do believe that both men may have played key roles in the coverup after the assassination. Why? Who really knows, but there may have been a decision by senior governmental officials to suppress evidence from the American people. It may have seemed like a wise choice at the time, given the chaotic mood of the nation. These leaders may have believed that, had the American public been told that rogue U.S. intelligence agents had murdered its president, there would have been rioting in the streets. But assuming that scenario is true, there is no reason today, more than thirty years later, to continue to withhold the truth.

Hoover certainly did not push for a full, thorough investigation to determine who really shot President Kennedy. But then again, here was a man who throughout the 1950s and 1960s continually argued that there was no organized crime or Mafia operating in the United States. Was he on the mob's payroll, as some researchers have claimed? Or was he, as British journalist Anthony Summers claims, compromised by the mob's possession of photographs showing him involved in homosexual activity? There can be no doubt that Hoover looked after himself and his agency first and considered the people's right to know the truth secondary.

While I have no doubt of Mafia involvement in the Kennedy assassination, I cannot believe it was the mob alone who carried this out. The crime bosses knew that if they did such an act and were ever caught or implicated, the American public would demand their immediate and total elimination, no matter what the cost. But with the inside assistance and protection offered by agents of the CIA, the Mafia felt safe from a government crackdown.

And there were those elements within the CIA who believed that when they looked at the American flag, they saw a deeper red, white, and blue than the rest of us see. These people knew that President Kennedy had expressed a desire to splinter the CIA. They believed that was not in the best interests of our country and took it upon themselves to stop John Kennedy from fulfilling his objective.

By the same token, although Castro and his procommunist supporters were delighted to see Kennedy killed, it is highly improbable that the Cuban leader had anything to do in advance with the assassination. Like the mob leaders, he knew that if he ordered Kennedy's elimination and the American public found out, his little island would have been turned into a huge Caribbean whirlpool from our bombers.

Can you imagine what would have happened if Lee Harvey Oswald had not been killed? How could the authorities have taken this case to trial? Based upon my legal training and experience, judges and juries would have run the government's prosecutors out of court.

"Your honor, we believe the victim was fatally shot in the head.

"No, your honor, we don't have the brain. We used to have the brain, but we got rid of it so the defense forensic pathologist would not be able to see it.

"Yes, your honor, we used to have autopsy slides and Kodachromes of the chest wounds, but they're not around any longer either.

"Yes, your honor, we did do experiments to try to reconstruct what we believe happened and those experiments prove us wrong, but we're certainly not going to repeat those experiments and we're going to do everything we can to keep the defense from repeating them.

"Yes, your honor, we do believe that the bullet was a magical missile that could stop in midair and make several acute turns."

What do you think any judge or jury in America would do upon hearing this kind of nonsense? They would be so inflamed and insulted that it would not take them ten minutes in the jury room before the entire case was thrown out of court on its merits.

In fact, such a mock trial was conducted in June 1992 by the Washington, D.C., Bar Association. The mock jury consisted of trial lawyers who attended the one-day seminar. Robert Blakey argued for the government that there were three bullets, one gun, and one gunman, Lee Harvey Oswald.

Testifying for the opposite side of the debate, I explained the "single bullet theory" to the panel of lawyers.

"This bullet passed through Kennedy's neck, knocked out four inches of one of Governor Connally's ribs, fractured a wrist bone, and lodged in the governor's thigh—all without suffering significant damage," I told the mock jury. "That's a rather amazing bullet. It becomes increasingly amazing as I grow older. In order for the single bullet to line up with both President Kennedy and Governor Connally, the Warren Commission concocted an unlikely series of body positions so that the bullet could inflict all those wounds. That's why it is necessary for the Warren Commission supporters to keep pushing Governor Connally over and over to his left. In another ten years, they will have him seated in his wife, Nellie's, lap."

The panel enjoyed the debate. While there was no formal jury deliberations or verdict, the judge presiding over the hearing did ask the lawyers on the panel for a show of hands, and more than three-fourths said they leaned toward the conspiracy theory and did not believe Oswald acted alone.

It's doubtful we shall ever know all the answers. However, the main question can still be solved. We can determine if there was only one gunman, or two or three and where they shot from. We can know who did it and why there was a coverup afterward.

Robert Russell may not have it, but I believe John F. Kennedy's brain is still out there somewhere. I doubt it was ever destroyed. Some person has it and a complete examination would reveal the answer to the first question. It may take a deathbed confession, but there are still people alive who have details about what really happened that day in Dallas. One day, they will enlighten the whole world.

The only other solution is exhuming the president's body. Even today, there are many things we could learn and mysteries we could solve by examining the body. Most importantly, the bones of the skull could be examined and it could be determined if the bullets came from the front, back, or side. It could tell us if there were more than two shots. An exhumation also would confirm or lay to rest any suspicions that the autopsy photographs were tampered with.

But the day the Kennedy family allows the president's body to be exhumed and examined is the day that I climb to the top of the Sears Tower in Chicago, jump off, and fly across the beaches of Lake Michigan. It's not going to happen. Throughout this entire case, the most amazing mystery to me has been the reaction of the Kennedy children. If I were ever killed in a mysterious manner, my children would not sleep until all questions were answered. They would raise holy hell. And yet the Kennedy children and the Kennedy family appear to have no interest in learning the truth about their father's murder. To me, this is completely incomprehensible.

In the fall of 1991, I once again journeyed to Dallas and spent several hours at Dealey Plaza. There are several fascinating places to visit in Dallas to learn more about the assassination of the president. The JFK Assassination Information Center, headed by Larry Howard, a key critic and researcher, has the best collection and organization of evidence that contradicts the Warren Commission's conclusions. It is located in a retail shopping center two blocks from Dealey Plaza. There is also a great tour bus that operates out of the center and takes visitors through every step Oswald is supposed to have made that day.

In my recent visit to Texas, I walked the motorcade route from Houston Street to Elm Street. At the time, due to the filming of *JFK,* Dealey Plaza was nearly identical to what it looked like in November 1963. I stood in the middle of Elm Street, in the exact spot where the president was shot. It's very much like a canyon in that once you start in, there's no way out. It's all one-way streets. I looked behind me, up toward the sixth-floor window where Oswald was allegedly standing. Tree branches partially blocked the way. I then glanced over to my right, at the fence at the end of the grassy knoll. It was in clear view. As I glanced over toward Houston Street, I saw the old city jail—the spot where Jack Ruby would be held for several years after killing Oswald. I then walked up to the sixth floor of the Texas School Book Depository.

The Dallas Historical Society has done a wonderful job of refurbishing the floor into a place where tourists and history buffs can relive that day in 1963. As I stared out the window of the sixth floor, the exact spot where Oswald supposedly stood, I looked out over Houston and Elm streets. Why did Oswald not shoot the president as the motorcade proceeded down Houston Street? The view was much clearer and straight on. Why did he wait until the president's car had traveled so far down Elm Street that his sight would have been sporadically blocked by tree branches? If Oswald had indeed been the lone gunman, why did he wait and seriously compromise his neurotic plan?

What this case needs is a special prosecutor—a person with integrity who is willing to sacrifice all to find the truth. The brain may never be located. The body will never be exhumed. A deathbed confession will likely never come. No governmental agency will ever admit to the truth. It will take the appointment of a person who is willing to fight all odds and who has complete authority to investigate the assassination without obstacles or roadblocks before this crime will ever be solved.

Yes, Lee Harvey Oswald probably was involved in the assassination attempt in some fashion, or knew something about it at the very least. He may have killed Officer Tippit that afternoon.

But from all the physical evidence I have reviewed, using all the forensic knowledge and experience I have, there is no doubt in my mind that Lee Harvey Oswald was not the lone gunman. Indeed, the hard evidence strongly indicates that he did not shoot at either Kennedy or Connally.

I do not believe the Department of Justice and its sister organization, the FBI, have any interest in solving this case. Both agencies demonstrated that attitude again in June 1993 when John Connally died of pulmonary fibrosis at the age of seventy-six. Before Governor Connally was buried, I joined a request by the Assassination Archives and Research Center of Washington, D.C., asking the FBI to recover the bullet fragments still lodged in his body.

"Subjected to neutron activation analysis and other scientific procedures, these fragments may be able to resolve the controversy as to whether President Kennedy was assassinated as the result of a conspiracy," we said in our request to Attorney General Janet Reno.

Amazingly, the Justice Department initially agreed it would be important for them to retrieve the fragments. However, when the Connally family rejected an FBI request to recover the bullet fragments, the agency did a total cop-out by completely dropping its inquiry. I know such a request may seem insensitive to the Connally family, but this was a matter of national public interest.

One day, the American public will know the truth about who killed their president and why. And I firmly believe it will be physical evidence that has yet to be released or tested that will give us those answers.

2
Evidence of a Second Gun:
The Assassination of Senator Robert F. Kennedy

The summer of 1968 was a wonderful time in my personal life. But it was also a period in which some great miscarriages of justice occurred, causing me and the country great pain.

As chief forensic pathologist of the Allegheny County coroner's office, I was being encouraged to seek election for the position of coroner the next year. But even more exciting was the birth of my fourth child and first daughter. Born on June 3, Ingrid had strands of her mother's blond hair and weighed seven and a half pounds. My family has always come first in my life, but I was doubly excited about the birth of my daughter.

These were the days when they kept mother and newborn in the hospital for a few days for observation. It was also before hospital and medical costs went through the roof.

After visiting the hospital late in the evening of June 4, I returned home with our three sons, David, Daniel, and Benjamin, to prepare for a trip to Washington, D.C., early the next morning, Wednesday, June 5. I was scheduled to speak to members of the Practicing Law Institute on the subject of medical malpractice. I was then to continue on to San Juan, Puerto Rico, to lecture at a seminar sponsored by the Association of Trial Lawyers of America.

About 3:00 A.M., I was awakened by the telephone. As chief

pathologist in Pittsburgh, I was used to early morning calls from the police saying there had been a mysterious death and my presence was needed. This time, however, it was my good friend and colleague Dr. Tom Noguchi on the telephone. In 1967, Tom had been named coroner and chief medical examiner of Los Angeles County, California, a very sought-after and controversial position. Before I could relay the wonderful news about my wife's giving birth to a beautiful baby girl, Tom interrupted. He had some bad news.

"Senator Robert Kennedy has been shot!"

I had gone to bed watching news of the California presidential primary, which projected Senator Kennedy as the likely victor. This win, the political analysts said, could guarantee him the Democratic nomination and pole-vault him past the Republican candidate, Richard Nixon, in the race for the White House.

"He's not been pronounced dead," Tom said, "but hospital officials have told me privately it's only a matter of time."

"You cannot let what happened in Dallas happen again," I interjected.

"I know," Tom responded. "That's why I'm calling. What plans should I make? Are there specific things I should do? Are you interested in flying out here?"

With my wife in the hospital, the three boys under my care, and my prior commitments to speak in Washington and in Puerto Rico over the next three days, I told Tom that an immediate trip to the West Coast was impossible. However, I made some specific suggestions during our forty-five-minute conversation.

"You need a go-between, a person that you can deal with reasonably, and a person whom the Kennedy family respects. That person is Pierre Salinger," I told him. Pierre Salinger was a California lawyer who had been a press spokesman and close confidant of President John F. Kennedy.

Salinger was a longtime friend of the Kennedy family. But he also knew the law and was likely to keep a level head, even in times of distress and chaos. After the shooting of President Kennedy, Secret Service and other federal officials had demanded that the president's body be flown out of Dallas immediately and that any autopsy be conducted at Bethesda Naval Hospital. I hoped that my suggestion would block any similar move in this instance.

My big concern was the federal government. Would federal

agents demand to take Senator Kennedy's body out of Los Angeles and back to Washington as they had with President Kennedy in Dallas?

"It would also be a good move," I suggested to Tom, "to contact the Armed Forces Institute of Pathology [AFIP]. I think it would be wise if you personally invited two or three of their forensic pathologists to fly to Los Angeles to act as observers as you do the autopsy. You have nothing to hide, and this would dispel any notion of conspiracy or coverup. Ask Dr. Pierre Finck, the chief of forensic pathology at the AFIP, to be a member of that team."

Dr. Finck had participated in the autopsy performed on President Kennedy four and one-half years earlier. Despite my repeated criticisms of the JFK autopsy, I considered Dr. Finck to be an honest man—a person who had learned much from the first Kennedy autopsy.

"With Dr. Finck and the other AFIP pathologists present, the federal government is less likely to hassle you," I said. "Make it clear that you are going to do the autopsy and that the body is not going to leave Los Angeles without an autopsy being performed, as required by law. You will also need to make it clear that you will permit no outside instructions on how to perform the autopsy. You have been doing this for several years and are a top-level professional."

Despite the fact that I had just been sleeping, my mind raced to think of other problems with the JFK autopsy that Tom could avoid with this one. That's when I thought of the confusion over the bullet wounds in the president's neck and head. Because of the tracheotomy performed by the surgeons at Parkland Memorial Hospital, the military pathologists were not even aware of the bullet hole in JFK's throat until more than a full day after the autopsy had been completed.

"You need to insist that the surgeons at the Hospital of the Good Samaritan who operated on Senator Kennedy in the emergency room are present when you are performing the autopsy," I told Tom. "These doctors should be there in the autopsy room to document any incisions they made in their efforts to save the senator."

After assuring Tom that no one could do a better job of handling this case than he, I said I might be able to fly to the West

Coast over the weekend. Unable to sleep, I spent the remainder of the early morning hours packing and watching the television news coverage of the shooting. From the descriptions of the wounds given by witnesses at the scene, I knew it would be a miracle if Robert Kennedy survived.

News reports had the senator from New York going into surgery at 2:30 A.M. Doctors said that his breathing and heartbeat were good, but that he had lost a lot of blood from three gunshot wounds. His condition was listed as critical. Three hours later, a team of surgeons announced that they had finished their operation and that they had removed several bullet fragments, including one from the brain. Kennedy remained unconscious and was moved into intensive care, where his condition was listed as extremely critical.

A suspect in the shooting had been placed under arrest, having been tackled by several people who had witnessed the shooting. As the morning wore on, police identified the man as Sirhan Bishara Sirhan, a twenty-four-year-old Palestinian immigrant who had moved to the United States with his family in 1957. Police also were looking for a young dark-haired woman, approximately twenty-five years old and wearing a polka-dot dress. She had been seen with Sirhan just before the shooting. Seconds after the shooting, witnesses outside the Ambassador Hotel saw this same woman running and screaming, "We shot him! We shot him!"

Three separate women would later come forward claiming they were that person. However, each was dismissed as seeking publicity or not fitting the appropriate description.

The medicolegal conference in the nation's capital at which I spoke went well, though everyone's mind was on the assassination of the man who very likely would have become the next president of the United States. Later that Wednesday, I had another telephone conversation with Tom, who said everything appeared to be in order. Senator Kennedy, he said, was still alive, though not conscious. His doctors were not optimistic. Because of the shooting, the seminar in San Juan was canceled, and I returned home to Pittsburgh early Thursday morning. That's when I learned that doctors had pronounced the forty-two-year-old Robert Kennedy dead at 1:44 A.M. on Thursday, June 6, 1968.

I was tempted to accept Tom's offer and fly immediately to Los Angeles to participate in the autopsy proceedings. But my wife, Sigrid, and daughter were coming home and I not only needed to be home with them, but I wanted more than anything to be with them.

On Friday, I again talked with Tom. He said the autopsy had been performed without any significant problems. Some federal agents had talked of taking the body out of Los Angeles and back to Washington, D.C., for the autopsy, but the preventive measures Tom and I had discussed put a quick end to such considerations. This time, it was appropriate for me to brag extensively about my new daughter. In the end, we decided I would fly to Los Angeles and go over the medical reports and photographs before Tom completed the final version of his autopsy.

Four days later, I spent the afternoon in Tom's office at the Los Angeles Hall of Justice, reviewing the autopsy photographs, the microscopic slide tissues, and the preliminary draft of his autopsy report. Everything seemed in order. Tom, as I had expected, had done a superb job. It was the most complete and detailed medicolegal autopsy report I had ever seen.

Senator Kennedy had been shot three times. The fatal bullet was most likely the first to strike him. The missile hit and entered him about an inch behind his right ear. It had a slightly forward trajectory. The bullet completely fragmented after impacting the senator's skull. While Tom was able to recover several very small fragments of the bullet, they were too small to be traced back to Sirhan's gun.

On Kennedy's right ear was a marking, like a tattoo, caused by burning gunpowder that exited the gun's barrel as the weapon was fired. The tattoo pattern was similar to those I had seen in many other homicide cases in which the victims were shot at point-blank range. This observation came straight from experience.

To strengthen this belief, the forensic laboratory, using infrared photography, had discovered large deposits of soot in the senator's hair. This soot is very similar to the soot that comes from a house's chimney. In the case of a pistol, it's carbon deposit from gunpowder that is ignited during the discharging of the bullet and is blown out the muzzle of the gun. From a handgun, soot can usually travel up to eighteen inches, but it barely shows up in lab tests because the soot disperses quickly after leaving the end of the gun's barrel. The amount found in Senator Kennedy's hair was dense, meaning the muzzle of the weapon that caused this wound was within an inch or two of his head.

Soot also was found in the examination of the microscopic tissue of the wound. The tissue slides clearly show the presence of soot inside the wound. No soot was found on the outside of the wound because the nurses had washed the wound area with a sponge shortly after Senator Kennedy was wheeled into the emergency room. This is not an unusual step in preparing a gunshot victim for surgery.

To obtain a more precise distance, Tom had police perform a classical "pig ears ballistics test." Using seven pig ears attached to fake skulls, police used a snub-nosed .22-caliber Iver Johnson Cadet revolver identical to the one used by Sirhan. On the first shot, the barrel was placed directly against the head one inch behind the ear. The gunman then moved back one-quarter of an inch and fired again. He pulled the gun away to a distance of one-half inch from the skull and again pulled the trigger. Shots also were fired at one, one and one-half, two, three, and four inches.

An examination of the tattoo patterns on the pig ears and of the marks on Senator Kennedy's ear showed an exact match at 1½ inches. Of course, every gun is going to fire differently, but this test confirmed that the gun must have been very close to the senator's head.

The autopsy photographs showed two other bullet wounds—both inflicted near Senator Kennedy's armpit. The first wound appeared to have entered toward the back of the right armpit and exited the front right shoulder. This slug was never found.

The third bullet struck about an inch from the other wound. But this bullet had gone in a different direction. It traveled sideways across Kennedy's body before lodging in the soft tissue at the base of his lower neck. During the autopsy, Tom had retrieved the slug from the senator's neck, which police were able to trace to Sirhan's gun.

A fourth bullet had gone through Senator Kennedy's clothing, but apparently did not touch his skin. The autopsy and the report were meticulously done. I told Tom he was to be congratulated.

That evening, we went to the Ambassador Hotel, the scene of the crime. We were joined by Karl Uecker, the hotel's maître d', and a Los Angeles County homicide detective working on the Kennedy assassination investigation. No person had a better view of what happened the night of the shooting than Mr. Uecker. Using his eyewitness and personal testimony, we reconstructed the events of that night.

Having watched the election returns from a private room in

the hotel, Senator Kennedy had just given a brief victory speech to thousands of people who had gathered in the ballroom celebrating the victory. "Let's go on to Chicago and win," he told the crowd, referring to the Democratic National Convention to be held in the Windy City a few weeks later.

Despite being only forty-two, Bobby Kennedy's political career had been incredible. His supporters found him charming, brilliant, and extremely devoted to the welfare of this country and to justice. After successfully managing his brother's presidential campaign, Bobby was rewarded by being named attorney general of the United States. When he was accused of nepotism, President Kennedy responded, "I can't see that it's wrong to give him a little legal experience before he goes out to practice law."

Indeed, Bobby Kennedy became a very good attorney general, recruiting some of the brightest young legal minds of the early 1960s, including James Neal, now a Nashville attorney considered to be one of the best trial lawyers in America, and Byron White, whom President Kennedy would later appoint to the U.S. Supreme Court, where he served until his retirement in June 1993. It was Bobby Kennedy who targeted organized crime and put Jimmy Hoffa behind bars.

Bobby Kennedy had been eating lunch at his McLean, Virginia, home on November 22, 1963, when he received word of his brother's assassination in Dallas. Emotionally devastated, he was standing at the airport when the presidential plane landed in Washington with the president's body. Friends say he was crushed.

The next year, Robert Kennedy was elected to the U.S. Senate from New York. In 1968, after President Johnson declared he was not running for re-election, Bobby Kennedy threw his hat into the ring. He was known more for his actions and ideas than for his political skills. Seldom did the general public get to see Bobby Kennedy's lighter side. In the presidential campaign, speaking to supporters in Fort Wayne, Indiana, he said that by voting him into the White House, taxpayers would save money. If he lost, he said, he and his family would have to go on some kind of public relief. "It will be less expensive," he said in a deadpan voice, "just to send us to the White House. We'll arrange it so all ten kids won't be there at once and we won't need to expand the place. I'll send some of them away to school and I'll make one of them attorney general."

Many political types who were close to Bobby Kennedy say he

had enjoyed running his brother's campaign considerably more than his own. Friends said that after his brother's death, he seemed to lose a bit of the fire that once burned inside him. Those same friends said they saw that fire return only once—the night he won the California presidential primary and stood victorious before the jubilant crowds.

Without any security guards, the senator then left the ballroom through a rear exit behind the stage and was walking through the kitchen corridor toward a separate room that was housing the press. Like his older brother, Bobby Kennedy hated tight security. He seemed to take pleasure in leaving behind those assigned to guard him. It immediately brought to my memory what the senator had told French writer Romain Gary. According to Gary, "He told me that sooner or later, he knew there would be an assassination attempt on his life. But he was willing to take that risk, as if it were his destiny."

Slowly, step by step, we re-created Robert Kennedy's final walk. Mr. Uecker played himself and guided us through what had occurred. Tom took on the role of Senator Kennedy and the detective stood in for Sirhan Sirhan. I stood back, watching, listening, and asking questions.

Mr. Uecker said he was leading the senator and his wife, Ethel, by the hand through the crowded hallway, which was lined with hotel employees and supporters. About thirty steps from the ballroom and about fifteen steps shy of the pressroom, the shots rang out.

"As we walked along, everybody wanted to shake the senator's hand, get his attention, or simply touch him," Mr. Uecker said in his German-accented English. "I don't think there were any security guards around."

Then we came to the exact spot where it happened. Mr. Uecker stopped.

"I was right here. Mr. and Mrs. Kennedy were one step behind me. I had ahold of them both when I first spotted him a few feet in front of me. He was standing at the edge of a kitchen worktable. At first, I believed he was a houseman, an employee of the hotel. Before I could focus on what was happening, there were gunshots, three of them, one after another. It sounded like Chinese firecrackers going off. I felt Senator Kennedy pull away from me, and I think I knew in my heart he had been hit, but I did not turn around and look. I instinctively jumped forward and grabbed the man with the gun around the neck.''

With the help of other witnesses, including professional football player Roosevelt "Rosie" Grier, Sirhan Sirhan, who stood only five feet, five inches and weighed 120 pounds, was wrestled to the ground and the pistol was pried from his hand. When Mr. Uecker finally did look behind him, he saw the senator lying on the concrete floor, his wife holding his bloodied head in her arms. Others were screaming for a doctor.

We were puzzled by what Mr. Uecker was telling us.

"From your description, it sounds as if Sirhan got no closer to Senator Kennedy than a couple of feet," I said.

"That's right," Mr. Uecker answered. "I was between the two of them the entire time, and my eyes were on Sirhan at all times. There is no way his gun got any closer than two or three feet. I am absolutely certain of this."

With that news, Tom and I just stared at each other. We knew Mr. Uecker was telling us the truth. But we also realized the forensic evidence told a completely different story. I would later learn that all the other witnesses, of which there were several dozen, supported Mr. Uecker's claim. Some even stated that Sirhan never got any closer to Senator Kennedy than five feet.

This was truly amazing. The forensic evidence, which is irrefutable, directly contradicted all the eyewitnesses. Forensic evidence does not lie. Sometimes it is subject to differing opinions. We are not dealing with mathematics, chemistry, or physics—the absolute sciences. But in terms of an entrance wound, there can be no question. In fact, there has never been any challenge to the forensic evidence in this case. The investigators simply refuse to address it!

All the while, the police stated they were still looking for the young woman in the polka-dot dress. Find her, I thought, and you may find the answer to our mystery.

As part of the re-creation, we tried to determine the path and trajectory of all the bullets. Starting with the fatal missile, we were again confronted with possible conflicts. From the autopsy photographs and report, I knew the bullet that entered behind the senator's right ear was shot from behind or beside him as he walked. Yet Mr. Uecker was saying that Sirhan was at all times in front of him. However, because there is no video recording of the

Robert Kennedy slaying, as there is of the John Kennedy assassination, we do not know the exact position of the senator when the bullets struck him. We don't know, for example, if Senator Kennedy's body or head was turned to shake a supporter's hand when the slugs struck him.

About two weeks later, I was back home in Pittsburgh, enjoying the new addition to my family, when I received a telephone call from Mary Bishara Sirhan, Sirhan Sirhan's mother. After a brief introduction, she went straight to the point.

"My son needs a good lawyer," she told me. "He needs some person who has courage, who is not afraid to stand up for what is right.

"Will you consider representing my son at his trial?" she asked me.

I was, to say the least, stunned. I was aware that Sirhan had already rejected two of the most prominent criminal defense lawyers in our country—F. Lee Bailey and Melvin Belli. The fact that Sirhan had turned down the services of two great trial lawyers and was selecting me was incredibly flattering.

Mrs. Sirhan spoke very broken English, which made it difficult to understand her at times. She said she had heard about my work on the assassination of President John F. Kennedy. From it, she said, she knew I was willing to stand up to the government and fight for the truth.

Indeed, from my trip to Los Angeles, during which I reviewed the autopsy files, and from the reconstruction and my interviewing of the key witness to the shooting, I felt this was a case that could be won in court. The authorities had charged Sirhan with the murder of Senator Kennedy. But I knew it was not that simple. I knew that the forensic evidence contradicted everything the state was saying, namely that it was Sirhan who pulled the trigger, firing the bullet that killed Robert Kennedy. From just the evidence I knew about, I believed that I could create enough reasonable doubt to thwart a first-degree murder conviction.

For about an hour, I listened intently to Mrs. Sirhan. Pain and fear could be heard in her voice. At this moment, she was nothing more than a heartbroken mother trying to save her son's life.

"He is a very good boy," she told me. "He must have been tricked or fooled into doing this. He would never have done this alone, not without some kind of encouragement or pushing from others." However, she never mentioned hypnosis. Many people theorize that Sirhan was under some type of hypnotic spell that night in Los Angeles.

Born in Jerusalem, the fourth of Mrs. Sirhan's five sons, Sirhan moved with his family to the United States in 1957. He was a very bright student, always ranking among the top students in his class. But because Sirhan's father had become physically abusive, frequently beating Mrs. Sirhan and the children, she took her family and moved out. The father eventually moved back to Jordan.

From 1964 through 1966, Sirhan attended Pasadena City College, where he was able to meet for the first time other Arabs living in the United States. He worked part-time as a gardener for those who lived near him. He also held a job as a clerk at a health-food store for several months. In school, Sirhan had joined several politically active Arab student groups. It was then that Sirhan became increasingly anti-Israel and pro-Arab. He openly showed his anger toward America's support for Israel. This, prosecutors would later say, was Sirhan's motive in the slaying. Robert Kennedy was a strong supporter of Israel.

At the end of our conversation, Mrs. Sirhan repeated her plea for me to defend her son against the charges that he and he alone had murdered Robert Kennedy.

"It's very tempting," I told her. "But I need some time to consider it. I need to talk this over with some of my colleagues and friends.

"You are aware that I am a Jew and I am very pro-Israel, aren't you?" I asked her.

That did not matter, she said. She believed my integrity would allow me to put my personal beliefs aside and defend her son to the best of my ability. As a card-carrying member of the American Civil Liberties Union, I knew she was right. Every person, no matter the crime they are charged with, has the right to a fair trial and the right to the best defense counsel in the land. The question was not could I do it, but did I want to. Should I do it? What was the right thing to do?

Less than a week later, I called Mrs. Sirhan and told her I had decided not to take her son's case. There were many reasons for me to accept—the intrigue and mystery, not to mention the notoriety. It is both disquieting and stimulating to think what might have happened had I accepted. I would have been able to reveal "the inside story" about Sirhan Sirhan.

But there were also many reasons for me not to take this case.

And it was more for Sirhan's sake that I turned it down than for my own. Not having practiced criminal law since leaving the Allegheny County district attorney's office in 1965, I did not think I could adequately defend Sirhan's rights in court. My schedule was very busy then and this case, being on the West Coast, would have consumed an incredible amount of my time and efforts—so much so that I would have had to cease doing everything else. I also took into consideration that I had little experience as a criminal defense attorney and I felt that Sirhan needed a lawyer who knew the ins-and-outs of the criminal justice system. And there was also the fact that I was in great sympathy with the Kennedy family. This fact alone would not have prevented me from defending Sirhan, but it certainly did play upon my mind and soul. In the end, I had to decline.

Sirhan Sirhan eventually was appointed a lawyer by the Court, Grant Cooper, an experienced criminal defense attorney. However, to my subsequent amazement, Mr. Cooper never once mentioned the incredible holes in the prosecution's case. Not once did he point out to the jury that the forensic evidence proves that Sirhan could not have been the person who shot the fatal bullet —this despite the fact that such evidence was already in the record. In his testimony before the grand jury that indicted Sirhan, Tom Noguchi testified that the weapon which fired the fatal bullet must have been less than an inch and a half from Kennedy's head when it fired. The defense attorney had a transcript of Tom's testimony, yet he never used it.

Nor did the defense pursue the possibility of a second gunman. Standing directly beside Senator Kennedy's right elbow when he was shot was a uniformed security guard named Thane Eugene Cesar, who was carrying a revolver. Mr. Cesar, according to his friends, was known to have right-wing political beliefs. Mr. Cesar admits to drawing his pistol when the shooting started, but he told police that night that he never fired the weapon. Amazingly, the handgun was never checked or tested for a possible ballistics match.

Months later, after witnesses to the shooting came forward and testified that they had seen the guard fire his weapon, authorities again questioned Mr. Cesar. Regarding the question of finally checking his gun, Mr. Cesar told police that he had sold it. In 1971, journalist Ted Charach wrote and directed a documentary about the case called *The Second Gun*. It was an excellent piece of work which I showed at the annual meeting of the American Academy of Forensic Sciences in Chicago in 1971.

Rather than pursue the possible involvement of Cesar, the defense conceded that it was Sirhan, but claimed that he was mentally incapable of premeditating and weighing the legal consequences of his crime in a mature and meaningful manner. Several expert witnesses for the defense told the jury that they believed Sirhan was a paranoid schizophrenic.

The jury did not buy the diminished capacity defense. Hardly any sane person would. Sirhan was convicted of the murder and was sentenced to die in California's gas chamber. However, in 1972, the U.S. Supreme Court struck down all death penalty sentences as unconstitutional. Sirhan's sentence, like that of all the other death row inmates, was commuted to life in prison. That's where Sirhan is today. All his appeals have been denied.

Looking back, I am sorry I did not accept Sirhan's case. Not for my own sake, but for the sake of justice. I would have hired an experienced criminal defense lawyer to assist me in preparing for trial and questioning the witnesses. But I would have made sure that the forensic evidence, which indicated without a doubt that someone other than Sirhan had fired the fatal bullet, would have been brought out.

There is no doubt that Sirhan Sirhan deserves a new trial. The most he is guilty of is attempted murder or conspiracy to commit murder. But it was not Sirhan Sirhan who killed Senator Robert Kennedy.

3

Chappaquiddick Revisited: The Death of Mary Jo Kopechne

A little more than a year after Robert Kennedy's assassination, Senator Edward "Ted" Kennedy held a party on Chappaquiddick Island in southern Massachusetts for six young women who had been members of his brother's staff. Known as "the Boiler Room Girls," the six women—all of them young and unmarried—had collected information for Robert Kennedy on delegates to the Democratic national convention in 1968 as part of Bobby's presidential campaign.

With his two brothers dead, a great deal of political pressure fell on Ted Kennedy. It was he to whom everyone turned to take up the gauntlet of causes and ideals that his brothers had preached and pursued. There had been immediate speculation that Ted Kennedy might step into the presidential race in 1968, filling the political void left by the deaths of his brothers. But at age thirty-seven, he publicly admitted he was not yet prepared for the White House. And he was right.

The weekend of July 18–20, 1969, would end in tragedy. It also would leave such a mark on Ted Kennedy that any future hopes of winning the presidency were dashed.

This was the kind of incident that major scandals are made of. A U.S. senator, who was married, had been driving down a dirt road late at night with a single, very attractive young woman. Both had been drinking. The incident went unreported for ten hours. Only a fiction writer could develop a scenario like that.

Chappaquiddick is a small, five-mile-long island east of, and partly connected to, Martha's Vineyard. A big raftlike ferry brings passengers and cars across from Edgartown, which is only a four-minute ride over less than five hundred feet of water. Among the women who attended the party was Mary Jo Kopechne, a twenty-eight-year-old former secretary to Robert Kennedy. After the senator's death, Ms. Kopechne took a job helping establish political campaigns with the Washington, D.C., firm of Matt Reese Associates. However, she kept in close contact with Ted Kennedy and members of his staff. Ms. Kopechne had devoted her life to politics. Like many young people her age, she believed in the vision and ideals put forth by the Kennedy brothers.

Late Friday night or early Saturday morning, Ms. Kopechne's life ended. She was a passenger in a car that was driven into the water off the side of a one-lane wooden structure roadway known by local residents as the Dyke. The roadway runs between Poucha Pond and Cape Pogue Pond. The wooden structure had replaced a dirt dike used to separate incoming ocean tides from the fresh water of the ponds. Senator Kennedy was the driver of that car. He escaped. She did not.

Much has been reported and written about the incident at Chappaquiddick. But there's very little new information or evidence. It has been analyzed endlessly by political gurus. Some said it was the blemish on Ted Kennedy's record that he would never outlive. Others said that the protection of Ted Kennedy demonstrated just how politically dominant his family was in Massachusetts.

All this may be true, but it was not my concern when I was asked by prosecutors in Massachusetts to look at this case. My goal was to determine if any evidence indicated foul play and to decide if Ms. Kopechne's body should be exhumed and an autopsy performed. As I reviewed the police records, I discovered a woefully inadequate investigation from the standpoint of the police and the medical examiner. Only after reading all the investigative files did I realize how severely this case had been botched. Sadly, it did not have to be this way. All the facts could have been uncovered and exposed. Had the medicolegal investigation been properly and thoroughly done, there would be none of the suspicions we have today. We would know the truth.

At first, the Edgartown, Massachusetts, authorities considered it a simple automobile accident that had ended in tragedy. The assistant medical examiner, Dr. Donald Mills, ruled that Ms. Kopechne's cause of death was drowning. However, no autopsy was ever done. Because the case involved the Kennedy family, few questions were asked.

The press angle on this incident was that another catastrophe had struck the Kennedy family. In fact, it was anything but the biggest news of the day. The *New York Times* gave the story a small box in the left corner of the Sunday, July 20, 1969, edition. Instead, the media and the nation were looking into space. Flying the *Apollo 11*, astronaut Neil Armstrong walked on the moon that very weekend, making the famous statement as he carried the American flag across the moon's surface, "That's one small step for man, one giant leap for mankind."

But to Senator Kennedy's dismay, the media focus did not remain skyward for long. Within days, reporters turned their attention to Chappaquiddick, and it was not friendly. The increased spotlight caused many local law enforcement officials—District Attorney Edward Dinis in particular—to question what had really happened that Friday night. Many reporters and some law enforcement officials discovered inconsistencies in Senator Kennedy's statements about what had occurred. The press also had become critical of how the investigation was handled—and rightfully so. Several local papers used their editorial sections to question whether or not the senator had been given special privileges. Others printed the inconsistencies, and some even demanded his resignation.

By the time the local district attorney, Mr. Dinis (*pronounced* Denise), decided the crash needed further probing, Ms. Kopechne's body was gone. Senator Kennedy's staff and the Kopechne family had had the woman's body flown for burial to Wilkes-Barre, Pennsylvania, her parents' home. The body had already been embalmed and buried when Mr. Dinis asked to have it examined again.

To have an autopsy performed, the prosecutor had to obtain a Pennsylvania judge's permission to exhume the body. However, both the Kopechnes and Senator Kennedy publicly opposed the exhumation, claiming that the police had already had their chance to thoroughly view the body and that nothing further would be learned from a complete postmortem examination.

The Kopechne family, which was very conservative and very religious, was afraid of what an autopsy might show. They thought it might disclose publicly whether their daughter was a virgin, whether she had had sex that night, or even the possibility that she was pregnant. Had semen been recovered, it would have been possible to identify her lover, which could have been embarrassing.

If Senator Kennedy was telling the truth about its being an accident, and I have never had strong reason to believe otherwise, then I have always wondered why he so vigorously opposed the exhumation and autopsy. An autopsy would have silenced many of his critics. But the position of the Kennedy staff was that an autopsy four months later would more cause grief than it would answer questions.

In late September 1969, I received a telephone call from prominent Boston trial lawyer F. Lee Bailey. Lee said he had been contacted by Mr. Dinis, who was looking for a forensic pathologist to review the Kopechne case to see if there was a legitimate forensic scientific need to exhume the body and perform an exhaustive autopsy.

"Before I give him your name, I wanted to check with you," Lee said. I told him I was willing to review the case file and discuss my opinion with Mr. Dinis.

The next day, Mr. Dinis called:

DINIS: Would there be any benefit to digging the body up now, after three or four months?

WECHT: I believe there could be, but I would have to review the medical examiner's report and see what his findings were.

DINIS: I will send all the medical and investigative reports to you immediately. However, no autopsy was done and there is very little documentation.

WECHT: How, then, did the medical examiner decide that the cause of death was drowning?

DINIS: From a purely external examination.

Biting my tongue, I avoided criticizing the local medical examiner. Mr. Dinis told me he had not entered the investigation earlier because the local police told him the crash looked clearly accidental with no evidence of negligence.

"If I checked into every car crash in my jurisdiction, my office would not have time to prosecute criminals in court," Mr. Dinis told me. "And I thought that if I took charge of this case, it would appear I was treating it differently just because it involved a United States senator—especially after I had been told there was no evidence of serious criminal wrongdoing."

I understood Mr. Dinis's situation. He was under extreme pressure. On one side, this was Massachusetts—a state the Kennedys owned politically. On the other, there was the news media, which kept coming up with flaws and gaps in the investigation. Somewhere in that morass, the search for truth and justice could be found.

When the file arrived a couple of days later, I was amazed at its thinness. There was almost nothing to it—the motor vehicle accident report, a five-page written report by Edgartown police chief Dominick Arena, a report on the external examination of the body by associate medical examiner Donald Mills, a limited toxicology report, and a three-paragraph statement written by Senator Kennedy.

According to the investigative report, a high school teacher and a fifteen-year-old boy who were fishing on Saturday morning, July 19, were the first to spot and report the car in Poucha Pond at about nine o'clock. It was completely turned over on its hood, totally submerged, and about ten feet from the bridge.

Chief Arena responded to the call for help. After borrowing swimming trunks at a nearby house, the chief dove into the water to see if anyone was trapped inside. However, the current from the tidal water was overpowering, and he was unable to dive down for a close look.

By 9:30 A.M., John Farrar, a scuba diver with the Edgartown Rescue Squad, had arrived. According to the police report, Mr. Farrar found the rear passenger window broken out. Sticking his head inside, he saw the body of a young woman. Her face was tilted upward, pressed into the footwell of the upside-down car. Her hands gripped the backseat, holding her in that position. Farrar reported that the woman's body still floated at the top of the car as he pulled her out, suggesting to him that she still had some air in her body. He felt that, in his experience, if there had been no air, the body would have sunk. As soon as he touched the woman, Farrar knew she was dead. Rigor mortis had already set in. By ten o'clock that morning, the body was out of the car and on dry land.

"Her head was in the floorboards where the last bit of air would have been," Mr. Farrar reported. "It appeared to me that she was holding herself up in that air to get the last bit of air. She would have to have been very conscious after the crash to get in that position to breathe the last pocket of air. There was no air pocket in the car when I arrived, but she could have been alive a good while after the car went off the bridge. If I had been called immediately after the accident, I think there's a good chance the girl could have been saved."

I thought these comments were damning. I searched the remainder of the reports for evidence supporting or negating Mr. Farrar's statements.

The medical reports were very superficial, almost nonexistent. Dr. Mills was not a pathologist, let alone a forensic pathologist. He was a local physician with no training in legal medicine or forensic pathology. Either he failed to recognize his professional responsibility in this case or he was well aware of what and who were involved in this tragedy and simply chose not to intercede.

The examination was purely external. Dr. Mills used his hands to search the body for trauma. He noted a pinkish foam around Ms. Kopechne's mouth, which he felt was a sign of drowning. Finding no visible evidence of trauma, such as bruises or marks on her body, Dr. Mills signed the death certificate declaring Ms. Kopechne's cause of death to be "asphyxiation by immersion," or drowning. From the amount of rigor mortis, Dr. Mills estimated the time of death to have been about "six hours or more" earlier. However, he did not take the body temperature, nor did he remove any vitreous humor (ocular fluid) to test potassium content—both of which might have helped to determine a more scientifically accurate time of death.

In newspaper clips I had received about the accident, Dr. Mills was quoted as saying that a "very moderate, very slight amount" of alcohol had been found in Ms. Kopechne's body. However, as I read the toxicology report, I saw that her blood-alcohol level was

.09, which would indicate consumption of about five or six mixed drinks. Most states today consider .10 to be legally drunk. In Canada and many European countries, the legal limit is .08 or even .05. Four shots of hundred-proof whiskey would give you a .10 blood-alcohol level. One shot of whiskey is equal to twelve ounces of beer or approximately four to six ounces of wine.

Of course, there's also a dissipation rate as long as you are alive, which is about .018 per hour. That must be considered when backdating alcohol levels.

All of this told me several things about the case. First, .09 should not be considered "very moderate" or "very slight." To me, this placed Dr. Mills's credibility in question. At the same time, .09 is certainly not inebriated to the point that a person would be unable to respond or react in a crisis. But it may have compromised Ms. Kopechne's sensory perception and motor reflexes and diminished her intellectual acuity and muscle coordination after the car tumbled from the bridge into the water. But it was clear evidence that Ms. Kopechne had been drinking. The police report said Senator Kennedy was the driver of the car. Had he also been drinking? If she had been driving, I would say that a .09 blood-alcohol level would be high enough to contribute to the crash.

As I searched through the police reports, I found nothing to indicate that Senator Kennedy had been given a blood-alcohol test. In fact, the whole process by which the authorities came to learn that Senator Kennedy was the driver of the car and how they dealt with him were very suspicious.

Around 9:30 that Saturday morning, Chief Arena sent the license tag number of the car to the Massachusetts Auto Registration Office for identification. Chief Arena was horrified when he learned that the car belonged to Senator Edward Kennedy. At first, he feared that it was a Kennedy family member who had died in the crash.

Thirty minutes later, the chief received a radio transmission that Senator Kennedy was at the Edgartown police station and wanted to talk with him. Still wearing wet swimming trunks, Chief Arena rode the ferry back to Edgartown. Arriving back at the police station, he found Senator Kennedy accompanied by his friend Paul Markham, the former U.S. attorney in Massachusetts under President Kennedy.

As the chief was starting to relate the finding of the body of a young woman in the submerged car, Senator Kennedy interrupted with some shocking news.

"I know," he said. "I was the driver of the car, and I'm here to make a full and complete statement."

Before Chief Arena could ask any questions, the senator said he wanted to write out his statement instead of giving it orally. That seemed satisfactory to the confused and stunned chief. A few minutes later, the senator presented the handwritten statement, which had been included in the file sent to me:

On July 18, 1969, at approximately 11:15 P.M. in Chappaquiddick, Martha's Vineyard, Massachusetts, I was driving my car on Main Street on my way to get the ferry back to Edgartown. I was unfamiliar with the road and turned right onto Dike Bridge, instead of bearing hard left on Main Street. After proceeding for approximately one-half mile on Dike Road, I descended a hill and came across a narrow bridge. The car went off the side of the bridge. There was one passenger with me, one Miss Mary ————, a former secretary of my brother Sen. Robert Kennedy. The car turned over and sank into the water and landed with the roof resting on the bottom.

I attempted to open the door and the window of the car but have no recollection of how I got out of the car. I came to the surface and then repeatedly dove down to the car in an attempt to see if the passenger was still in the car. I was unsuccessful in the attempt. I was exhausted and in a state of shock.

I recall walking back to where my friends were eating. There was a car parked in the front of the cottage and I climbed into the back seat. I then asked for someone to bring me back to Edgartown. I remember walking around for a period and then going back to my hotel room. When I fully realized what had happened this morning, I immediately contacted the police.

According to Chief Arena's report, Senator Kennedy then refused to answer any questions and left the police station. As I read on, the inconsistencies in Kennedy's statement became obvious.

From his many visits to Chappaquiddick, he certainly must have known the island's roads. His claim that he did not realize he had made a wrong turn did not seem very credible.

Senator Kennedy's statement that he and Ms. Kopechne, whose last name he could not remember when he wrote his story, had left the party at 11:15 P.M. was also contradicted. A deputy sheriff named Christopher "Huck" Look had seen the very same car after 12:45 A.M. that night while he was on patrol. The car had driven past him going in the opposite direction of the dyke where the car was found. Even though it was dark, Officer Look said he had gotten a good look at the vehicle and there was no doubt this was the same car.

Nowhere in his written statement did Senator Kennedy ever mention the party on Chappaquiddick. Nor did he mention any drinking. The chief did not ask him to take a blood-alcohol test. By the time the police did learn about the party, the next day, the Kennedy staff had left the island, sending the workers home and telling them not to say a word.

From Chief Arena's description of the senator that morning, the claim that he had been in a state of shock did not appear credible. He appeared very calm, cool, and collected during his meeting with the chief. There was no medical evidence to ever support Kennedy's statement that he had been in a state of shock.

Because the senator had admitted to leaving the scene of the accident and not reporting it for about ten hours, Edgartown police finally charged him with "leaving the scene of an accident" —a misdemeanor offense. Kennedy pleaded guilty to the traffic violation and received probation.

When Mr. Dinis called me seeking help, the powers that be were clamoring for more information and investigation. There was strong suspicion—though little evidence to support it—that Senator Kennedy had been drinking when he drove the car off the bridge. If he were intoxicated, then Massachusetts law is clear: he could be held criminally liable for Mary Jo Kopechne's death and face being convicted of manslaughter.

Then there were Mr. Farrar's comments that Ms. Kopechne may have been alive for a period of time after the crash and that if Ted Kennedy had sought help immediately, she might have been saved. If it could be proven that she had lived for thirty minutes or an hour, then Senator Kennedy's failure to seek help would constitute neglect and possibly make him legally guilty of manslaughter in Massachusetts.

After reviewing the entire file, I called Mr. Dinis and told him I thought there should be an autopsy.

"I don't know what we'll find," I told him. "Most likely, it will prove that she indeed drowned. But at least we will know for sure."

Drowning was then and remains today a diagnosis arrived at through exclusionary means. There is nothing in the submerged body that medically and scientifically confirms that a death is due to drowning. When a forensic pathologist finds a body in the water, the only way to know for sure it is a drowning is by medically ruling out injury (such as a gunshot wound, stabbing, or blow to the head), disease, other trauma, or poisoning. Just because there is water in the lungs and stomach, which was all Dr. Mills based his diagnosis on, does not necessarily mean that death was caused by drowning. If a dead body is thrown into the water, some of that water may seep into both the stomach and the lungs.

Based on this news, Mr. Dinis filed a petition in Luzerne County Court in Pennsylvania to have the body exhumed and to have an autopsy performed. Mr. Dinis asked if I would testify at the hearing. If he were successful, he also asked if I would supervise the exhumation and perform the autopsy. I agreed.

In October 1969, Luzerne County judge Bernard Brominski heard evidence over a three-day period from both sides. The sole purpose of the hearing was to determine what, if anything, could be learned from an autopsy four months after the body had been buried.

Under direct examination by Mr. Dinis, I told Judge Brominski exactly what I had told the prosecutor earlier.

WECHT: An autopsy should have been performed back then when the accident occurred, and it should be performed today for the same reasons. As a medicolegal investigator, you cannot pick and choose which cases you want to review. You either have a medicolegal investigative system that routinely, uniformly, thoroughly, and adequately performs autopsies in cases of sudden, violent, suspicious, unexplained, unexpected, and medically unattended deaths, or you have something less than acceptable. The whole idea is to make certain you are not missing something. If you make a determination based on who the person is and your personal feelings about the circumstances or people involved, then obviously the system is compromised.

DINIS: What about the pink foam found in Ms. Kopechne's throat? Doesn't that prove drowning?

WECHT: The pink foam was created when blood mixed with the air trapped in her body. While the pink foam is certainly consistent with drowning, it is in no way diagnostic of drowning.

DINIS: Why is an external examination of the body not enough to determine drowning as the cause of death?

WECHT: We in forensic pathology spend a lot of time on the external examination and we should. But that is only the beginning. To consider the external examination the end of the medicolegal investigation is absurd, a throwback to the antiquated system where the local butcher or baker is the coroner calling all the shots and making the decisions.

DINIS: But if other injuries had caused death, would they not have been visible to the eye?

WECHT: No, not always. You can have very extensive internal injuries without any evidence of external trauma. You can strangle a person to death and leave no visible marks.

DINIS: If the body is exhumed and you do the autopsy, would there be any way to tell how long Ms. Kopechne lived after the crash?

WECHT: If she had lived only a few minutes, less than five or ten minutes, then there would be no way to tell. However, if she continued breathing for more than thirty minutes, then the autopsy would show microscopic changes in the tissues. So, if she survived under the water for any lengthy period of time, it is possible that an autopsy today would show that.

DINIS: If she had survived for a few minutes after the crash, would she have experienced any pain?

WECHT: The question of pain and suffering is one I am asked about a lot in drowning cases. The answer is, until you are unconscious, there's a tremendous amount of emotional pain and suffering. Physically, it's not like a cut on the skin. But there is certainly pain. It's like when you are under water and you try holding your breath for as long as you can, it feels like your lungs are going to burst. That tightness in the chest is incredibly painful. And it would last until such time as the person became unconscious.

DINIS: How long can the brain survive without oxygen?

WECHT: About four to six minutes, unless the body is experiencing a hypothermic condition. Then it would be longer. We have all heard the stories of people who fell into icy waters and were submerged for a substantially longer period of time and survived. It's because the cold water causes the body to go into a self-preserving hypothermic condition. In the Kopechne case, if there had been an air pocket and she found it and breathed in all the oxygen until the air was replaced by carbon dioxide, then she was probably conscious while experiencing her own asphyxiation.

DINIS: Taking into account the fact the body has been in the ground for several months and has been embalmed, how likely is it that an autopsy today would tell us what the cause of death was?

WECHT: In this particular case, I think there would be an excellent opportunity to arrive at a quite substantial valid medical opinion with more than a reasonable degree of medical certainty.

During the lunch recess, Mr. Dinis, a state policeman, and I were eating at one of the better restaurants in Wilkes-Barre when Judge Brominski, a highly respected jurist who handled the case with dignity and fairness, walked over to our table. I will never forget what he said.

"You know, gentlemen," began Judge Brominski, a large, stocky man who had played college football, "what they are saying about me is not true. Just because I'm Polish does not mean I will grant your petition for an autopsy but deny the order for the exhumation!"

Judge Brominski, a veteran judge in a predominantly Catholic community, was up for reelection that year. Months later, in a written opinion, the judge denied the prosecutor's motion for the exhumation and the autopsy, pointing out that it was likely that the autopsy would show Ms. Kopechne indeed had drowned and there was no reason to put the family through so much personal anguish and misery again.

Despite all the unanswered questions in the case and senseless obstructionistic tactics by Senator Kennedy, I have never asserted that Ms. Kopechne's death was anything other than an accidental drowning. I felt then and I believe today that the best thing for Senator Kennedy would have been to cooperate and agree to have the autopsy performed. It would have eliminated the rumors of foul play that continue to this day. But by not immediately seeking help after the crash, and by not fully cooperating with law enforcement and telling the truth, Ted Kennedy brought much of the pain he has suffered because of this incident on himself.

Several years later, in the fall of 1979, I was in my bathroom shaving when one of my children yelled up the stairs, "Dad, there's some guy named Kennedy on the phone and he wants to talk with you."

Ten years had gone by and I was now chairman of the Democratic party in Allegheny County, a major player in the state Democratic party, and a member of the Democratic National Committee. Senator Kennedy was calling to ask for my political support in his presidential bid. It was clear to me that incumbent president Jimmy Carter was in deep political trouble and was sure to be defeated by Ronald Reagan in the 1980 election. I told Kennedy I would support him for the Democratic nomination because I believed he had a better shot at beating Reagan than did Carter.

While it is almost impossible to defeat an incumbent president from your own party in the primary, I honestly believe that had there been no Chappaquiddick crash, Edward Kennedy would have beaten Carter. In a sense, the Edward Kennedy case is more tragic than those of his two brothers. All three had a vision of how to make the world a better place. Sadly, Jack and Bobby Kennedy never had the chance to make that dream come true. However, the fact that Ted Kennedy had the opportunity, but because of his own actions would never be permitted to deliver, is even more sad.

There is a key lesson to be learned from the case at Chappaquiddick. Every jurisdiction needs an established medicolegal investigative office. If there had been a forensic pathologist, trained and experienced and with a knowledge of the law, an incident like Chappaquiddick would have been avoided.

However, this case is far from unusual. All across the country, especially in small towns, there is a desperate need for people experienced in forensic sciences. In fact, there are some rural areas where not only is the coroner or medical examiner in a county not a forensic pathologist, but he or she is not even a hospital pathologist. And in a few places, the person in charge of the medical investigation is not even a medical doctor.

I have long favored abolishing the office of coroner—an elected position—in favor of an appointed medical examiner system in which a person must be a forensic pathologist to hold the job.

In one county in the mountains of eastern Kentucky—I am sure it is not an isolated case—every four years the residents elect a coroner to investigate their deaths. Every election year, the same two people run for the office. They are not experienced medico-legal investigators, pathologists, or even doctors. They are the directors of the two local funeral homes. The one that gets elected coroner automatically gets a hand up on the competition because he gets to steer the family of the deceased toward his funeral home.

This is completely unacceptable. Who knows how many murders disguised as suicides or accidental deaths occur and these people would not have a clue as to the difference. All they are concerned about is making money. One day, I hope this will all change. But until it does, the Mary Jo Kopechne cases will leave us longing for more information.

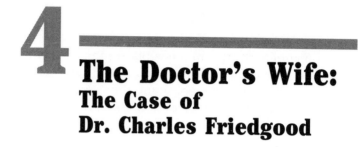

4

The Doctor's Wife:
The Case of
Dr. Charles Friedgood

Police officer Bill Glandt was in his squad car Wednesday afternoon, June 18, 1975, when a call came across the radio at 1:30, of a possible DOA in a neighborhood near where he was patrolling. As an officer with the Kensington, New York, Police Department for twenty years, Patrolman Glandt recognized the address—47 Beverly Road—as being in the community of Great Neck, an upper-middle-class residential neighborhood on Long Island. Within two minutes, he was at the scene.

As he pulled into the driveway of the lavish eighteen-room, three-story brick home, Officer Glandt was greeted by a hysterical woman speaking Spanish and broken English. Through all the screaming, crying, and language barriers, he was able to decipher that she was Lydia Fernandez, the maid, plus a few other key words.

"Upstairs. Mrs. Friedgood. Bed. Dead."

Racing to the second-floor master bedroom, Officer Glandt found a woman lying in bed, mostly covered by a white sheet, but apparently nude. With Mrs. Fernandez at his heels crying uncontrollably, he walked over to the woman he later learned was Sophie Friedgood. Her right hand was up above her head. Reaching out, the officer took hold of the woman's wrist and attempted to get a pulse. There was none. Her body was cold, her fingers stiff.

"She's dead," Officer Glandt told Mrs. Fernandez. Immediately, the maid jumped onto the bed on her hands and knees and began crying and chanting: "Mrs. Friedgood, Mrs. Friedgood."

After removing the maid from the bedroom, Officer Glandt tried to call for a doctor—several lived in the neighborhood. However, it was Wednesday afternoon, which meant that few doctors would be at home or at their office. Instead, they were on the golf course. He telephoned a local ambulance service and a funeral home to come take care of the body. He also had Mrs. Fernandez call the woman's husband, Dr. Charles Friedgood, a surgeon in Brooklyn. The ambulance paramedics arrived shortly before two o'clock. After checking the woman's vital signs and finding none, the paramedics said there was nothing more they could do. Only a doctor could make an official determination of death.

Dr. Friedgood arrived at the house about 2:15 P.M. As he stepped from his 1974 white Cadillac, Officer Glandt introduced himself, told him that his wife was dead, and offered condolences. As Officer Glandt led Dr. Friedgood up to the master bedroom, he said he had tried locating a physician to pronounce death, but had been unsuccessful. That's when he noticed a small brown leather case and some white form papers in the doctor's hand.

Upon entering the room, Dr. Friedgood walked over to his wife, turned her body on its back, pulled the sheet down, and listened to her chest for a heartbeat. Finding none, he pulled her body close to his, hugging her. The officer noticed tears streaming down the physician's face and watched as he kissed his wife on the lips. After holding her body in his arms for two or three minutes, he laid her down on the bed and quickly left the room.

Officer Glandt gave the doctor a few minutes to himself in the next room before approaching him again.

"The reason I have these death certificates," Dr. Friedgood said, waving the white sheets of paper at Officer Glandt, "is that I'm expecting a patient to die."

Somewhat taken aback by the statement, Officer Glandt could only nod in acknowledgment.

"When I left this morning for work about eight-thirty, my wife was complaining about a severe headache and not feeling well," Dr. Friedgood continued. "My God, I should have realized there was more to it."

A few minutes later, Officer Glandt overheard Dr. Friedgood

on the telephone with the funeral home telling them to come pick up the body. "I have death certificates," he said, "but they are New York City death certificates, and I do not know if they are good in Nassau County. Well, when you respond, bring the proper forms and I will sign them."

That indeed happened. Dr. Friedgood signed the death certificate and listed the cause of death as a "cerebral vascular accident," which is a stroke. This seemed acceptable to the police and paramedics at the scene after Dr. Friedgood told them that his wife had suffered a severe stroke fifteen years earlier. Citing his family's Orthodox Jewish beliefs, Dr. Friedgood arranged for his wife's body to be flown to Hazelton, Pennsylvania, where her family had a burial plot. Under the laws of Orthodox Judaism, burial should take place within twenty-four hours of death and autopsies are to be avoided.

The next morning, as Kensington police chief Raymond Sickels reviewed his officer's report on Sophie Friedgood's death, a knot developed in his stomach. Something was wrong with this case. There was the matter of Dr. Friedgood signing his own wife's death certificate and his rush to have the body shipped back to Hazelton, Pennsylvania, for burial. True, it was mere suspicion, but enough to bring the case to the attention of the district attorney and the medical examiner of Nassau County.

By noon, Long Island authorities had contacted Dr. Friedgood, asking his permission to fly the body back to New York for an autopsy. Citing religious reasons, Dr. Friedgood rejected their request. However, he said he would permit the Luzerne County coroner, Dr. George Hudock, to perform an autopsy. But there was one condition: Dr. Friedgood would attend the autopsy himself, and there could be no one from Nassau County in attendance. Dr. Hudock agreed.

Dr. Hudock met Dr. Friedgood at 7:30 P.M. on Thursday, June 19, at St. Joseph's Hospital in Hazelton, where he performed many of his autopsies. As Dr. Hudock prepared for the autopsy, Dr. Friedgood informed the pathologist that his wife had suffered a CVA, a stroke, when she was thirty-three.

"Combining her history with the fact that she apparently died so suddenly indicated to me that the most probable cause of death was a CVA," Dr. Friedgood explained to Dr. Hudock. "What do you think?"

Dr. Hudock nodded in agreement and began the autopsy, describing his findings and observations into a microphone on a tape recorder. Sophie Friedgood was forty-eight years old. She stood five feet, one inch tall. She weighed 150 pounds. There was no evidence of trauma to her head. However, he noted black and blue marks on both her arms and her buttocks.

"Do you know the cause of these bruises?" Dr. Hudock asked Friedgood.

"I believe they were caused postmortem [after death] as the body was being picked up and handled by the undertaker," Dr. Friedgood answered.

Dr. Hudock again nodded. However, he would later write on his report that he believed there was a good chance those marks or bruises were caused before death. Opening up the brain, Dr. Hudock noticed an old scar on the left side of the brain—this caused by her first stroke. But as he searched the brain tissue, he could find no evidence of any acute or recent hemorrhage or CVA in the brain to account for the death.

After explaining that there was no evidence to support a claim that Sophie Friedgood had died of a stroke, Dr. Hudock asked Dr. Friedgood, "May I proceed with the examination?"

"Go right ahead, Doctor. Do whatever you have to do to find the cause of death," Dr. Friedgood responded calmly. "But do not send any specimens back to Nassau County because they are trying to railroad me."

Dr. Hudock proceeded with the autopsy, taking organ samples from throughout the body. After completing his work, Dr. Hudock announced that he had found nothing to indicate what the cause of death might have been. However, he planned to run tests on the various specimens he had retrieved from Mrs. Friedgood's body.

Several days later, those lab tests came back and showed a lethal amount of the painkilling drug Demerol in Mrs. Friedgood's system. Nassau County and Luzerne County officials obtained a joint court order allowing them to exhume Mrs. Friedgood's body two weeks later. This time, they found what they believed to be five needle marks on Mrs. Friedgood's arms, buttocks, and chest where the Demerol had been injected.

On August 5, Charles Friedgood was indicted by a Nassau County grand jury on charges he had murdered his wife. He was arrested at his Brooklyn medical office and taken to jail, where he was held on $1 million bond.

At first glance, *State of New York* v. *Charles Friedgood* seems no different from many of the homicide cases we read about every day in the newspaper. However, I can honestly say this was one of the most bizarre cases I have ever been involved in. It had everything great mysteries are supposed to have—money, sex, international travel, drugs, and, of course, murder. But few of the cases I have been involved in have had the many interesting twists of the Friedgood case.

In June 1975, my career and personal life could not have been going better. All my children were into baseball. In fact, Ingrid was one of the first girls to play Little League baseball in Pittsburgh. My second son, Danny, though, was the star baseball player. That year, as always, my wife took the children to our summer house in Connecticut. Sometime in late June the baseball coach in Pittsburgh called and said their team had made the playoffs and they really needed Danny to pitch. As if we were in a movie, we flew Danny back to Pittsburgh, where he pitched a two-hitter, hit a home run, and helped his team win the championship!

At work, I was in my fifth year as coroner of Allegheny County. Establishing the office as one of the premier forensic science departments in the nation was my goal. By 1975, I was fully engulfed in my research into the assassination of President Kennedy.

I was at work one afternoon in August 1975 when I received a telephone call from New York attorney John Sutter, who told me he had a client who had been charged with murdering his wife. He needed an expert in forensic pathology to review the medical evidence. Police believed that his client, Dr. Charles Friedgood, had killed his spouse of twenty-five years by injecting her with a lethal dose of the painkilling drug Demerol.

"This case," Mr. Sutter said, "will rise and fall on the medical testimony. It's a very odd case, and there's an awful lot of circumstantial evidence stacked against us. However, it's my belief that the medical evidence is on our side and may actually clear my client of any wrongdoing.

"I believe that the time of death will be a major factor in this case," Mr. Sutter told me. "My client says his wife was alive when he left for work at eight-thirty or nine that morning. However,

Nassau County officials believe she was dead long before that time. If we can prove that Dr. Friedgood is telling the truth, I don't see how we can lose this case."

Before agreeing to take the case, I laid down some simple ground rules to Mr. Sutter: "Send me everything you have on the case and I will review it thoroughly. However, I will call it as I see it. There will be no bending or twisting my opinion to fit a particular scenario. My findings will be exactly what the evidence shows and no more."

He concurred, and a few days later I received a package in the mail from Mr. Sutter. Enclosed, I found police investigative reports, the autopsy reports and various other medical reports, and some newspaper clips about the incident. I soon discovered the lawyer was not exaggerating—this was a very strange case.

The investigative reports were full of details about the Friedgood family. Charles Friedgood was a very successful Brooklyn surgeon. At age fifty-seven, he and his wife, Sophie, who was forty-eight, lived in a luxurious home in Kensington, Long Island. They had met in 1948 at a Philadelphia hospital where she was working as a medical assistant and he was doing his residency. He had come from a poor family; her father was a wealthy Orthodox Jewish shoe manufacturer in the small coal-mining town of Hazelton, Pennsylvania. Almost immediately, they began dating and fell in love. A year later, they married.

The young couple moved to Brooklyn, where Dr. Friedgood opened a medical practice. Long hours combined with his natural skills brought almost instant success. It was obvious he cared about his patients, and they about him.

Home life had been just as wonderful. The couple had six children in their first eight years of marriage. As the children grew old enough to go to school, Mrs. Friedgood, described by friends as a vibrant, sweet, loving person, enrolled in law school. The family seemed to have it all.

Then, in 1960, Mrs. Friedgood, at age thirty-three, suffered a stroke. For many months, she was confined to a wheelchair. And when she finally could walk again, she did so with a noticeable limp. It was about this time that she began drinking heavily. Friends and family say her personality changed dramatically. She became somewhat abusive toward her husband and the children.

Numerous examples of such abuse were listed in the materials

I received from Mr. Sutter. There was the time the family agreed to meet for dinner at 7:30 at an Italian restaurant on Long Island. Everyone was on time, except Dr. Friedgood. He finally arrived at 8:30, saying he had been delayed at the office. "In front of dozens of people in that restaurant, Mrs. Friedgood began making an incredibly embarrassing scene," a friend of the family was quoted in the newspaper as saying. "She was screaming at him for being late. It was quite humiliating to him. But he stood there, apologized, and said nothing."

I read in the police investigative reports that sometime in the late 1960s, Dr. Friedgood began having an affair with Harriet Larsen, an attractive registered nurse who worked for him for several years. He had met Ms. Larsen, who was fourteen years younger than Mrs. Friedgood, while attending a medical seminar in Denmark, her native country. She moved to New York a year later and worked at Dr. Friedgood's office. By 1974, Miss Larsen had moved back to Denmark, but she had already given birth to two of his children—a boy and a girl. Mrs. Friedgood apparently became aware of the affair in the early 1970s and made it the subject of her many tirades.

While all of this is great stuff for a daytime soap opera, I did not consider any of it proof that the doctor had murdered his wife. The same could be said for his decision to sign Mrs. Friedgood's death certificate. Such an action is professionally unwise, but certainly not illegal. Assuming for the moment he did kill his wife, it would have been incredibly stupid for him to sign the death certificate because that would have sent up an immediate red flag. If he had planned this elaborate scheme to kill his wife, why didn't he simply call up a physician who lived down the street and, with tears in his eyes, ask one of his golfing buddies to come over and sign the death certificate? Had Dr. Friedgood not signed the death certificate, there probably would never have been a homicide investigation into the death of his wife. All that being said, it was still not evidence that Charles Friedgood had murdered his wife.

As I turned to the various medical reports, my first job was to determine the cause of death. Dr. Friedgood had listed a stroke, which taking into account his wife's previous stroke, was a completely reasonable assumption as the cause of death. But Dr. Hudock, whom I knew to be an experienced pathologist and coroner, had found no evidence of a recent stroke in the brain tissue. A cerebral vascular accident, therefore, was out of the question.

As I reviewed the toxicology report, any doubts I may have had as to what caused the death of Sophie Friedgood were quickly put to rest. The level of Demerol found in Mrs. Friedgood's body was more than 600 milligrams—twice the amount needed to cause death. Demerol is a synthetic drug similar to morphine which depresses the central nervous system, leading to sedation, sleep, and, in heavy doses such as this, coma and death.

A good medical examiner learns to follow certain paths to make sure not to get ahead of himself. It would be very easy to assume that, because Charles Friedgood was a doctor and had access to Demerol and needles, he had made the injections. But you must evaluate and consider every piece of evidence in an objective fashion. There were several potential scenarios to explain how the Demerol could have made its way into Mrs. Friedgood's body. It was possible that this was a suicide and that Mrs. Friedgood had ingested the Demerol. Or she could have injected the drug herself. It's the medical examiner's job to check every possibility and leave no stone unturned.

There was no question in my opinion that Demerol poisoning was the cause of death. Did she swallow the drug or was it injected? That was answered quickly when the second autopsy revealed five injection marks on both arms and the right buttocks. However, those are all places where self-injection is physically possible.

But the likelihood of suicide was significantly diminished when I noticed on the autopsy report that there was evidence that a needle had been inserted through the lower chest wall between the ribs. The ribs overlie and protect the liver on the right side. The autopsy report stated that specimens from Mrs. Friedgood's liver had been taken. I immediately called my old friend and colleague Dr. Leslie Lukash, who was chief medical examiner of Nassau County, New York, and asked him if he would put aside a small specimen for me to examine as well. He readily agreed. Through the years, I have been consulted in several cases in Nassau County, and I have always found Dr. Lukash and his staff to be extremely professional and courteous. I wish I could say the same about some of my other forensic pathology contemporaries. Too many times, medical examiners and coroners become very defensive and even hostile if you question their findings.

When I later tested the liver specimen for Demerol, I found that there were very high amounts throughout the organ. In the area of the needle tracks, the level of Demerol increased by tenfold. That proved the Demerol had been directly injected into the liver.

It also told me something else. The amount of Demerol injected into the liver was so high that Sophie Friedgood was most likely unconscious, in a coma, or possibly already dead before the injections had been completed. Therefore, the Demerol could not have been self-injected, eliminating suicide as the manner of death. Add that finding to the police investigative reports, which said the first officers at the scene searched the room but found no evidence of any hypodermic needles, and you have a scenario that rules out self-injection.

The fact that the cause of death was a lethal dose of Demerol, a prescription drug, and that it was administered by injection, certainly pointed to Dr. Friedgood. This homicide was committed in a manner unlike most—a shooting, stabbing, or strangulation— where almost any average Joe could be the perpetrator. Here we had a case in which the killer apparently had some knowledge of medicine and used it on his or her victim. So while all this so far was just circumstantial evidence, it carried with it strong overtones of an ominous nature for Dr. Friedgood.

That's when I came across what Mr. Sutter had said would be the central issue in the case—the estimation of time of death. During the autopsy, Dr. Hudock discovered Mrs. Friedgood had a full stomach. According to eyewitnesses and Dr. Friedgood's own statement, the Friedgoods ate dinner the evening before her death at about eight o'clock at Lundy's, a seafood restaurant in Brooklyn. Mrs. Friedgood had eaten fish, a baked potato, green salad, and clam chowder. These were the exact items found in her stomach. Further examination showed no food particles in the small intestines—the place food goes after leaving the stomach. All this meant that the digestive process had just begun.

Using this analysis and the generally accepted understanding that it normally takes a full stomach about four to six hours to empty, Dr. Hudock set the time of death at about twelve midnight to two in the morning, which would have been approximately four to six hours after the Friedgoods had eaten dinner.

I generally accept the time frame set forth in Dr. Hudock's

conclusion. However, I hesitate to establish a definite time of death based solely on stomach contents. And I certainly would not be comfortable sending a man to prison based upon that finding alone. There are too many variables that can speed up or slow down the gastric emptying process. Stress, fever, constipation, even room temperature are factors that can delay the digestion of food for hours.

Another major factor in slowing down the digestive system is alcohol consumption. According to her friends, Sophie Friedgood could consume substantial amounts of alcohol.

"Sophie would never have injected herself," a friend told police. "She didn't even like to take pills, only booze. Sophie liked martinis and white wine. Soave Bolla was her favorite wine. She was not a lush, but more of a social drinker. 'Where's my martini? Where's my lemon?' she used to say when she visited my home. She had a bossy way about her. After she drank her first martini, though, she was lovely."

At the Tuesday evening dinner at Lundy's, the Friedgoods were joined by a retired real estate developer, Boris Rudoff, who had known the couple for twenty-seven years. In his statement to police, Mr. Rudoff said that while he was there, Mrs. Friedgood drank two martinis and a half bottle of white wine. "There's no doubt," he told authorities, "that she was intoxicated."

But there was one more question about the stomach contents that no one seemed prepared to answer conclusively: are we sure that the meal at Lundy's was the last time Sophie Friedgood ate? Both Dr. Friedgood and the maid, Mrs. Fernandez, told me about Mrs. Friedgood's habit of not being able to sleep late at night, of her sitting in front of the television and snacking until the wee hours of the morning. Add to that Mrs. Fernandez's statement to police that she found an empty but dirty dinner plate in front of the television set when she arrived Wednesday morning for work, and the scenario became very complicated. And there was Dr. Friedgood's statement that his wife brought home a doggy bag from Lundy's. Could the food found in her stomach have been eaten early Wednesday morning?

There was other evidence that Sophie Friedgood may have been alive after 9:00 A.M. For example, there was the statement Mrs. Fernandez gave to police detailing what she saw and heard the morning that Mrs. Friedgood died.

About ten to ten-thirty A.M., I was sleeping in the downstairs. I listen and Mrs. Friedgood walk. She walk with an impediment, like she was lame with one foot. I had been sick with hay fever that day and was napping on and off. About nine-thirty, I hear the radio playing and I go up and check on Mrs. Friedgood. She was laying on her side facing the door. At one o'clock, I check on Mrs. Friedgood again because she get a phone call. This time, Mrs. Friedgood laying on her stomach. I try to wake her but could not. I loved Mrs. Friedgood very much. It's very hard for me to talk about her.

Mrs. Fernandez, who was in her late fifties, came to the United States from Santo Domingo in 1967. When I heard her testimony at Dr. Friedgood's trial in November 1975, she had a translator interpreting many of her comments. I thought her statements about hearing Mrs. Friedgood's footsteps and noticing that her employer had radically changed her position in bed certainly bolstered Dr. Friedgood's claim that his wife was alive when he left for work at 8:30 A.M. But that was not all Mrs. Fernandez would reveal. The maid said she picked up the telephone about 9:30 and heard Mrs. Friedgood talking.

After this statement was made public, two women came forward to announce they had called the Friedgood house that morning after 9:30, and both said they had spoken with Sophie Friedgood.

Lillian Ruiz, a medical assistant at the Brooklyn health center where Dr. Friedgood performed surgery, said that she called for Dr. Friedgood at his home about 9:30 A.M. to check his schedule. But it was Mrs. Friedgood who answered the phone, Mrs. Ruiz said. "I had met and spoken with Mrs. Friedgood several times and I knew her voice," Mrs. Ruiz said in her statement to police. "There's no doubt, it was Sophie Friedgood I talked to."

Anna Harvey, a former patient of Dr. Friedgood's, also came forward saying she called his house about 9:55 A.M. and spoke with Mrs. Friedgood. Mrs. Harvey said she had talked with Mrs. Friedgood before and recognized her voice, and she, too, was sure that it was Sophie Friedgood on the other end of the telephone line.

I wasn't sure how good Dr. Friedgood's alibi was after 8:30 A.M.—and it was not my job to find out—but it appeared he certainly had a winnable case at this point.

But there are other ways to estimate time of death besides stomach analysis. For example, what was the condition of the body when it was found?

I carefully read over the statements of the first three people who observed Sophie Friedgood's body: Officer Glandt; Edward Currivan, a medical technician; and James Abramo, the funeral home director.

Officer Glandt said that Mrs. Friedgood's body was cold and that her fingers were stiff. However, he was able to move her hands and arms to check her pulse. But his most important statement was that he noticed a discoloration on Mrs. Friedgood's cheek. But when the autopsy was performed twenty-four hours later, the discoloration had disappeared. To me, this meant Mrs. Friedgood could not have been dead for twelve hours as the Nassau County authorities claimed.

The discoloration is called livor mortis, and it occurs after death when the blood settles in the lower portions of the body as a result of gravity. This is one of the universal and traditional methods of determining time of death. Livor mortis begins within an hour or so after death and usually takes more than six to eight hours to become fixed. The fact that the discoloration dissipated in this case indicated that Mrs. Friedgood had not been dead long enough for the blood to have become permanently fixed in that area of her body.

I thought it also very interesting that neither Officer Glandt, nor Mr. Currivan, nor Dr. Friedgood—all of whom examined the body prior to 2:20 P.M.—said he had seen any livor mortis or discoloration on Mrs. Friedgood's back. The discoloration on her back is to be distinguished from the discoloration on her cheek. So no one reported any livor mortis on Mrs. Friedgood's back until 3:30 P.M., when Mr. Abramo of the funeral home arrived. He and others reported seeing such discoloration in the back region at that time.

Mr. Abramo also told police that when he arrived at 3:30 to remove the body, rigor mortis, which is the stiffening of the body after death, had already set in. Rigor mortis generally begins about one to two hours after death and takes eight to twelve hours to become fixed.

On October 8, 1975, Dr. Charles Friedgood went on trial for murdering his wife. Sixty witnesses testified for the prosecution, including Dr. Hudock and Nassau County medical examiner Dr. Leslie Lukash. Both men gave their estimated time of death as between midnight and 2:00 A.M. There was no argument at the trial about the cause of death—Demerol poisoning by injection.

On December 7, Mr. Sutter called me to the witness stand. Slowly, I told the jury of my findings and conclusions. I went over the testimony of Dr. Hudock and Dr. Lukash regarding the stomach contents and reiterated my concern as to the accuracy of their estimations. And I relayed to the jury my interpretation of the observations of the body by those who had first arrived at the scene.

SUTTER: Taking all those factors into consideration, what is your conclusion as to the time of death?

WECHT: It is impossible to make an exact determination as to the time of death. All I or anyone can do is give you a range. The body was found around 1:00 P.M. and Officer Glandt made his observations between 1:30 P.M. and 2:15 P.M. It's my opinion that she died about two or three hours prior to that. It's possible that she died as many as four hours earlier. I would estimate the time of death to have been between 10:00 A.M. and 1:00 P.M.

SUTTER: What do you think of the opinion that she could have died as early as midnight or 2:00 A.M.?

WECHT: I think that it clearly misinterprets the medical evidence in this case. First, we have no firm idea as to when she ate last. Second, there are so many variables that can make the stomach analysis as means of determining time of death completely off base.

SUTTER: Is there anything else your review of the autopsy revealed?

WECHT: Yes. The medical evidence is clear and convincing that Mrs. Friedgood was murdered. But I also believe the medical evidence tells us there was probably more than one assailant.

An incredible hush came over the courtroom. This was the first news of multiple assailants. You can always tell when you say something quite unexpected, exciting, or titillating because the reporters in the press gallery begin writing down your comments at a furious pace. Even the prosecutor, Nassau assistant district attorney Stephen Scaring, showed a look of surprise at my comment.

SUTTER: And what leads you to make such a comment?

WECHT: She had deep bruises on her arms and in various spots throughout her body that strongly suggested a struggle. She obviously tried to fight off her attacker. I believe the bruises indicate that one person held Mrs. Friedgood down while a second person injected her with the Demerol. I definitely lean toward the belief that two people were involved in this crime.

I felt my testimony had gone over rather well. The jurors had nodded their heads in apparent understanding as I explained various medical terms and concepts to them. One of the newspaper reporters covering the trial wrote that "Dr. Wecht did to the state's evidence what the Pittsburgh Steelers did to the New York Giants last Sunday." My Super Bowl champion Steelers had trounced those guys from the Big Apple quite convincingly the previous weekend.

Mr. Sutter followed my testimony with that of Dr. Alfred Angrist, a noted pathologist and professor at the Albert Einstein College of Medicine. Dr. Angrist's testimony was, I thought, particularly fascinating because he had trained and taught Dr. Lukash, the Nassau County medical examiner. And now Dr. Angrist was testifying against his former student.

ANGRIST: Dr. Lukash was one of my boys. I respect him. He's a good man.

SUTTER: After reviewing the medical evidence in this case, what do you think of the possibility that Sophie Friedgood died about twelve hours before her body was found?

ANGRIST: She surely did not die at 2:00 A.M. She died much later than that, much later. The maximum it could have been was three or four hours before the body was discovered.

But I soon discovered that the prosecution was steering the trial away from the medical evidence and emphasizing the circumstantial evidence. They were also trying to assassinate Dr. Friedgood's character by bringing up his past run-ins with the law.

In 1964, he had been indicted in Brooklyn on charges of performing an illegal abortion, including a first-degree manslaughter charge after a woman died from an abortion allegedly performed by Dr. Friedgood. This was before abortions were legalized in New York. However, the case was dismissed by a judge after he learned that all the evidence was obtained through an illegal wiretap.

A couple of years later, Dr. Friedgood was convicted on three federal income tax evasion charges involving more than three hundred thousand dollars. He was sentenced to two years' probation.

In 1972, Dr. Friedgood's business partner in some real estate transactions charged the doctor with having him kidnapped and drugged. The man claimed Dr. Friedgood was trying to force him to sign a $510,000 promissory note. However, the case was dismissed because of a lack of evidence.

And at the time of Mrs. Friedgood's death, Dr. Friedgood was one of thirteen doctors under investigation by the New York State Assembly's Health Committee Task Force on Institutional Medicaid Costs. The government panel had targeted Dr. Friedgood and his medical group for alleged fraud involving Medicaid benefits.

While all of this did much to undercut Dr. Friedgood's character, it had nothing to do with the question of whether he killed his wife. Accordingly, Nassau County Supreme Court judge Richard Delin declared most of this testimony inadmissible and instructed the jury to ignore such evidence when it came up.

However, many of Dr. Friedgood's own actions involving the death and the period immediately after his wife's death looked very suspicious. His signing of the death certificate and his ordering the body to be buried immediately were instant red flags, even though both were explainable. But there were other things that raised the eyebrows of even his supporters and family members.

One week after Mrs. Friedgood died, Dr. Friedgood showed up at the office of the family's stockbroker wanting to sell a considerable portion of their stocks and securities. George Bapis, a broker with E. F. Hutton, told the jury that Dr. Friedgood supplied him with a letter dated June 10, signed by Sophie Friedgood, authorizing the sale of $49,543 of stocks and securities listed in her name. Mr. Bapis testified that the Friedgoods owned stocks jointly and separately, including shares in companies such as AT&T, IBM, and Con Edison.

The next day, June 26, Dr. Friedgood again dropped by Mr. Bapis's office. This time he wanted the stockbroker to sell $92,240 in stocks and securities in his name. Because Dr. Friedgood was such a regular customer, Mr. Bapis said the two visits did not alarm him.

That same day, Dr. Friedgood forged his wife's name on documents giving him access to her private safe deposit box at a Long Island bank. Inside the box, he found an envelope containing three letters, his passport, and a nude photograph of Harriet Larsen. In Sophie Friedgood's handwriting on the photograph was the word *whore.*

It was two days later that Assistant District Attorney Scaring received a call from Friedgood's son-in-law Abraham Menache, who was married to Dr. Friedgood's youngest daughter, Dvorah. Mr. Menache had a tip for the prosecutor: Dr. Friedgood is at New York's Kennedy Airport preparing to leave the country. Immediately, Mr. Scaring called the New York Port Authority and asked that a check be made at all the airlines for a passenger named Charles Friedgood.

Sure enough, they found Charles Friedgood listed in the computer for a BOAC flight bound for London. As the jumbo jet was preparing to take off, authorities boarded the airplane and confronted Dr. Friedgood. He had a one-way ticket to London and a black briefcase in his hand. He was carrying no other luggage with him. Confiscating the black briefcase, police discovered more than $650,000 in bonds, securities, and jewelry inside. Although he was not arrested, Dr. Friedgood was escorted from the plane and was required to give up his passport. Mr. Scaring told the jury that Dr. Friedgood was fleeing the country to rendezvous with his lover, Harriet Larsen, in Denmark. Mr. Sutter tried to explain the incident to the jury by saying that Dr. Friedgood was taking the bonds and securities to London to place them in a bank account where they would be unnoticed by U.S. authorities when it came time to calculate the inheritance tax. However, the expression on the faces of the jurors was that of disbelief and sarcasm.

Much of the strong circumstantial evidence against Dr. Friedgood came from his own daughters and their husbands. When he took the witness stand at the trial, Mr. Menache and the other son-in-law, Dr. Jack Cook, admitted giving police several tips that led to Dr. Friedgood's arrest and indictment.

However, neither man should have been casting stones. Mr. Menache admitted that he and Mrs. Friedgood never got along and had many heated arguments. Mrs. Friedgood had in fact stated publicly several times that she did not like Mr. Menache. He was against everything she believed in. He maintained the idea that a family and family gatherings were outdated and useless. To Mrs. Friedgood, her family was everything.

Similarly, Dr. Cook and Mrs. Friedgood had a long-running feud. Family members told of many occasions when Dr. Cook or his wife would storm out of the house in a rage. Several times Mrs. Friedgood had rejected his request to borrow money. Dr. Cook and his wife, Beth, actually sued Mrs. Friedgood for fifty thousand dollars, demanding that she release money Mrs. Friedgood had set aside for her children in a trust fund.

SUTTER: You knew that if your wife's mother were dead and her husband was convicted of the murder, you and your wife's share of the inheritance would be greatly increased?

COOK: I don't think I ever really thought about it.

SUTTER: Isn't it true that you told other people that you wanted to be the administrator of Sophie Friedgood's estate?

COOK: I was prepared to do it, and I was asked to do it, and was urged by some family members to do so.

SUTTER: Have you ever told any of your friends that you wished Mrs. Friedgood dead?

COOK: No.

SUTTER: Did you ever tell a friend that you were going to have Sophie Friedgood committed to a mental institution?

COOK: No, I did not.

SUTTER: Did you ever tell a friend that she was like a cancer and that when you have a cancer, you want to get rid of it?

COOK: No, I never said that.

One by one, Mr. Scaring called to the witness stand each of Dr. Friedgood's four daughters and one of his sons. The impact of having five children testify against their father was probably more dramatic in the jurors' minds than the words they spoke. While each told of their love for their mother and father, they gave the courtroom an incredible insight into the Friedgood family. In the end, it is very likely that it was the testimony of Dr. Friedgood's daughters that influenced the jury's decision making.

Each of the five children testified that he or she was aware of Dr. Friedgood's extramarital affair with Miss Larsen. Some even said they did not resent him for the relationship. The girls discussed the abuse their mother put them through after she suffered her stroke. She would call them terrible names, including "cow-face," "fat pigs," "ugly," and "horse-face." She would hit them for having messy hair or holes in their blue jeans.

The Friedgoods' youngest daughter, Dvorah, who was twenty-two when her mother was killed, probably gave the greatest insight into the relationship between Dr. Friedgood, his wife, and their children. I read the following statement she made to the Long Island newspaper *Newsday* with fascination. She had made similar comments to the jury during her testimony, but it was not as clear and concise as the interview she gave to the newspaper:

I thought [mother] hated me. I looked at my father as the good guy because he never yelled at me. Instead, he always played the mediator. He always complimented us. He could make you believe you were great. He could give you a lot of confidence. When I would go out, he would leave a note in my wallet: Have a good time.

And when my mother would yell at him, he never expressed any emotion or anger. He would just say nothing. Instead, his face went through contortions, and my heart went through contortions for him.

At my high school graduation from Great Neck South, my father arrived an hour late, and he brought Harriet. They sat by themselves in the bleachers. My mother was so furious that she threw her shoe at them. She called her a whore. I thought [mother] was brutal. And through it all, my father said nothing. He only smiled. Because I was so angry at my mother in those years, I was fond of Harriet. I thought of her as this wonderful woman who made my father so happy. I wanted him to run away with her. Though my father never admitted it, I always assumed she was his mistress. Later, when she became pregnant, I wrote [Harriet] a letter complimenting her on her "maturing belly."

Only later did I realize it was my mother who really loved me.

The children had obviously turned against their father and believed he was their mother's killer. Four of the five openly showed disdain for him on the witness stand. They refused to look at him. Only Esther, who was then in her twenties, expressed her support and love for her father. The second of the Friedgood children to testify at the trial, Esther had a law degree and had married Richard Zaretsky. They were living in Florida. However, she had flown to New York to be with her father after her mother's death.

As Mr. Scaring began asking her questions, it was clear that she did not like or want to testify against her father. But under a court order, she was forced to tell the jury about the afternoon of June 22—the day the police came to the Friedgood house with a search warrant. This might have been the most damaging testimony of the trial.

SCARING: Please tell us what happened that day and about a conversation between you and Dr. Friedgood.

ESTHER ZARETSKY: When the police came to the door, they handed my father a copy of the search warrant. They stated they needed to search the premises. After reading the search warrant, my father pulled me aside and began speaking to me in Yiddish. I told him I don't speak Yiddish and asked him to speak in Hebrew. He said he couldn't speak Hebrew. In a very soft voice, he whispered the words, "Upstairs, file cabinet, bottle syringe."

SCARING: And what was your reaction?

ESTHER ZARETSKY: I walked over and told my sister, Beth, to go up and get the items and hide them. But she said she was too afraid and would not.

SCARING: And what happened next?

ESTHER ZARETSKY: I walked upstairs myself, looked in the file cabinet in my dad's den, and found two bottles, a syringe, and a prescription of Empirin.

SCARING: What did you do with these items?

ESTHER ZARETSKY: I hid them in my underwear until the police left.

SCARING: And then what?

ESTHER ZARETSKY: Later, I took the bottles to the sink to wash my fingerprints off and I noticed the word *Demerol* on the side in raised letters. I put all the items in a bag and hid it in a closet. I told my father and my sister where it was.

On cross-examination, Mr. Sutter had a few questions of his own that Mr. Scaring had not asked:

SUTTER: Your father told you, did he not, that when he saw the search warrant and realized that they were looking for Demerol and needles that he remembered the old vial lying upstairs and he became afraid?

ESTHER ZARETSKY: Yes, that's what he told me. I asked him why, if my mother had died from it, what was it doing lying up there in a drawer. He said it was just an old vial that he remembered being there for so long.

SUTTER: And he became afraid when the police came looking for that substance?

ESTHER ZARETSKY: Yes. There has always been a variety of drugs and needles in our house for as long as I can remember. It looked like a pharmacy. After all, he was a doctor.

I noticed that unlike the other children, Esther did stop and talk with her father after her testimony. They hugged. She kissed him on the cheek and then she left. It was obvious that it pained her incredibly to have to testify against her father.

In her testimony, Mrs. Zaretsky said that when she checked on the bag containing the needles and bottles three days later, it was gone. She thought her father had taken the items from the closet.

However, it was not her father who had retrieved the bag, but her sister Toba, who had married Larry Press and moved to Forestville, California. It was Toba, at age twenty-six the oldest daughter, who had called the police about the bag. She was Mr. Scaring's next witness.

SCARING: When your father found out you had turned the items over to the police, what was his reaction?

TOBA PRESS: My father told me he was very disappointed with me. He told me that I had opened the lid. If I hadn't said anything, nobody would have known. I should have kept it a secret, he told me. He said Esther had told me to keep it a secret and I should have and that I was trying to put him in jail.

SCARING: What was your response?

TOBA PRESS: I told him I just couldn't hold on to that any longer and that I just had to tell the truth and to find out what happened. It was a very angry, uncomfortable conversation.

The twelve-week trial ended without Dr. Friedgood taking the witness stand. On December 15, the jury of eleven men and one woman found Charles Friedgood guilty of murdering his wife. Judge Delin sentenced him to twenty-five years to life in prison. "You were motivated by greed and lust," Judge Delin told Friedgood at the sentencing. "Greed for your wife's jewels and lust for your mistress."

The Friedgood case was much like the assassination of Bobby Kennedy. While Sirhan Sirhan was undoubtedly involved in the murder attempt, the medical evidence strongly suggests there is more to the story. In the case of Charles Friedgood, I believe he or whoever committed this crime possibly had an accomplice. I also stand firm in my opinion that Sophie Friedgood did not die until after 10:00 A.M.

But I have never said that I thought Charles Friedgood was innocent of this crime. I simply do not believe it happened the way the prosecutor and police say it happened. It may be a case of the authorities having the right man, but the wrong theory.

Another reason why I believe Friedgood lost his case was because he did not present the jury with an alternative explanation or theory. There are two schools of thought when defending someone in a murder trial. The first is "the victim deserved to die and my guy was the man for the job." Sophie Friedgood may not have been the most lovable person in the world, but she was no monster or queen of terror. There can be no question that she did not deserve to be killed. So that line of defense was ruled out.

The second defense is this: "Find somebody else to blame for the crime whom the jury will hate worse than you." Friedgood's lawyers, I believe, had an opportunity to do this with the two sons-in-law, Abraham Menache and Dr. Jack Cook, both of whom had had many angry fights with the victim and who had sued her for an inheritance. Being a physician, Dr. Cook had just as much access to Demerol as Dr. Friedgood. Before a jury will find a person not guilty, the jurors must feel that the defendant was framed by the police or that it is possible that someone else committed the crime. I would like to make it clear that there was no evidence that either man played any role in the death of their mother-in-law. However, simply pointing out that they may have had motive or opportunity could have created enough doubt in the jurors' minds to gain a "not guilty" verdict for Dr. Friedgood.

In the summer of 1991, I was in New York City and arranged to drop by Sing-Sing State Prison in Ossining, New York, to visit Dr. Friedgood. We sat and chatted for more than three hours about his case and how he was doing. He was in remarkably good health and was involved in teaching many of the inmates various subjects, such as math and English. Fifteen years after his conviction, Dr. Friedgood continues to proclaim his innocence. He told me he is asking that he be released from prison and sent to work with the poor and needy in Israel to serve the remaining time of his sentence. I think that would be a humane decision, and I hope the New York State Parole Board will give serious consideration to his plea.

5
Victim or Murderer?
The Case of
Jeffrey MacDonald

To those who knew him as a friend and co-worker, Jeffrey MacDonald was always kind, considerate, a loving, caring father, and the hardest working, most dedicated physician they had ever met. He was quarterback of his Long Island high school football team, king of the senior prom, and was voted both "most popular" and "most likely to succeed." He graduated at or near the top of his classes at Princeton University and at Northwestern University Medical School.

But to the Federal Bureau of Investigation and investigators for the army, he is a murderer—a man who, with no thought of mercy or love, used a wooden club, a knife, and an ice pick to brutally kill his pregnant wife and two young children in 1970.

Because of the savagery and horror of what happened to MacDonald's family, and because the person suspected of committing this horrifying act was a well-respected doctor and a captain in the army's special forces, the Green Berets, the case grabbed the attention of the national news media. There were extensive articles in the *New York Times,* and all the television networks ran dramatic stories depicting what happened. This is how I and millions of other Americans learned about and followed this bizarre tragedy.

Though the terrifying event occurred during the early morning hours of February 17, 1970, Dr. MacDonald did not stand trial until August 1979, which is when I became officially involved. Days before the case was scheduled to begin, I received a call from Bernard Segal, a prominent criminal defense lawyer who was representing Dr. MacDonald.

"I know I should have called you before this, but is there any way I could persuade you to fly to North Carolina and review the physical and forensic evidence in this case?" Mr. Segal asked.

I agreed to meet him the following week at the motel where he and Dr. MacDonald and other members of the defense team were staying in Raleigh, North Carolina—the site of the trial. Meanwhile, I asked if he would send me whatever information he could about the case. Within two days, a large package from Mr. Segal arrived at my office in Pittsburgh. It contained a brown notebook filled with police reports, autopsy records, and a detailed summary of the evidence gathered by police. Over the weekend, I read through the entire four-hundred-page notebook with fascination.

When cases are tried several years after the alleged criminal act occurs, the ability of medicolegal investigators who are brought in to determine what happened is severely limited. In this case, it was nine years later. All I had to go on was the evidence that had been collected by the original authorities in 1970.

The more I read, the more disturbed I became. The military police who investigated the case had botched the whole thing. The investigation was messy, evidence had been destroyed, and proper records had not been kept. In fact, the medical evidence in this case—my primary source of information—was slim to none. Yet my hands were tied by what the military investigators had done nine years earlier. The investigative file may have been four hundred pages thick, but the details it brought to light regarding what really happened that night were quite meager.

About 3:45 A.M., February 17, 1970, military police received an emergency call from 544 Castle Drive in Fayetteville, North Carolina. The house was located on the grounds of Fort Bragg—the largest army base in the United States.

A few blocks from the house, Military Police Officer Kenneth Mica, driving an army jeep, saw a young woman in her twenties wearing a "floppy" wide-brimmed hat standing on a street corner in the rain. However, Mica gave her only a casual glance. His thoughts were on responding to the call for help a few blocks away.

When Mica and other military police officers arrived, they broke down the front door. The scene inside made several of them physically sick. As they entered the house, they noticed bloodstains throughout the living room. A coffee table lay on its side, magazines were scattered all over the room, and a flower pot was standing straight up, but the flower it held was on its side—all these were signals that made it appear that there had been a struggle in the living room.

Running through the house, the MPs first searched the master bedroom, which resembled a war zone. Blood was everywhere. They found Dr. MacDonald lying on the floor. He was wearing the torn bottoms of his pajamas, but no shirt. Next to him lay his twenty-six-year-old wife, Colette. His head was on her left shoulder. Both appeared to be dead. But as the officers checked for a pulse, they discovered that Dr. MacDonald was alive. By two-way radio, the MPs summoned an ambulance. One of the officers heard a faint whisper come from Dr. MacDonald.

"Check my kids. How are my kids?"

While one MP stayed with Dr. MacDonald, two others scrambled down the hallway. Officer Mica was the first to enter the bedroom of two-year-old Kristen. She had no pulse. The little girl with blond curls had been stabbed with a knife seventeen times and speared with an ice pick fifteen times.

When the MPs checked the bedroom next door to Kristen's, they found five-year-old Kimberly lying in bed dead. She had been struck on the head three times with a club and stabbed ten times with a knife.

Returning to the master bedroom, the officers discovered that Dr. MacDonald, who had lost a significant amount of blood from being hit in the head and stabbed several times, had passed out. Mrs. MacDonald had been gouged twenty-one times with an ice pick and clubbed so many times that her skull had been fractured. Above the headboard of the couple's bed was the word PIG written in their own blood.

Using mouth-to-mouth resuscitation, the MPs revived Dr. MacDonald. He was very weak and his teeth were chattering, but he told them that four "hippie" intruders—three men and a woman—had broken into his house and committed these awful acts.

"I can't breathe," he told the officers. "How are my children? I heard my kids crying."

The MPs asked him if he knew the intruders. He did not.

"But they kept saying, 'Acid is groovy. Kill the pigs,' " Dr. Mac-Donald said.

At the hospital, he was treated for a puncture wound to his right lung, several stab wounds to his abdomen and his left arm, and bruises on his forehead.

The Jeffrey MacDonald case captured my attention from day one because of another famous murder investigation in which I was involved at that time—the Beverly Hills slayings of glamorous actress Sharon Tate and three of her friends by the so-called Charles Manson family. At the time, I was the coroner of Allegheny County, having been elected the year before. When Tate and her friends were brutally murdered on August 9, 1969, Dr. Thomas Noguchi, the chief medical examiner of Los Angeles, called to ask me to be an official consultant to him in the case.

As in the MacDonald case, the Beverly Hills victims had been beaten and stabbed. On the front door, a word was written in the victims' blood—PIG.

The next day, the Los Angeles killers struck again, this time at the home of Leno and Rosemary La Bianca, who lived in the Los Feliz section of Los Angeles, an upper-middle-class neighborhood. They, too, were stabbed. Written in blood on the walls was DEATH TO PIGS. And on the refrigerator door in the kitchen were the words HELTER SKELTER.

Through solid police investigation and analysis of forensic evidence, authorities arrested known hippie and drug user Charles Manson and his followers for the murders. When I heard that Fayetteville, North Carolina, had a large hippie community, my initial thoughts led me to wonder if the MacDonald slayings were copycat crimes. I watched with interest to see what evidence would turn up.

Six weeks after the tragedy at Fort Bragg, the U.S. Army Criminal Investigation Division officially advised Dr. MacDonald that he was a suspect in the murder of his wife and two children. Here's what the military investigators believe happened:

Dr. MacDonald discovered that his youngest daughter, Kristen, had wet the bed and he became violently angry. His fury was unleashed when his wife, Colette, began defending their child. Dr. MacDonald then picked up a club and struck both his wife and his daughter in a moment of uncontrollable anger. Interestingly, the detectives never found the "club" that was used in the slayings and they never identified what type of club it was. Within moments, he returned to his senses and realized he needed to make it look like they had all been victimized. That's when, according to the MPs, he killed his other daughter, Kimberly, and wrote the word PIG in their blood.

Investigators said that in order to make it appear as if he too had been attacked, Dr. MacDonald hit himself in the head several times and stabbed himself in the stomach and side with a knife and ice pick. This claim would become the principal allegation I would focus on. Were Dr. MacDonald's wounds self-inflicted? I would need to review closely the medical reports from 1970 and take a firsthand look at Dr. MacDonald's scars and hear from him exactly how he was attacked.

Military investigators said there were several oddities that made them believe the scene they saw the night of February 17 was staged. First, there was the overturned coffee table in the living room that appeared to have been placed on its side and not knocked over in a struggle as Dr. MacDonald had claimed. The investigators also found among a cluster of magazines thrown on the floor the March 1970 edition of *Esquire,* which featured an article on the Manson slayings titled "Evil Lurks in California." Added to this was the fact that a friend who had visited MacDonald's house just days before the slaying told police that Dr. MacDonald had shown him the article on the Manson family. The friend said Dr. MacDonald was completely fascinated by it.

On May 1, 1970, Dr. MacDonald was officially charged with the murder of his family. To defend himself, Dr. MacDonald hired Bernard Segal, a nonmilitary lawyer with an excellent reputation in handling high-profile homicide cases. To save time and money, Mr. Segal notified the army that he planned to challenge the charges against his client at the preliminary phase of the military judicial proceedings. The preliminary hearing turned into a full-blown trial at which more than four months of testimony and evidence was presented to a military judge.

More than fifty witnesses testified at the hearings. In addition to Officer Mica, who had seen the woman, two other people testified that they had seen two or three men and a woman with long, stringy, blond hair wearing a floppy hat and carrying a lit candle near the MacDonald house shortly before the murder. The night of the attack, Dr. MacDonald told the MPs the woman was wearing a floppy hat and held a candle in her hand. That woman was identified as twenty-year-old Helena Stoeckley.

Ms. Stoeckley lived with her family just a few blocks away from the MacDonald residence. A third witness who lived next door to Ms. Stoeckley testified that he saw her return home at about 4:00 the morning of the murder. The car she got out of, the witness said, had three men inside.

On the witness stand, Ms. Stoeckley did not deny she was in the MacDonald home the night of the murders, but said she could not account for her actions between midnight and 4:00 A.M. because she had used mescaline, a hallucinogen, given to her by a soldier. And, she said, she had injected herself six or seven times earlier that day with heroin and opium, had smoked marijuana and hashish, and had taken a heavy dosage of barbiturates and LSD—all of which she had gotten from soldiers on the base or fellow hippies.

"I'm not sure what I did," Ms. Stoeckley told the court.

She admitted she owned a floppy hat, high boots, and a shoulder-length blond wig—items that Dr. MacDonald and other witnesses described a woman at or near the murder scene as wearing.

"Didn't you tell me yesterday you saw a body on the couch and you were holding a candle?" Mr. Segal asked.

"It was only like in a dream or something like that," Ms. Stoeckley answered.

Mr. Segal informed the judge that Ms. Stoeckley had given him answers completely different from those she gave the day before when she had admitted to being at the doctor's house and watching the murders take place, even describing them in detail. The defense lawyer also pointed to several witnesses who were prepared to testify that Ms. Stoeckley had confessed to them she was in the MacDonald house and had seen the stabbings.

It was later learned that Ms. Stoeckley was considered a reliable informant for narcotics officers investigating drug use and sales in and around the military base. I thought it quite ironic that when it was to the benefit of authorities, Ms. Stoeckley should be believed. But when it was to the detriment of police, she was a wholly unreliable witness!

Mr. Segal also told the military court that candle wax drippings were found in the MacDonalds' carpet the morning after the slayings. Tests showed, he said, that the wax did not match that of any of the candles found in the MacDonald home. This was significant because both Dr. MacDonald and two other witnesses said the woman in question was holding a lit candle.

In the end, the judge ruled that Jeffrey MacDonald had nothing to do with the murder of his family and ruled that he be freed immediately. The military judge also told the MPs to turn all evidence regarding Ms. Stoeckley over to civilian authorities and suggested that she be investigated for the three murders.

For several years, the case lay dormant. Dr. MacDonald completed his military service in July 1971 and moved to Long Beach, California, where he became director of emergency services at St. Mary Medical Center until 1979, when he was again put on trial for the murders of his wife and children. Throughout the military hearings, his wife's mother and stepfather supported him fully. Publicly, they stated he was a loving, caring husband and father, and they never believed he could have done such a horrible thing.

But sometime in 1972, after Dr. MacDonald had moved to California to begin a new life and started dating women again, Colette's stepfather changed his mind and started a relentless crusade to have the investigation into Dr. MacDonald reopened. By 1975, the stepfather had found a sympathetic ear with federal prosecutors and the FBI in North Carolina. The case was reopened and Dr. MacDonald was eventually indicted for the murder of his wife and daughters. This time, however, it was not the military that would hear the evidence but a federal judge and jury.

Dr. MacDonald's lawyers challenged the new charges on two grounds: double jeopardy, meaning that it is unconstitutional to try someone a second time on a criminal allegation after that person has been previously cleared or acquitted of that charge. Second, the attorneys argued that because no new evidence had surfaced since the original military hearings nine years earlier, to bring charges against Dr. MacDonald in 1979 violated his Sixth Amendment right to a fair and speedy trial. Both arguments went all the way to the U.S. Supreme Court, which ruled in favor of the prosecutors, clearing the way for the trial in 1979. In denying Dr. MacDonald's appeal, the Supreme Court disagreed with the argument that Dr. MacDonald could not get a fair trial because too much time had passed between the date of the slayings and the trial. No more specific reason was given.

The first Monday in August 1979, I arrived in Raleigh, North Carolina, and met with Mr. Segal and Dr. MacDonald. That first night, Dr. MacDonald spent several hours with me alone, going over the events surrounding the night he was attacked and his family murdered. Though he shed no tears in our conversation, I could tell by the tone of his voice and his expressions that it troubled him immensely. I found him to be quite sincere and believable.

Dr. MacDonald told me he babysat the children that night while his wife, Colette, attended a University of North Carolina psychology class. Shortly before his wife returned home, he gave the girls a glass of orange juice and put them to bed.

Colette, who was five months pregnant, arrived home around 10:00. The couple spent about an hour or so watching television together. Feeling a little bit of discomfort, Colette took a Benadryl to help her sleep and went to bed around 11:30. Because he had taken a nap earlier that evening, Dr. MacDonald said, he stayed up to read a detective novel, wash the dishes, and clean the kitchen, before finally heading to bed about 2:00 A.M.

When he went into his bedroom, he discovered that Kristen, the two-year-old, had crawled into bed with her mother and fallen asleep. He also found that she had wet the bed, soaking the sheets on his side of the mattress. Dr. MacDonald said he carried Kristen back to her own bed. After grabbing a quilt and a pillow, he headed for the living room couch to sleep for the night.

"To the best of my knowledge, Colette did not wake up when I took Kristen to her own bed," Dr. MacDonald told me. "I went to sleep on the couch, not because Colette and I had had any sort of argument or fight, but because I did not want to wake her up by changing the sheets on the bed."

An hour or so later, while sleeping on the couch, Dr. MacDonald said he was awakened by the screams of his wife and his daughter Kimberly.

"I remember Kimberly yelling, 'Daddy, Daddy, Daddy,' " he said. "When I jumped up off the couch, I was met by four people at the end of the couch. Two were white males, one was a black male and the fourth was a white female. The black male had a large club and started swinging it at me. The other two males had a knife and an ice pick."

The white female, he said, wore knee-length shiny boots, a floppy hat, had long, blond hair, and carried a candle. Dr. Mac-

Donald told me he tried to fight the intruders, but was struck several times in the head and abdomen. The blows to his head knocked him unconscious.

"I don't remember much," he told me, "but I remember hearing the woman say, 'Acid's groovy, kill the pigs.' "

Dr. MacDonald told me that when he regained consciousness later, he discovered his hands were tangled in his pajama top, which had been ripped by the knives and ice pick. As he got up to check on his family, he had trouble breathing. Once he made it to the master bedroom, he found Colette lying on the floor on her back with a knife in her chest. She was not breathing. He pulled the knife out and covered his wife with his pajama top and tried giving her mouth-to-mouth resuscitation. But when he felt her wrist and legs for a pulse, he found none and knew she was dead.

He stumbled into Kimberly's room, where his oldest daughter lay in bed. She had no pulse. Again, he tried unsuccessfully to give CPR. He then went to Kristen's room and repeated his action.

That is when he called the operator for help.

I found Jeffrey MacDonald to be an extremely intelligent, thoughtful person. He looked me in the eye in answering every question I posed and was not evasive in any manner.

Because Dr. MacDonald was not deeply depressed in the months following his wife's death, his wife's parents later accused him of lying about what happened. True, I did not find him an incredibly emotional person. He did not cry uncontrollably. Nor did he beat on his chest in agony. But he was a physician and a Green Beret. He was a tough guy who had been taught by his father and his army superiors not to show emotion. And beyond that, how do you measure suffering anyway? Do you count the number of tears or days in mourning to decide how much pain a person is feeling?

As I studied his psychological profile—that of a well-educated, successful, balanced person—I found that it did not fit the profile of a person who would suddenly snap, kill his wife and kids, and then regain his composure enough to try to cover it up. People who have these kinds of angry, violent outbursts tend to display such behavior more than once in their lives. That kind of person is known to slam a fist into a door, throw household objects, or verbally threaten people. But Jeffrey MacDonald had never displayed any of these actions either before or after that night in 1970.

Still, there were some unanswered questions that troubled me. Why were his wife and two children so brutally murdered while he received comparatively fewer and less serious injuries? This led to the central issue—were his wounds self-inflicted?

This was not the first time in my career that this question had been a controversy in a murder investigation. A local district attorney who was prosecuting a man charged with killing his wife had come to me a few years earlier asking me to examine four stab wounds on his client. The man was claiming he and his wife had been attacked, but the police believed the man had killed his wife, then stabbed himself. From reading the surgeon's report at the hospital where he was being treated and from examining the suspect's injuries at the hospital, I noticed that the wounds were parallel in nature and had a downward direction on the skin. Based on these findings, I concluded that his wounds had most probably been self-inflicted—meaning the whole thing was staged. The man was found guilty of murder.

That is the position the military investigators and FBI agents took in the MacDonald case. They claimed that because of his medical knowledge and training, Dr. MacDonald knew how to strike himself in the head and stab himself in the abdomen without killing or seriously endangering himself.

Personally, I thought this ludicrous. Even the most knowledgeable physician cannot be positive how the body will react to a stab wound. How do you know for sure what blood vessel the knife will strike? It's not like using a measuring stick on an open cadaver.

With his lawyers present, I asked Dr. MacDonald to unbutton his shirt so I could examine the scars on his chest and stomach. But there was a huge difference between this case and the earlier one. In the previous case, I was able to inspect the wounds when they were fresh, within days of their being inflicted. In the MacDonald case, however, it had been nine years since he had been stabbed. I looked at the scars, hoping to see some indication of direction or angle of the knife as it entered his body. But the wounds were so old, I was unable to tell anything conclusive from the personal examination.

I also reviewed the medical reports from the morning he was rushed to the hospital and compared the findings to the story he told me. But once again, I discovered that neither the police nor the medical officials who treated Dr. MacDonald had examined the wounds he received with regard to the angle of entrance or the depth of penetration. This lack of detail frustrated me tremendously.

Many things can be learned from the angle, direction, and depth of a stab wound. If it came from one angle, you could tell if the attacker was taller or shorter than the victim. A particular direction of the knife wound may tell you if the victim was on her hands and knees, if she was crawling or lying down. The depth of the wounds can sometimes suggest the strength of the attacker. But none of these observations were made in the original investigation. And nine years later, because of decomposition, it would have done no good at all to exhume the bodies.

While I was positive about the wounds being self-inflicted in the previous case, I could not be so sure in this case. There was nothing that convinced me that Dr. MacDonald's wounds had been self-inflicted or were the result of multiple attacks by an assailant. Because my opinion was that there was nothing conclusive either way, Mr. Segal decided I should not testify at Dr. MacDonald's trial.

No case has ever troubled me more than this. The medical evidence simply was not there. All investigators had to go on was circumstantial evidence, which, while it may be admissible and enough for a conviction, is never enough to satisfy me from a forensic or physical evidence standpoint. I like hard evidence that I can examine through a microscope and test.

After spending three days with the doctor and his attorneys, I flew back to Pittsburgh disappointed that I was unable to testify. I did follow the trial through the newspapers, which printed large portions of the testimony. The most damaging new evidence against Dr. MacDonald came from an FBI crime laboratory expert named Paul Stombaugh. Stombaugh had performed a time-consuming experiment which he claimed proved Dr. MacDonald was lying about what happened the night his family was murdered.

Stombaugh told the jury that he had folded Dr. MacDonald's pajama top in a nearly identical fashion to the way it was found on Colette MacDonald's body by the MPs. When that was done, he said, he discovered forty-eight knife and ice pick holes in the shirt that matched perfectly the location of the twenty-one wounds that Mrs. MacDonald received. More simply stated, according to Stombaugh's interpretation, the pajama top that Dr. MacDonald claimed was ripped and torn by intruders in the living room was actually cut at the same time Mrs. MacDonald was fatally stabbed. This new testimony pointed directly at Jeffrey MacDonald as the person who killed his wife.

Though the defense attorneys brought in their own experts to attempt to refute Stombaugh's dramatic testimony, the damage was done. After six weeks of hearing evidence, the jury took six hours to return a verdict of guilty. The judge sentenced Dr. Mac-Donald to three consecutive life prison terms. He is now serving that sentence at a federal prison in Oregon.

Did Jeffrey MacDonald kill his wife and two children? My gut instinct after meeting with him and reviewing all the physical evidence is no. Is it possible that he committed this horrible crime? It is certainly within the realm of possibility. The weight of the evidence does lean against him. In the minds of the jury and of most Americans, he did it. But there is something in my heart that makes me want to believe that no matter how angry he could get, Jeffrey MacDonald could never have brutally murdered his own beloved children. Only someone under the influence of mind-altering drugs, or a true psychopath, could commit such a heinous act.

6
Covering Up for the King:
The Death of Elvis Presley

I have never worked harder than I did in 1979. While still running the Allegheny County coroner's office, the number of requests for me to speak at legal and medical conferences and to be on television programs and radio talk shows skyrocketed. Most of the requests came as a result of my involvement in two cases, one being the JFK assassination.

There was another major case that captured a great deal of my interest and the attention of the general public in those years. I was in my office late one evening in August when my secretary notified me that Charlie Thompson from the ABC television show *20/20* was on hold. Anticipating an invitation to be on the program to discuss Kennedy, I picked up the receiver. But it was not the president Mr. Thompson wanted to talk about; it was the "King."

"Listen, we are going to be doing a special program on the death of Elvis Presley, and we need a forensic pathologist to review the medical reports we have obtained and interpret them for us," Mr. Thompson told me. "After you've had a chance to look them over, we would like to send a camera crew and a reporter to Pittsburgh to interview you as to your findings.

"However," he continued, "we will need for you to keep this completely confidential until after the television show airs."

I agreed, and within a few days, I had received a detailed tox-icology report and had begun reviewing it. Rumors had floated about for years that Elvis was a heavy drug user. However, his publicist denied such accusations and portrayed the singer as a clean-cut, good ole country boy from Tennessee who loved singing gospel music as much as anything secular. This was an opportunity for someone not involved in the music business or connected with the original Elvis investigation to review the records and deter-mine fact from fiction. I was lucky enough to be that person.

My task in this case was simple: review the toxicology report (the findings on what substances were present in his body when he died) and compare it to the final autopsy report. I was then to determine if there were any disparities, contradictions, or irregu-larities in the medicolegal investigation. Though my participation in the case lasted only a few weeks, the inside view of how the death of Elvis was handled was clear and it was not pretty.

I must admit I was never a big fan of the King of Rock 'n' Roll and his music. But as a former musician (I played classical violin for many years), even I could recognize his talent and energy. His voice was incredible. I recall the day he died, August 16, 1977. His death was the lead story on the television news. Reporters detailed the singer's last few hours. At midnight, he and his twenty-year-old fiancée, Ginger Alden, had been to the dentist. This strange late-night visit to a health care professional, security guards for Presley said, was necessary to avoid the constant flocking of fans. At 5:00 A.M., Elvis wanted to play racquetball, so the couple hit the lighted courts at Graceland mansion for about two hours. Dressed in blue pajamas, Elvis kissed Ginger good night and said he was going to read for a while in the bathroom. She awoke that afternoon and Elvis was still not in bed. She called out his name, but there was no answer. When she opened the bathroom door, she found her lover face-down on the shag carpet. At first, she thought he had fallen off the toilet seat and banged his head. She called Graceland security, and there were attempts to resuscitate Presley, but they were unsuccessful. Elvis Presley was dead at the age of forty-two.

That night, all the networks showed thousands of people dressed in black gathering around Graceland in Elvis's memory. Millions of people around the world who loved and adored Elvis prayed that their idol had not died of illegal drug use. If he had, they feared, his image as the greatest entertainer of all time would most certainly be tarnished and quite possibly ruined.

But what stands out the most to me about August 16, 1977, was the statement given to reporters by Memphis medical examiner Dr. Jerry Francisco about Elvis's death. After the autopsy had been completed, Dr. Francisco answered reporters' questions about Presley's untimely death.

FRANCISCO: The results of the autopsy are that the cause of death is cardiac arrhythmia due to undetermined heartbeat. There are several cardiovascular diseases that are known to be present. One is a mild degree of hypertension that had been under treatment for some time, and there was hardening of the arteries of the heart. The two diseases may be responsible for the cardiac arrhythmia, but the precise cause was not determined.

REPORTER: When will we know the exact cause of death?

FRANCISCO: It may take several days. It may take several weeks. It may never be discovered.

REPORTER: Rumors are flying that drugs were involved. Will you address that?

FRANCISCO: He was using medication to control his high blood pressure and for a colon problem, but there is no evidence of any chronic abuse of drugs whatsoever.

What kind of nonsensical diagnosis was that, I thought, as I watched the press conference on television. What Dr. Francisco basically had said was that Elvis died because his heart stopped beating. We all die when our hearts stop. The question is, what caused the heart to stop? What a ridiculous statement for an experienced forensic pathologist to make.

But this was not my case, I concluded, and I therefore thought no more about it until Mr. Thompson called me in 1979. As the months rolled by after Elvis's death, Dr. Francisco refused to make public the autopsy and toxicology reports. He claimed that the autopsy was not performed at the direction of the Memphis district attorney and that therefore the autopsy and toxicology reports were not part of an official investigation. The autopsy, Dr. Francisco said, had been performed at Baptist Hospital in Memphis by their pathologists. Furthermore, Dr. Francisco told reporters, he was merely an advisor and bystander at the autopsy and had not assumed jurisdiction of the case in his official capacity as medical examiner.

However, when various pathologists at Baptist Hospital told news reporters in October 1977 that they believed drugs, and not an irregular heartbeat, had killed Elvis, Dr. Francisco held a press conference to denounce those findings, declaring that Elvis's death was caused by hypertensive heart disease and coronary artery disease. The medical examiner said the University of Tennessee Medical School in Memphis had done a thorough toxicological analysis and had found no reason to believe that drugs had contributed to the singer's death. "Drugs played no role in Elvis Presley's death," he repeated numerous times.

What Dr. Francisco did not know was that Baptist Hospital on the night of the autopsy had prepared a separate identical sample of all specimens to send off to a private toxicology lab. One set was given to Dr. Francisco and one set was sent by a Baptist Hospital pathologist to Bio-Sciences Laboratories in Van Nuys, California, one of the most respected toxicology labs in the nation. Chemists at Bio-Sciences came up with completely different results from those reported by Dr. Francisco.

Somehow, Charlie Thompson had obtained a copy of the Bio-Sciences lab report, and that's what he sent me. To read and understand the clinical-pathological significance of a toxicology report, you must understand the language. Therapeutic is the level at which the drug is designed to be effective—in other words, the appropriate amount. Toxic levels are considered to be dangerous and potentially life-threatening. The third category is lethal, which is self-explanatory.

What I found in their toxicology report stunned me. I read it through carefully. I knew that if I was asked direct questions, I would have to give very accurate, specific answers. That had never bothered me before and it did not bother me this time. However, I knew there would be major consequences resulting from this interview.

A few days before the program was scheduled to air on *20/20*, ABC reporter Geraldo Rivera arrived at my office in Pittsburgh with Mr. Thompson and a camera crew to do the interview. I had met Mr. Rivera five years earlier on this same show when he was doing a program called "Who Killed JFK?" After some small talk and pleasant conversation, when all the cameras and lights were in place, and the cosmetics that I hate so much had been generously applied, the questioning began.

RIVERA: Dr. Wecht, how did Elvis Presley die?

WECHT: I believe that Mr. Presley died as the result of a combined drug effect. Various drugs, all of which are known to be central nervous system depressants, collectively caused his heart and lungs to be depressed. The brain controls the activities of the heart and lungs involuntarily. When the brain is depressed by multiple drugs, such as happened in this case, in my opinion, the heart and lungs will not function properly.

RIVERA: What specific drugs are we talking about?

WECHT: There were several drugs involved here. The principal offender in this case was codeine, which is a pain reliever but is known to have a central nervous system depressant effect. Other drugs included Valium, a tranquilizer; Valmid, Placidyl, phenobarbital, and butabarbital—all sedatives. These are all drugs we commonly refer to as "downers." It's incredible that all of these drugs should have been given to a patient simultaneously.

RIVERA: How would you have labeled the cause of death, if you had been in charge of the case rather than Dr. Francisco?

WECHT: I do not believe, based upon the postmortem levels of these various drugs, that it was suicide. It seems almost definite that it was an accidental death.

RIVERA: In what way did the drug levels reflect on the type of medical care that Elvis was receiving?

WECHT: If one physician prescribed all these drugs, then it was below acceptable standards of care. I would consider this to have been poor, unacceptable, and potentially dangerous medical care. If the drugs were prescribed by two or more physicians, then I would say each physician was at the very least not sufficiently diligent, and perhaps worse, somewhat negligent in having failed to ascertain what other drugs might have been prescribed by other physicians. It is a cardinal concept in medicine that before you prescribe a drug that has a brain depressant effect, you find out whether the patient is taking other drugs that might have a similar pharmacological effect.

RIVERA: Did the level of codeine kill Elvis Presley?

WECHT: The level was significant by itself. It could have resulted in death. It was at a near-fatal level. On the other hand, if he had been taking it for some time, he would have built up some tolerance. Codeine does not usually cause death by itself, although it can. Most codeine deaths that we see are, as in this case, those situations in which other drugs having a depressant effect upon the brain have also been ingested together with codeine. That can result in death.

RIVERA: Were the doctors that were attending to the health of Elvis responsible for his death?

WECHT: I think this would be a bona fide medical malpractice case that would certainly require further study and possible legal action. It was not good medical care. In a situation resulting in harm or death to a patient, such an odd array of drugs prescribed from one physician in particular, or two or more, could possibly be sufficient foundation for a medical malpractice or professional negligence lawsuit.

RIVERA: Being a lawyer as well as a forensic pathologist, will you analyze the manner in which Dr. Jerry Francisco has handled the Elvis Presley case?

WECHT: Look at the facts. Here we have a forty-two-year-old man —and let's forget for a moment that he's Elvis Presley. A man is suddenly found dead and you have no reason to suspect any prior life-threatening circumstances. That kind of situation would universally be a medical examiner's or coroner's case. But what happened? An autopsy was requested by the hospital. I think Dr. Francisco's explanation of his role in the autopsy and why it was not conducted at his office leaves much to be desired and raises questions about whether he acted properly in this situation. Instead, Dr. Francisco claims he did not want to transport Presley's body across the street from the hospital to his office because a crowd was gathering outside. He tells us that the private autopsy was done under the auspices of the hospital and that he was only there as a consultant. So he's saying that the case was not under the jurisdiction of the medical examiner. But while the autopsy was still being performed, he held a news conference to give the cause of death. It's inconsistent.

There are other problems—not only with conclusions drawn from the autopsy but with the procedures employed. For example, the sequence of events following the autopsy—the haste with which Dr. Francisco declared that Presley had died of heart disease—casts doubt on that diagnosis. The microscopic slides from the autopsy would have taken at least twenty-four to forty-eight hours to be prepared. Similarly, the toxicology reports that would indicate whether drugs were involved could not have been completed that quickly. Those analyses would take days.

Yet Dr. Francisco immediately held a news conference giving the cause of death as cardiac arrhythmia. Cardiac arrhythmia is something a pathologist cannot see when he or she is doing an autopsy. There are only two ways one can make that diagnosis— in a live person with a stethoscope held to the chest or with an electrocardiogram. When you examine someone after death, nothing will tell you he had an irregular heartbeat just before he died. For Dr. Francisco to be giving such a diagnosis when he had no information about Elvis's condition prior to his death, and without the benefit of the microscopic sections and toxicologic analysis, is incredible.

When the program aired September 13, 1979, on ABC's *20/20*, with tens of millions of American homes tuned in, I announced to the public for the first time that Elvis had not died of heart disease as all of us had been led to believe. It was drugs that killed the singer—a combination of about ten depressants working together had negatively affected his central nervous system and caused his heart to simply stop pumping.

This condition is commonly termed "polypharmacy," and usually refers to a situation where two or more doctors are prescribing medications for one patient and fail to check with each other. Before you know it, the patient is taking four or five or six drugs at the same time. And the patient does not realize that Drug A should not be taken with Drug B. But the physicians should know and should take every precaution to prevent such an occurrence.

I recently testified in a wrongful death case in Virginia in which an elderly woman with a hip fracture had died under mysterious circumstances. The death had occurred after an apparently successful operation and a relatively uneventful postoperative recovery period. The woman also had an alcohol problem. Three internists, two orthopedic surgeons, and a psychiatrist were simultaneously prescribing medications for her when she suddenly died. The autopsy showed that she had died from an overdose of depressant drugs that affected her central nervous system. The sad thing is that despite all the technology and understanding of drugs we have today, polypharmacy cases continue at an alarming rate.

Just days after the television program aired, a judge in Tennessee ordered that the entire Elvis autopsy report be released to the public. It confirmed all my suspicions. The autopsy, which was performed with a fine-tooth comb by the pathologists at Baptist Hospital, revealed several things that directly contradicted what Dr. Francisco had claimed the autopsy had found.

In his statements to the press, Dr. Francisco said Elvis's heart was twice the size it should have been, and that this irregularity indicated hypertensive heart disease. However, the Baptist Hospital pathologists weighed Presley's heart at 520 grams. Elvis stood nearly six feet tall and weighed in the neighborhood of 235 pounds. A normal heart size for a man Presley's height and weight would be about 350 to 400 grams. The autopsy also stated that the pathologists searched the heart muscle for evidence of scarring and found none. There was no retention of salt and water, which would have indicated congestive heart failure. They found no evidence supporting congestive heart failure and moved on.

Next, the doctors slowly and systematically dissected the coronary arteries, which supply oxygen-filled blood to the heart muscle. They searched diligently for a fresh blood clot, hardened arteries, or an obstruction of any kind that might have triggered a heart attack. None was found.

The upper right chamber of the heart, which receives the blood from the veins, and then the other three chambers, were the next to be examined and dissected. But all the pathologists could find was that Elvis had a very mild case of high blood pressure, one that was nowhere near serious enough to have killed him. The examination of the brain showed no clots, infarcts, or aneurysms. No signs of a stroke.

The bottom line was that even after the autopsy had been completed, there was still no anatomic basis to determine the cause of death. The toxicology report would not be back for another forty-eight hours. Despite this knowledge, Dr. Francisco voluntarily spoke to reporters and announced his opinion.

The same night I heard Dr. Francisco's original statements to the media, I also saw Dr. George Nichopoulos, Elvis's personal physician for ten years, being interviewed. Dr. Nick, as he was affectionately called, had long, bushy white hair and wore diamond rings on his fingers and gold chains on his wrists and around his neck. He quickly agreed with Dr. Francisco's findings and dismissed any rumors of drug use by his patient. "If he had been taking cocaine, I would have known about it," he told reporters.

A couple of weeks after my appearance on *20/20*, a federal grand jury sitting in Memphis subpoenaed all the autopsy and toxicology records in the Elvis Presley case. The panel issued an extensive indictment against Dr. Nichopoulos for overprescribing drugs to Elvis and various other people, including singer Jerry Lee Lewis. The investigation showed that in the seven months prior to Elvis Presley's death, Dr. Nichopoulos had prescribed more than fifty-three hundred tablets of various stimulants and downers to the singer-idol.

The medical board that licenses and regulates doctors suspended Dr. Nichopoulos's license to practice medicine for three months. To fight the criminal charges, the physician hired perhaps the best trial lawyer in the South, and among the best in the nation—James Neal.

If anyone could rescue Dr. Nichopoulos, it was Mr. Neal. Neal graduated from Vanderbilt University School of Law in 1959, and two years later he was hired by Attorney General Bobby Kennedy to prosecute Jimmy Hoffa. Neal did and won. Later, he was called upon to prosecute the key figures in the Watergate scandal. He did and they were convicted. Now, Neal had become a big-time defense attorney in Nashville, Tennessee, and he was exactly what Dr. Nichopoulos needed.

As a defense, Mr. Neal argued that his client did indeed supply all the prescription drugs to Elvis, but he did it out of compassion for the singer. Neal said that Dr. Nichopoulos was actually trying to save the man's life. Elvis Presley was a drug addict, and if he had not gotten his drugs from Dr. Nick, he would have gone out on the streets and obtained more dangerous drugs, Mr. Neal told the jury. At least Dr. Nichopoulos was able to keep a watchful eye on Elvis and was actually trying to wean him off drugs slowly, the lawyer contended.

I considered this a rather disingenuous defense, to say the least. It was like telling the judge that the bank was going to be robbed anyway, so I robbed it first because I knew I wasn't going to kill anybody and I planned on giving some of the money to the poor! If Dr. Nichopoulos was so concerned, if Dr. Nichopoulos was such a good friend of Elvis, if Dr. Nichopoulos had treated his personal patient properly, he should have fought tooth and nail to get Elvis into a detoxification program. If all those things were true, as Dr. Nichopoulos claimed, then he should have staked his friendship, his job, and his income on getting Elvis professional help. He should have said, "Elvis, I cannot stand to see you destroy yourself. I love you. You have to do it this way or I cannot be your doctor. I want to be your friend, but it cannot go on like this." In my opinion it was his own ego and personal greed—the fear of having Elvis fire him—that kept Dr. Nick from doing what he must have known was medically right and necessary.

This contention on my part takes nothing away from James Neal. It was the only defense available, and he made the most of it. The jury acquitted Dr. Nichopoulos. This trial was an example of a lawyer not necessarily having the better argument but being the better arguer—a technique that makes great trial lawyers.

As for Dr. Francisco, I have no personal knowledge what his motive was to cover this case up. There was obviously nothing criminal in his actions. Maybe he, too, was a fan of Elvis Presley and was convinced that by declaring that the singer had died of drugs, he would have tarnished the image that brought millions of tourists to Memphis every year.

The final page on the Elvis Presley death and autopsy was written in 1991 when Dr. Eric Muirhead, the chief of pathology at Baptist Hospital in Memphis back in 1977, went public for the first time about the case. Dr. Muirhead, a highly respected pathologist who actively participated in and supervised the Presley autopsy, said he knew from day one that Elvis had not died of heart problems as Dr. Francisco first stated.

"I should have stepped forward that first day and corrected it," he said. "I'm truly sorry I did not."

The opinions I had expressed on national television twelve years previously had finally been confirmed by the person in the best position to know the truth.

7
Slave to Love:
Jean Harris

There are those cases where you know—you know without a shadow of a doubt—that someone is guilty or not guilty. And then, for some reason, the opposite verdict is reached.

No question about it, Lee Harvey Oswald could not have been the only gunman in the assassination of President John F. Kennedy. I am just as confident that Sirhan Sirhan was not the lone assassin in Senator Robert Kennedy's death.

In the same vein, I am willing to bet my house against a hut that Jean Harris was telling the truth when she said the shooting of her longtime lover and friend was an accident. And my certainty is not based on a gut feeling or some intangible emotional thought; it's based on physical evidence.

I met Mrs. Harris in the fall of 1980. She had already been accused of shooting and killing Dr. Herman Tarnower, the famous physician who wrote *The Complete Scarsdale Medical Diet*. I had read about the case in the newspapers, in which she was referred to as "The Diet Doc Killer." Mrs. Harris was headmistress at the socially prominent Madeira School for Girls in McLean, Virginia, a suburb of Washington, D.C.

Dr. Tarnower's book had gone to the top of the *New York Times* best-seller list in 1980. The diet was so popular that you could walk into many restaurants and tell the waiter or waitress you were on the Scarsdale Diet and they would bring you a special menu. I had read reviews and excerpts of the book, but knew nothing of Tarnower personally, except that he was a successful cardiologist and a respected physician. Two weeks after his slaying, his book reached the number one spot on the best-seller chart.

I first became interested in the Jean Harris case a few days after the shooting. The *New York Times* wrote a series of long articles detailing how Dr. Tarnower and Mrs. Harris, fifty-seven, had been longtime friends and lovers. However, on March 10, 1980, Mrs. Harris, in a jealous rage over an affair the sixty-nine-year-old physician was having with his much younger nurse, shot him four times with a .32-caliber pistol.

Police and prosecutors said the evidence was clear and convincing—Jean Harris had committed deliberate, premeditated murder. In fact, she had even confessed. Given interviews with Dr. Tarnower's friends and the authorities, it sounded like an open-and-shut case.

Several weeks later, I received a call from a good friend, Professor Herbert MacDonell, a nationally renowned criminalist who specializes in reconstructing crime and accident scenes. Herb and I had worked closely on several cases, including the Black Panther shoot-out in Chicago.

Whenever Herb and I got together on a case, controversy and mystery were not far off. So I did not hesitate to agree to participate in the Jean Harris investigation.

Within days, Joel Arnou, Mrs. Harris's lawyer, had in my hands a copy of the autopsy reports, medical and crime scene photographs, and a summary of the case. After spending a couple of days reviewing the documents, I flew to New York, where I was to meet with Mrs. Harris, and Herb and I were to check out her story.

When I'm hired by a defense attorney whose client is pleading not guilty, I never ask the lawyer or the defendant if he or she is indeed guilty of the crime. That is not my job. My job is to review the physical evidence, which includes autopsy reports and photographs, crime scene photographs, and any physical evidence. Sometimes I even request permission to examine the body, including asking that it be exhumed if it has already been buried. I even consider it my prerogative to attempt to reenact the crime as police say it happened and as the defendant claims the events occurred to see which is more likely to be telling the truth. But it is never my job, whether I am working for the prosecutors or defense lawyers, to go out and quiz witnesses or do my own secret, all-encompassing probe of a crime.

By the same token, I seldom turn down an opportunity to talk to and question a defendant. Since Herb and I were being asked to reenact the crime, getting Jean Harris's version firsthand was very important.

The first time I ever laid eyes on Mrs. Harris was in the office of Mr. Arnou in White Plains, New York. For the better part of a morning, Mrs. Harris told her story. A petite woman of maybe five feet, two inches, I did not find her a warm person. Neither did she make any attempt to win me over. She struck me as a very frank person who did not appear to be creating fiction. But even then, I considered her story self-serving. Though I tried to be open-minded, I recalled the many newspaper articles I had read and my early conclusion of her probable guilt played heavily on my mind. As I sat listening to her, I just wasn't sure she would ever be able to convince me it was an accident. And if she could not convince me—an individual she was paying to be on her side—then how in the world did she think she could convince a jury?

Here is the story Jean Harris told me:

Mrs. Harris first met Dr. Tarnower, or Hy, as she called him, at a dinner party in December 1966. A friend had arranged for the pair to meet.

She agreed to meet the doctor and, in fact, had a grand time. She and Dr. Tarnower, both recently returned from visits to Russia, spent much of the evening comparing notes, each trying to one-up the other.

Several weeks went by without her hearing from him. Mrs. Harris said she was tempted several times to pick up the telephone and call him. She refrained. She had enjoyed his company and found him intellectually stimulating, but concluded he was not as impressed with her.

On a Thursday afternoon in January 1967, she received a book on the history of Israel. Attached was a note: "It's about time you learned about Jews." Signed, "Hy."

Roses arrived a few days later. Next came candy. Soon he was calling her regularly, setting up plans to travel abroad together. Their relationship began to blossom.

"Hy was a very bright, interesting man," Mrs. Harris told me.

"Hy did everything in his own good time. He hated appearing eager. I realized then he was totally self-centered, but I enjoyed his company. He loved money and people with money and had become the doctor of many very wealthy people. He was devoted to them and they to him. He liked it that I was bright and attractive—a woman who made him look good."

As a couple, Mrs. Harris said, they were extremely compatible —intellectually and sexually. After less than a year of dating, Dr. Tarnower proposed marriage in May 1967. Mrs. Harris, who had two children from a previous marriage, was deeply in love and readily accepted. Days later, he gave her a huge diamond ring.

But within a few months, Dr. Tarnower began expressing doubts about their marriage plans. As she pressed him for a wedding date, he put her off. Finally, he told her he no longer wished to marry.

"Hy was about fifty-five then, and down deep in my heart I knew that if he had not married by then, he would probably never marry," Mrs. Harris said. "So I wrapped the ring up in a package and mailed it to Hy with a short message: 'You ought to give this to Suzanne—she's the only woman you'll ever need.' "

Suzanne was Suzanne van der Vreken, Dr. Tarnower's live-in housekeeper. It was she Dr. Tarnower depended upon completely. Her husband, Henry, was Dr. Tarnower's chauffeur.

Even after the decision not to marry, their relationship continued. Together, they shared many trips abroad and many weekends in his spacious six-bedroom estate in Westchester County near White Plains, New York. For Mrs. Harris, being with him and being his companion was clearly enough.

"I was aware of his many flings, but he always kept coming back to me," Mrs. Harris explained to me, "and, at the time, that was enough."

Both strong-willed, opinionated individuals, they tended to debate a lot, but it seldom descended to what would be considered arguing. Richard Nixon was a favorite subject.

The couple attended a dinner party in 1974 at the Westchester County home of Dr. Tarnower's good friend Seymour Topping, an editor at the *New York Times*. The subject eventually shifted to Watergate.

"I bet Nixon resigns and I hope the son-of-a-bitch resigns," Mr. Topping spoke up.

"I think he's going to have to step down," Mrs. Harris added.

Dr. Tarnower, silent after Mr. Topping's statement, turned to Jean and said, "Jean, I cannot believe you would make a stupid statement like that."

"One of Hy's friends asked me one time why I let him put me down the way he does," Mrs. Harris continued. "I guess my ego was strong enough that I didn't feel put down. Besides, the friends I grew up with all insulted each other. To me, that was a sign of true friendship."

On her next visit to Mr. Topping's house, Mrs. Harris claimed her revenge. In front of all the guests who had heard Dr. Tarnower badger her the month before, she pointed out a newspaper, framed and hanging in the den. NIXON RESIGNS, the headline screamed. She would remind Hy of that on each subsequent visit.

Their relationship staggered on through the early and mid-1970s.

In 1977, Mrs. Harris, who had been headmistress of the Thomas School in Rowayton, Connecticut, from 1971 to 1975, accepted the headmistress position at Madeira. She was probably the ideal person for the job—a well-educated, kind of lofty and strong-willed individual. The students at Madeira were daughters of members of Congress, lobbyists, and business leaders. When such powerful parents inquired about why their little Suzy did not graduate top of her class or why Joan did not get the lead in the school play, it took someone with great integrity and self-confidence to be honest. As Mrs. Harris noticed the erosion of her relationship with Dr. Tarnower, her time in the office escalated. Always a workaholic, she was routinely spending eighteen hours a day, six, sometimes seven days a week in the office.

"I told Hy that I knew I could do the job, but I'm just afraid I'm going to drop from exhaustion," she told me. "That's when he handed me a little white pill. He told me that he took them and they helped him on the long workdays. I asked him what it was and he said Desoxyn. Within minutes of taking it, I felt peppier."

Mrs. Harris said she would take a 2 or 5 mg tablet of Desoxyn every day, and that Dr. Tarnower mailed them to her. This shocked me. Desoxyn is a controlled substance, a methamphetamine. In street terms, it's known as "speed."

The fact that Dr. Tarnower prescribed this kind of addictive drug in such a situation told me his medical ethics were less than exemplary. As a knowledgeable physician, he knew what Desoxyn could do. *The Physicians Desk Reference* clearly points out that it is "habit-forming." I knew Desoxyn was frequently used as an appetite depressant during the 1970s, but examining Mrs. Harris, who weighed slightly over one hundred pounds, told me the prescription was not for dietary purposes. Dr. Tarnower, I concluded, was not a wonderful, caring, sensitive individual.

After 1977, Mrs. Harris saw her quality time with Dr. Tarnower evaporating. She knew his sexual escapades with other women had been increasing, but she was as addicted to him and his companionship as she was to Desoxyn. When she wasn't with Dr. Tarnower, she worked.

"Hy's house was the only place I did not work morning, noon, and night," she said, discussing her frequent visits to Dr. Tarnower's Westchester home. "It was kind of a refuge for me."

Mrs. Harris told me she seldom brought up his seeing other women—and then only in a light vein. "I had no right or standing to be judgmental," she said. "It was his life."

As they did during most Christmas seasons, Mrs. Harris and Dr. Tarnower spent the 1979 winter holidays at the home of friends in Florida, Arthur and Vivian Shulte. Not having the financial resources of the others in gift buying, Mrs. Harris took a considerable amount of time writing a personalized Christmas card for the trio that parodied "The Night Before Christmas." While it was addressed to all three, it was also designed to point out to Dr. Tarnower in a humorous way that she knew of his other affairs. I believe she was actually trying to solicit a specific response from him—possibly embarrassment, a confession, or simply laughter. Whatever it was, and I don't believe even she knew, the poem itself was very humorous and displayed Mrs. Harris's wonderful creative skills. When she showed it to me, I could not hold back the laughs. The card's cover is titled "A Very Merry to Vivian and Arthur and Herman."

Twas the night before Christmas,
When in part of the house
Arthur was snuggling
With Vivian, his spouse.
In the guest room lay Herman, who, trying to sleep,

Was counting the broads in his life—stead of sheep!
On Hilda, on Sigrid, on Jinx, on Raquel,
Brunhilda, Veronica, Gretel, Michelle;
Now Tania, Rapunzel, Electra, Adele;
Now Susie, Anita—keep trucking, Giselle.
There were ingenues, Dashers, Dancers and Vixens,
I believe there was even one Cupid—one Blitzen!
He lay there remembering, with a smile broad and deep
Till he ran out of names, and he fell fast asleep.
(Let me mention, my darling, if this muse were inclined
Toward unseemly thoughts, or an off-colored mind,
It wouldn't be easy to keep this thing refined!)
But 'tis the time to be jolly—and very upbeat
And for now that's not hard because Herman's asleep!
Beside him lay Jeannie, headmistress by Jiminy,
Who was waiting for Santa to come down the chimney.
A huge stocking they'd hung by the hearth, those four sinners
In hopes St. Nick would forgive and they'd all end up winners.
Would he leave them a prize or a well-deserved switch?
And how would they know which switch went to which?
But for now they were all snuggled all safe in their beds
While visions of dividends danced through their heads.
Then all of a sudden there arose such a clatter,
Herm woke from his sleep to see what was the matter.
And with Jeannie obediently three paces back,
They tip-toed to the living room to watch St. Nick unpack.
He smiled to himself as he looked at their list
And thought to himself, "What an ironic twist!
I know perfectly well they've been gambling and boozing
But they're likable sorts—so it's rather confusing.
I'll leave them some bauble to match their uniquenesses
And cater a bit to their favorite weaknesses!"
Nick looked to the left and the right once or twice,
"That Vivian's a marvel—she sure keeps it nice,"
He said as he left her some sugar and spice.
Then he added a ten-karat bauble or two
And a bunch of hard books he knew she'd get through.
"Yes, sir, she's a bright one—a real cerebellum,
The place is in good hands with Viv at the helm.
It's no problem leaving some goodies for her

But what can I give to that rascal Arthur?
He has lots of golf balls and ties and nice socks
There's one thing he could use—complete with the locks,
But there just wasn't any room in the sled for Fort Knox.
I'll start with this book—it'll cheer the poor feller
Now he too shall have his very own best seller.
And one little thing more he can have while Viv snoozes
A very small jug of his favorite boozes.
Now let's see—there's Herman—with Tarnower for monika
It seems to me he got his best stuff for Chanukah.
I see at the top of his long list of druthers
He wants a handicap one point higher than Arthur's.
But a handicap's something old Nick can't be cutting,
Herm'll just have to stop gambling on Arthur's great putting.
But here's one little thing I know he will use,
If his evenings are lonely he'll have no excuse.
Here's some brand-new phone numbers in a brand-new black
   book
(I'm not quite the innocent gent I look!)
This book holds the key, and the hope, and the promise,
Of a whole bunch of fun, with some new red-hot mamas.''
Then he put in a couple of more odds and ends
Of stuff he wanted to leave for his friends,
Some of it useful, some of it funny
Remembering it's always the thought, not the money!
Then grabbing his sack up the chimney he rose,
Herman and Jean returned to their room on tiptoes.
If they'd been nonbelievers, now they really had proof,
You could still hear the fellow up there on the roof.
And the warmth that they felt, say the heart really melts,
This Santa Claus feeling is just—something else!

   Mrs. Harris told me she could handle most of Dr. Tarnower's affairs, but his relationship with Lynne Tryforos, his thirty-seven-year-old administrative nurse, bothered her immensely. He should have ended it immediately, she believed. A very attractive woman and divorced mother of two, Mrs. Tryforos had slowly replaced Mrs. Harris as Dr. Tarnower's regular companion during the late 1970s.
   According to Suzanne van der Vreken, the doctor's house-

keeper, Mrs. Tryforos would sleep with Dr. Tarnower during the week and Mrs. Harris would come for the weekends. Those were not his only two women, she pointed out, just his two favorites. When Dr. Tarnower knew one was coming over for the evening, Mrs. van der Vreken says they used to "run around the house picking up the other woman's clothing."

The two women were never there together and only saw each other once or twice. But each made it clear to the other that she intended to be Dr. Tarnower's sole lover and only companion by playing adult pranks on the other.

"She would call me in the middle of the night, never giving her name, but I knew who it was," Mrs. Harris said.

Exactly one week after Mrs. Harris presented her personal Christmas poem to the physician, the couple were drinking coffee at the Shultes' Florida home when she noticed a small classified advertisement at the bottom of the front page of that day's *New York Times*: "Hy. Happy New Year. Love Lynne."

"I was appalled at how low and tasteless it was," Mrs. Harris told me. "I remember Hy saying he hoped none of his friends sees it. I didn't mention I was one of his friends and I saw it. But, in a very sarcastic tone, I did say, 'Herman, why don't you have her use the Goodyear Blimp next year—I think it's available.'

"I told him to stop messing up so many women's lives and just mess up mine," she continued. "He liked that line. But marriage was not what I required, just his interest and affection."

The winter of 1980 was the most difficult for Mrs. Harris. Two years earlier, she had purchased a Harrington and Richardson .32-caliber handgun at a sporting goods store near her school. The pistol had a two-inch barrel and shot six bullets. She told her friends it was for her own protection, and she reminded everyone that there had been a murder on campus a couple of years earlier.

"I had become frightened by the exhaustion of my work," she confided. "The gun was like a security blanket. If things got too bad for me, if the pressures got to be too much, the gun was my way out, it was my avenue of instant relief."

In March, everything seemed to fall apart. Four prominent seniors at Madeira were caught with marijuana seeds and drug paraphernalia. After meeting with the students and telling them they had to learn to be responsible, Mrs. Harris suspended them. Instead of being outraged at their daughters' activities and supporting the school's disciplinary procedures, the parents protested Mrs. Harris's punishment and demanded her immediate resignation. Even many faculty members publicly opposed her actions.

Add to this one other problem: she had run out of Desoxyn and had been unable to get in touch with Dr. Tarnower for a new prescription. She perceived the world collapsing around her. Despite her intellect, appearance of self-confidence, and take-charge personality, Mrs. Harris had begun to doubt the value of her own existence and, more specifically, she believed she was not up to the task for which Madeira had employed her.

By midweek, the students had left the campus for three weeks of spring break and Hy had agreed to send her another vial of Desoxyn through the mail. But when Saturday arrived and the pills had not, Mrs. Harris was at the end of her rope.

Within forty-eight hours, she decided, her life would be over.

She called in two of her school employees and they witnessed her signing a new will. After collecting her belongings and putting a few financial deeds in order, she went home and loaded her untested pistol. Off her back porch, she test-fired the weapon—it triggered easily, just as she had hoped. This was the first time she had ever fired a weapon in her life. But when she tried to shake the spent bullet shells or casings out of the gun's cartridge, they would not fall out. After bullets are fired, the shells expand and are not as easily removed from the pistol. Instead of reading the directions on how to load, unload, and reload the weapon, Mrs. Harris used a small ice pick to push the spent shells loose. If she had read the directions, she would have learned of the ejector rod on the pistol, which automatically removes the used shells. This point is very important to keep in mind.

Finally, Mrs. Harris called Dr. Tarnower and told him she was coming to visit him in New York that evening.

Before her departure, Mrs. Harris, with suicide in mind, knew she had several last-minute chores. I thought it incredible that a woman about to end her own life was so organized and believed in detail to such a degree that she would sit down and carefully write good-bye letters to her two sons, to several friends, to Dr. Tarnower, which she sent certified mail, and to school officials.

With the pistol in her purse, she drove up Interstate 95 from Washington to New York, rain pouring down the entire five-hour trip. The weather fit her mood perfectly. She stopped only once, for fuel on the New Jersey Turnpike near the George Washington Bridge. Every mile of the way, she recalled, bizarre, very intense thoughts rapidly scurried through her mind.

Not all of her memories that night were bad. There were the many trips she had taken with Dr. Tarnower—to Kenya and Ceylon, journeys to Nepal and through the Khyber Pass into Afghanistan, vacations to Bulgaria and Paris. Their annual two-week winter hiatus to Florida. It was all wonderful to think about.

Before she knew it, the five-hour drive was over. Mrs. Harris pulled into the driveway of Dr. Tarnower's two-story white brick, very modern home about 11:00 P.M. Nearly all the lights were off. His blue Cadillac was in the driveway. Built in 1958, the spacious home on Purchase Street is in an exclusive part of Westchester County, about ten miles from Long Island Sound, fifteen miles from the Hudson River and famed Sing-Sing State Prison, and less than five miles from the Connecticut line. The house sits on 6.8 acres of land and sold in 1980 for five hundred thousand dollars. There were no street signs at the end of the long driveway, no numbers, no mailbox, nothing to tell people this was the home of Dr. Herman Tarnower. According to Mrs. Harris, he liked it that way.

Dr. Tarnower's home overlooks a duck pond with a small island displaying a concrete statue of Buddha, which he purchased on one of his many trips abroad. Beside the pond were daffodils. The doctor had once told her that this is the place where he would like to have his ashes scattered. With that thought in mind, Jean Harris decided it would be the exact spot where her life would end as well.

Regarding what happened that night on Purchase Street, here's what Jean Harris told me:

The darkened house confused her. He knew she was coming. She had a key, but did not need to retrieve it from her purse after she discovered that the side door—the entrance Dr. Tarnower and she used most frequently—had been left unlocked.

Shutting the door quietly, Mrs. Harris tiptoed through the foyer to a circular staircase that led to Dr. Tarnower's bedroom. As she entered the room, Dr. Tarnower was already in bed asleep. She begged him to sit up and talk to her, but he barely acknowledged her entrance.

She immediately went into the bathroom, where she found

Mrs. Tryforos's green satin negligee. Enraged, she threw the negligee and many other items, including hair curlers, from the bathroom across the room, breaking a window.

Mrs. Harris kept throwing things—shaving cream, aftershave, soap, a comb. If it was on the bathroom counter, it was soon flying across the bedroom.

Dr. Tarnower, now obviously angry, grabbed his lover of fourteen years and slapped her twice, both times very hard and in the face.

"Hit me again!" Mrs. Harris cried out. "This time, make it hard enough to kill me."

At this point, it didn't matter any longer to her. If he wouldn't kill her, she would do it herself, as she had planned.

"My intent at that moment was to walk out and finish the job," she told me. But when she picked up her purse from the edge of the bed and felt the weight of the handgun, she impulsively decided to take it out right then and there.

"No, Jean," Dr. Tarnower shouted. He reached up to grab the pistol just as she pulled the trigger. The gun fired, the shot "echoing like a tremendous clap of thunder," Mrs. Harris recalled.

It took a couple of seconds for her to realize she was not dead. In fact, she remembered being aware that the bullet had wounded Dr. Tarnower's hand before she consciously thought about her own survival.

Dr. Tarnower had grabbed the gun away from her as it fired, she told me. The bullet went clear through his hand. Cursing under his breath, the physician took the gun into the bathroom where he washed his wound.

A few seconds later, he returned with the gun and tried calling for medical help, but the phone in his bedroom was not working.

"Please give me the gun," Mrs. Harris begged, now in tears. "Let me die or kill me yourself."

"Jesus, Jean. You're crazy. Get out of here," Dr. Tarnower replied. Those words echoed through her mind. She would never forget them, preying on her like an eternal damnation.

That's when she saw the pistol lying partially under the bed and fell on her knees to get it. Dr. Tarnower, his hand bleeding from the first wound through his palm, "lunged" toward her, she said, grabbing the pistol away.

As he picked up his intercom phone to have Mrs. van der

Vreken call for medical assistance, Mrs. Harris, catching the physician off guard, seized the handgun from Dr. Tarnower's grasp.

In reaction, Dr. Tarnower leaped up, his hand grabbing the weapon, and struggled with her to take it away.

"For a split second, I felt the muzzle of the gun against my stomach. I had my finger on the trigger and I pulled it," she told me. "It exploded against me and my first thought was that it did not hurt at all—I should have done this a long time ago."

The rest remains a blur to Mrs. Harris. In the struggle, the gun fired three more times, striking Dr. Tarnower's upper right arm, right shoulder, and the right part of his chest. The fifth bullet missed completely. She has no memory of the third or fourth shots.

Mrs. Harris told me she remembered getting up and that Dr. Tarnower was no longer chasing her or trying to wrestle the gun away. She slowly examined her own body, discovering that she had not been wounded at all. All the bullets had struck her lover.

"I put the gun to my head and pulled the trigger and it just clicked," she explained. She shook the gun to test fire it and it "exploded against the headboard of the bed." Aiming the gun at her head, she again pulled the trigger and "shot and shot and shot, but it just clicked."

Realizing that the "servants," as Mrs. Harris referred to Dr. Tarnower's housekeeper and gardener, were downstairs and had heard the shots and would be coming upstairs any second, Mrs. Harris began searching through her purse for more bullets, which she finally found. When she could not get the empty shell casings out of the gun's chamber, she began banging the pistol against the bathtub, hoping to loosen the cartridges. Instead, the gun's cylinder finally broke and fell off.

"No one person has ever had this much bad luck," she remembered thinking to herself. "If I cannot even kill myself, what good am I?"

As Mrs. Harris walked back into the bedroom, she noticed Hy had moved onto the guest bed next to his own. She picked up the phone, but it was still dead.

"I helped Hy back over to his bed," she said. "He didn't look like he was dying. He looked exhausted. I looked into his eyes and he looked into mine. We were both in a state of shock that something this ugly and sad could happen between two persons who never argued over anything except the use of the subjunctive.''

Realizing she needed to phone the police, Mrs. Harris shoved the pistol into her handbag and raced down the stairs, calling out to the servants, "I'm going for help." She knew of a pay phone at the community center less than half a mile away.

As she pulled into the center, a police car with flashing blue lights drove by. Immediately making a U-turn, Mrs. Harris followed the officer back to the house.

"Hurry! Please hurry," she pleaded with the officer. "He's been shot."

On the steps to the house stood Mr. van der Vreken hysterically pointing at Mrs. Harris: "She's the one. She did it."

That was Mrs. Harris's complete testimony to me, and, to be honest, it seemed very suspicious. She was claiming it was all an accident. Do you shoot someone four times and miss a fifth shot if it's an accident? Why does she not remember shooting bullets three and four? Why did she pull out the gun in front of him in the first place? I considered these questions as I listened to her story—and trust me, there was a great deal of skepticism on my part.

The police and prosecutors told a different story. The shooting was no accident. Mrs. Harris went into the house that night in a jealous rage, found Dr. Tarnower in bed and pulled out her gun. It was as simple as that.

And the fact is, such a story under the circumstances is quite believable. The police had a suspect and they had a motive for murder.

In our criminal justice system, we have what's known as the presumption of innocence—a person is innocent until proven guilty. This means that the defendant in a criminal case has to prove nothing; the police and prosecutors bear the burden of proving that the defendant committed the criminal act. In the Jean Harris case, the prosecutors had enough evidence to show that Mrs. Harris fired the shots. Mr. and Mrs. van der Vreken saw her fleeing the scene. Mrs. Harris even confessed to several police officers that night that she had pulled the trigger. The gun, with her fingerprints on it, was found in her car. And the motive— which, keep in mind, prosecutors are not even required to develop or prove—was pretty darn strong: a lover of fourteen years replaced by a much younger woman becomes angry and decides that if she cannot have the man, then no one will.

With the state's case seeming so strong and with Mrs. Harris adamantly denying she intentionally murdered Dr. Tarnower, Herb MacDonell and I realized the difference between her going to prison or going home probably depended upon the two of us proving she was telling the truth about the facts of that night—not such an easy task since I wasn't so sure I believed her myself.

The best place to start our search for the truth (or as close as we could get to it), Herb and I agreed, was at the Tarnower house itself, where we could examine the scene and reconstruct the shooting. The couple who had purchased the house were sympathetic to Mrs. Harris and allowed us to use Dr. Tarnower's bedroom extensively.

Using the autopsy photographs and diagrams of the wounds as well as the photographs of the crime scene taken the night of the shooting, we were able to determine the direction each bullet was traveling when it struck Dr. Tarnower's body. For several hours at the scene, Herb and I took turns playing Mrs. Harris and Dr. Tarnower in an effort to reenact the actions of that evening to see if Mrs. Harris's story had any legitimacy to it at all. I would go to the spot where Mrs. Harris claimed she stood and Herb would stand where she said Dr. Tarnower was. We then used string to trace from the spot where she said the barrel of the gun was pointing to where Dr. Tarnower was standing. Time after time, the string matched perfectly with the trajectory or path the bullets were traveling in order to match the wounds to Dr. Tarnower. Using the string and positions the couple were in according to Mrs. Harris, we were able to reasonably explain every shot that was fired. On the other hand, as I examined the autopsy reports showing Dr. Tarnower's wounds to the clavicle and side, and compared them to the theory developed by the police and prosecutors, I came to the conclusion that in order for the state's theory to be true, the bullets fired at Dr. Tarnower had to originate from the ceiling. Combining all this with what we knew about where Dr. Tarnower's body had been found and his height compared to Mrs. Harris's height, and the angles and trajectories of the bullets as they struck him, led us to one conclusion: it very well could have happened the way Jean Harris said it did.

There was nothing that pointed to incredible gyrations or bodily contortions. All that was required was a dynamic constantly moving scenario with two people struggling over control of a weapon.

The next day, I visited the Westchester County medical examiner's office to review the autopsy findings, X rays, and more photographs. At the time, nothing unusual stood out at me. Dr. Louis Roh, the deputy medical examiner who performed the autopsy, mentioned nothing out of the ordinary. While I was generally satisfied with the autopsy and the job Dr. Roh had done, the more I read the police reports, the less thrilled I became with the way the police had handled the investigation. The bottom line: it was inept, incomplete, and lacked any serious political, literary, or artistic value. In other words, as the following list supports, it was obscene:

- Evidence had been moved the night of the shooting before crime scene photographs could be taken—an absolute no-no in a homicide probe.
- The blankets and sheets on Dr. Tarnower's bed were wadded up and thrown into a bag immediately after the shooting—possibly altering bloodstains.
- Forensic testing was never done on the sheets.
- The sheets were not marked to know which end was at the top and which was at the bottom, which was the right and which was the left.
- The murder weapon was not immediately dusted for prints—if it had been and Dr. Tarnower's prints also had appeared, then Mrs. Harris's claim that he held the gun for a short period would have merit.
- Police did not properly secure the scene of the shooting. Proper police procedure is for no more than two or three detectives to be in the room at one time. That night, more than nineteen people were in the room, including the housekeeper, the gardener, and the prime suspect.
- Police failed to properly take fingerprints from the telephone in Dr. Tarnower's bedroom. Instead, the police handled the phone themselves. Mrs. Harris claimed that Dr. Tarnower was on the phone when she picked up the gun a second time, but when forensic experts dusted the phone's receiver, all they found were prints from police officers who had responded to the scene.
- Several pieces of key evidence were missing. The most significant was the throw rug on the floor where the struggle

took place. Examination of the rug could have shown bloodstain patterns, which would have indicated exactly where Dr. Tarnower was and whether he walked to the bathroom to wash his hand wound, as Mrs. Harris claimed. In other words, the rug would have acted as a map of what had occurred that evening between Dr. Tarnower and Mrs. Harris. According to police, the rug was rolled up by Mr. van der Vreken and given away. It could not be located.

• Police improperly allowed Mrs. Harris to wash some of the blood off her blouse and did not take the blouse for evidence. The bloodstains could have shown how the splatter occurred.

• No photographs were taken of Mrs. Harris's physical condition or clothing. Detectives readily admitted that Mrs. Harris had a severe black eye and a bruise on her face from the two times Dr. Tarnower slapped her.

I could go on and on. Simply stated, it was a very shabby investigation.

As I continued reading the police and autopsy reports, it hit me that no medical personnel reached Dr. Tarnower until more than fifteen minutes after the shooting occurred. If a paramedic or EMT had arrived a few minutes earlier, the bleeding might have been stopped and the doctor might have survived. Was this Jean Harris's fault? I read on.

The police reports said that Mrs. van der Vreken called emergency 911 at 10:56 P.M., while Mrs. Harris was still upstairs with the physician.

DISPATCHER: White Plains police.

MRS. VAN DER VREKEN: Dr. Tarnower. Purchase Street. Send somebody. [Combine the housekeeper's hysterical state and her broken English, and these were the only words that could be understood.]

DISPATCHER: Is this an aid call?

MRS. VAN DER VREKEN: Something terrible has happened.

When the operator asked for an address, the phone call was terminated from Mrs. van der Vreken's end. As police frantically searched for a Tarnower on Purchase Street, Mr. van der Vreken called in and a different dispatcher took the call.

"Doctor, Purchase Street" stuck out in the operator's mind, but Mr. van der Vreken hung up before more information could be obtained.

Five minutes later, Mrs. van der Vreken phoned again and the first dispatcher answered. But the housekeeper was so upset that the police could get no details from her. Instead of hanging up the receiver this time, Mrs. van der Vreken dropped it on the floor and walked away, leaving the dispatcher shouting into the phone, "Hello. Hello. Hello."

While monitoring Mrs. van der Vreken's phone line, the dispatcher contacted the telephone company to get an immediate trace on the phone call.

POLICE DISPATCHER: I need this information; people need an ambulance.

TELEPHONE COMPANY OPERATOR: I have to get somebody.

DISPATCHER: This is an emergency.

OPERATOR: Just hold on.

DISPATCHER: Somebody is doing something to them; there was a shooting.

The officer was transferred from a phone operator to a night supervisor, then to the phone company's service manager in charge—all taking a considerable amount of time.

While on hold, the White Plains dispatcher learned from nearby Harrison police that they were aware of the location and were sending an officer to the scene.

Even then, because there are no signs or mailboxes indicating house numbers along Purchase Street, police and medical technicians had a difficult time locating the house.

The first officer at the scene found Dr. Tarnower in his bloodied pajamas slumped over one of the two twin beds. He was on his knees, with both arms hanging toward the floor and his head against the headboard. The officer reported finding no pulse but said that after the doctor was given oxygen, he began breathing again. Dr. Tarnower was transported to St. Agnes Hospital, where he was pronounced dead.

As a forensic pathologist who has examined tens of thousands of bodies, I firmly believed that if Dr. Tarnower had received the necessary medical attention a few minutes sooner, he could have, and I emphasize *could have*, survived the wounds.

Everything appeared to be shaping up for the defense of Mrs. Harris until just a few days before the trial was set to start. George Bolen, the thirty-four-year-old assistant district attorney prosecuting this case, telephoned a key expert witness for the defense—an action that is considered highly unethical. Mr. Bolen claimed he had received a Christmas card from Dr. Henry Ryan, a former Westchester County medical examiner and now the chief medical examiner of Maine, and simply decided to call him to say thank you. Although Mr. Bolen was well aware that Dr. Ryan was a witness for the defense, he inquired about Dr. Ryan's testimony during their phone conversation. If a defense lawyer did this, he or she would be brought up on disciplinary charges, possibly disbarred or suspended.

It was during this phone conversation that Dr. Ryan told Mr. Bolen about some particles he had found in the X rays of Dr. Tarnower's chest. What those particles were, he said, he had no idea. Possibly bone or cartilage.

But this insight gave Mr. Bolen, who had become literally possessed with getting a conviction in this case, the idea that the particles just might be bone fragments from Dr. Tarnower's hand. If it were true, it would mean that Mrs. Harris was standing up, pointing the gun at Dr. Tarnower, and preparing to fire when he held out his hand in a defensive position. If this were true, it would completely blow out of the water Mrs. Harris's claim that it was all an accident.

That same day, Mr. Bolen called Dr. Roh and told him of his new scenario and asked the medical examiner to check again and see if this were true. Lo and behold, Dr. Roh's review found that, by George, it was bone fragments that would match the fragments from Dr. Tarnower's hand.

As the trial began on November 21 in White Plains, defense attorney Joel Arnou, Mrs. Harris's principal lawyer, knew it would be an uphill battle. The prosecutors had stacked the deck. Over the next sixty-four days, the jury heard from thirty-three witnesses for the state and fifty-eight for the defense. More than four hundred exhibits were introduced as evidence. Every day, the courtroom was packed with news reporters, friends, family, and everyday citizens who wanted a glimpse of the drama. Murder was on everyone's mind. On the night following the opening of the trial, the famous "Who Shot JR?" episode of the CBS television show *Dallas* aired. While the trial was in progress, Beatles star John Lennon was fatally shot.

One by one, the prosecutor called his witnesses. Police detectives testified how Mrs. Harris told them the night of the slaying that she was responsible.

Harrison police lieutenant Brian Flick: "I do remember her telling me that it was ironic that the doctor was dying and she was living because he wanted to live and she wanted to die."

Mrs. van der Vreken presented the court with a daily diary she had kept during her sixteen years of employment at Dr. Tarnower's residence. In it, she detailed each houseguest, including information about whether the guests, mostly female, were simply there for dinner or whether they also spent the night with the physician in his bedroom. According to the diary, Jean Harris had been there sixty-three times in 1977, forty-nine times in 1978, twenty-six times in 1979, and four times in 1980. All of this contributed to the prosecution's theory that Mrs. Harris killed Dr. Tarnower because she had been scorned.

The other woman, Lynne Tryforos, had been Dr. Tarnower's dinner guest the very night of the shooting, Mrs. van der Vreken said.

As the state's star witness, Dr. Roh testified that the "four gunshot wounds were not consistent with a struggle over the gun, but more consistent with defensive wounds."

Dr. Roh: "If a person holds his hand up in a defensive position, it lines up perfectly with the wound Dr. Tarnower suffered in the chest. It could not have happened" the way Mrs. Harris said.

With that seemingly damning evidence, the state rested its case.

Joel Arnou, Mrs. Harris's lawyer, elicited testimony from his first several witnesses to develop the relationship between Dr. Tarnower and his client. Several witnesses described how Mrs. Harris had become "despondent" in recent weeks because of the pressures of her job.

More than a week into the defense testimony, Mr. Arnou called

out my name as his next witness. Everyone knew I had been studying the autopsy reports over and over since Dr. Roh's startling
revelation that bone chips from Dr. Tarnower's hand were found
in his chest.

ARNOU: After reviewing the autopsy reports and photographs and
the physical evidence in this case, what is your scientific
conclusion?

WECHT: These wounds were not the kind one sees when the victim
is being shot at for the purposes of killing. The wounds are more
consistent with a struggle than a homicidal attack. A person who
usually intends to kill aims the gun at the heart, stomach, or head.
The absence of any blood splatters on Dr. Tarnower's face or neck
also dispels the defensive position theory.

ARNOU: What about the particles that have been discovered in Dr.
Tarnower's chest?

WECHT: I have reviewed the same materials Dr. Roh has reviewed
and I too believe there are foreign particles lodged in his chest.
However, I am 100 percent convinced they are not from the hand.
Skin from the hand and palm area has completely different cell
structure than skin from any other part of the body and there is
no sign of that type of skin here. In my opinion, one of the particles in the chest is a piece of cartilage that most likely came from
the collarbone, which a bullet also hit. The other two particles in
the chest are collagen, a universal substance also known as con-
nective tissue, which is found throughout the body. There are
absolutely no particles in the chest that can be traced to the hand
or the palm.

ARNOU: When you visited the crime scene, did you discover any
bloodstains?

WECHT: Yes. About ten months after the incident occurred, Herb
MacDonell and I were reviewing police photographs when Herb
saw something in the picture of the glass door where one of the
bullets struck, but because the photograph was underdeveloped,
we could not determine what it was. After obtaining the negatives,
Professor MacDonell had the scene further developed and we
agreed there appeared to be small bloodstains on the aluminum

frame of the glass door in the cardiologist's bedroom where the bullet exploded against the window. In a subsequent visit to the crime scene, we were shocked to find that while the window had been replaced, the stains on the frame were still there. We took samples and examined the stains and they indeed turned out to be bloodstains that matched Dr. Tarnower's.

This meant one thing: the bullet hole in the glass and the bloodstains on the frame were consistent with the gun's having been fired through Dr. Tarnower's hand and then striking the window.

The new evidence absolutely wiped out Dr. Roh's and the prosecution's contention that the same bullet that went through Dr. Tarnower's hand went into his stomach. Not only was this not a defensive wound, but Mrs. Harris was more likely telling the truth than the prosecutor, I concluded.

As I examined Dr. Tarnower's pajamas, I noticed that the bullet holes in the shirt did not match the wounds the physician suffered, meaning he was moving when the bullet struck and not sitting on his bed in a defensive position as prosecutors claimed.

There was no doubt in my mind: Jean Harris did not intentionally shoot to kill Dr. Tarnower. The more Herb and I probed her story and reenacted her claims, the more it fit what she was saying. This is very important because she had no way of knowing how to make up a story that would work out perfectly. This was not some ordinary shooting where anybody with reasonable intelligence can think of a dozen ways to tell police how the person was accidentally shot.

It would take a skilled forensic pathologist and criminalist hours, if not days, to sit down at a drawing board to come up with the scenario of somebody's being shot four or five times and having it work out.

After I exited the witness stand and discussed the case with the defense attorneys, they were confident of an acquittal. But to add support, Mr. Arnou called some of the best experts in the land to back me up.

Dr. Henry Ryan, the Maine pathologist, also testified that he found no palm tissue in Dr. Tarnower's chest.

Drs. Alfred Angrist and Michel Janis, both professors at Albert Einstein College of Medicine in New York, each told the jury that he could not find anything similar to hand or palm tissue in the victim's chest.

And Dr. Albert Ackerman, a nationally renowned expert in dermatopathology, after giving jurors a blackboard lesson on the cellular structure of hand and palm tissue, emphatically proclaimed that no such tissue was found in Dr. Tarnower's chest. "I even went over my findings with Dr. Roh and his associates and at no time did they disagree with me," Dr. Ackerman testified.

Dr. Roh was the only person the state had saying these were defensive wounds and that cartilage from the hand was found in the chest. But then again, he also testified that hair and fingernails are living tissue. If you have taken Biology 101, you know that is simply not true.

If the jury had been polled when I stepped down from the witness stand, I believe they would have allowed Jean Harris to go home a free woman. But there was one more witness to be called, and this witness would be the most destructive of all to her case. The witness was Jean Harris.

The first two days on the stand went very well for her. Mrs. Harris was very much in control—sad when she needed to be and humorous when necessary. But by day three, she was beginning to look worn out. Her answers grew sarcastic. She took on the attitude of "Why should I have to be here? Who has the right to sit in judgment on me?" And it got progressively worse over the next five days.

She was only able to account for three of the five gunshots: the wounds to Dr. Tarnower's hand and shoulder and the lone bullet into the bed's headboard. With Mr. Arnou's assistance, Mrs. Harris took the jury through the events of that night just as she had done with me weeks earlier.

The cross-examination by Mr. Bolen, whom Mrs. Harris had obviously grown to despise, was not simple or easy. There were instances in which the two stared at each other, neither blinking, for minutes at a time.

BOLEN: Isn't it a fact that the doctor told you that day that he preferred Lynne Tryforos over you?

HARRIS: No!

BOLEN: And in a phone conversation the morning of March tenth, did he tell you that you had lied to him and cheated on him?

HARRIS: No indeed. That would be a strange word from him. [She was referring to his numerous lady friends.]

BOLEN: And did he tell you that you were going to inherit two hundred thousand dollars?

HARRIS: No, he did not. [In fact, in his will Dr. Tarnower left Mrs. Harris and Mrs. Tryforos each $200,000.]

BOLEN: Didn't he say, "Goddamnit, Jean, stop bothering me"?

HARRIS: No! Is this going to go on forever?

BOLEN: And isn't it true, Mrs. Harris, that you intended to kill Dr. Tarnower and then kill yourself because if you couldn't have him, nobody else could?

HARRIS: No, Mr. Bolen. That's not true.

As a final touch, Mr. Bolen introduced as evidence the letter Mrs. Harris had written Dr. Tarnower and mailed to him just before she left her Virginia home for Purchase Street. Mr. Bolen claimed the evidence clearly showed Mrs. Harris's bitter contempt for Dr. Tarnower and his new lover. Defense attorneys argued that the note demonstrates their client's desire to die but no resolution to harm Dr. Tarnower.

To me, the letter demonstrated two things: Mrs. Harris's weakness for Dr. Tarnower and the way he had humiliated her. He was to turn seventy years old the following week and was to be honored for his many professional contributions to the American Heart Association by the Westchester Medical Society. But instead of taking Mrs. Harris, he had chosen Mrs. Tryforos. The more I read the fifteen-hundred-word letter, the more I felt Mrs. Harris's frustration.

Hy,

I will send this by registered mail only because so many of my letters seem not to reach you—or at least they are never acknowledged so I presume they didn't arrive.

I am distraught as I write this—your phone call to tell me you preferred the company of a vicious, adulterous psychotic was topped by a call from the Dean of Students ten minutes later and has kept me awake for almost thirty-six hours. I had

Dr. Wecht has been a consultant in many celebrated cases, including those of Mary Jo Kopechne, Elvis Presley, and Robert F. Kennedy. His analysis of the evidence suggests new interpretations of their deaths. (AP/Wide World Photos)

President John F. Kennedy taking questions during a press conference. Dr. Wecht demonstrates that JFK was not the victim of a lone gunman and that the single bullet theory is technically impossible.
(Larry Howard, JFK Assassination Information Center)

BELOW: The site of the JFK assassination. In the upper right-hand corner is the Texas Schoolbook Depository from which Lee Harvey Oswald, according to the Warren Commission, shot JFK and Governor John Connally. The presidential motorcade was proceeding down Elm Street, the uppermost street shown in the photo.
(Larry Howard, JFK Assassination Information Center)

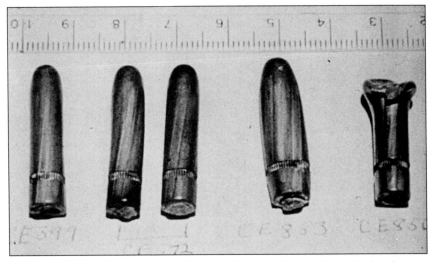

ABOVE: Evidence from a test performed for the Warren Commission in 1964 at the Edgewood Army Arsenal in Maryland. Bullet #1 to the far left is the stretcher bullet (the "magic bullet"), which is in near-pristine condition. Bullets #2 and #3 were shot into cotton wadding. Bullet #4 was shot through a rib of a goat carcass to demonstrate what a bullet would look like after it broke Governor Connally's rib. Bullet #5 broke the distal end of the radius in a human cadaver to simulate the fracture in Governor Connally's right wrist. According to the Warren Commission, the stretcher bullet broke both Governor Connally's rib and radius and yet emerged without any significant deformity. (Josiah Thompson)

BELOW: The remarkable path of the "magic bullet," as shown by the Warren Commission. (Josiah Thompson)

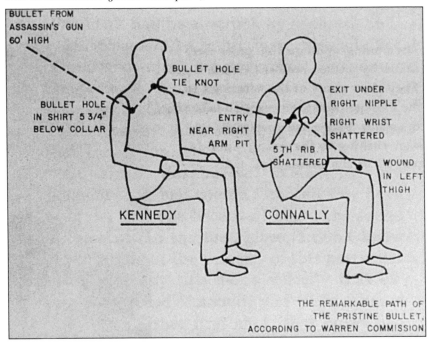

In 1982 Claus von Bulow was convicted of attempting to murder his wife by lethal injections of insulin. A year later, Dr. Wecht was hired by von Bulow's lawyer, Professor Alan Dershowitz, to re-examine the evidence. *(Newport Daily News)*

Jean Harris was convicted in 1981 of killing her lover, Dr. Herman Tarnower, the Scarsdale Diet doctor. However, as Dr. Wecht discovered, the accidental scenario described by Jean Harris was physically plausible. (Jean Harris)

A Green Beret captain and medical doctor, Dr. Jeffrey McDonald was convicted in 1970 of killing his wife and two children at their home on the grounds of Fort Bragg in Fayetteville, North Carolina. Dr. Wecht analyzed the crime scene and Dr. McDonald's wounds to probe his account of having been attacked by unknown assailants. (*Raleigh News & Observer*)

BELOW: Dr. Charles Friedgood being arrested for the 1975 slaying of his wife. After examining the medical and physical evidence, Dr. Wecht found that the case against Dr. Friedgood was scientifically untenable. (*Long Island Newsday*)

A clean-shaven Delbert Ward (center) poses with brothers Roscoe (left) and Lyman (right) on April 14, 1991, at a party celebrating Delbert's acquittal one week earlier. (John Haeger/*Oneida Daily Dispatch*)

This small, messy shack, without running water, heat, or electricity, was the dwelling for the four bachelor recluse Ward brothers of Munnsville, New York. (William B. Sullivan)

ABOVE: Andrew "Dominick" Diehl in a happier moment: smiling for the camera in North Carolina in November 1985. (Courtesy of the Diehl family)

LEFT: Only four months before Andrew's death, the Diehl family poses happily for a newspaper feature outside their bus at Virginia Beach's Indian Cove Campground. Andrew is standing in the top right-hand corner. The Diehls' natural children are the four dark-haired boys standing to Andrew's right in the top row. (Patty DiRienzo/*Virginia-Pilot and Ledger-Star*)

Dr. Wecht, testifying in Karen Diehl's murder trial in Virginia Beach Circuit Court on July 14, 1987, leans toward the jury to explain an essential autopsy photo. (Kenneth Silver/*Newport News Daily Press*)

Jack Allan Davis, Jr., in his high school yearbook photo, taken a year and a half before his death at Indiana University of Pennsylvania. (Courtesy of Elaine Lynch) BELOW: This view from the top of the 22-step stairwell in which Davis' body was found illustrates the near impossibility of his having tumbled all the way to the bottom of the second landing or from atop the wall. (Indiana County Coroner's Office)

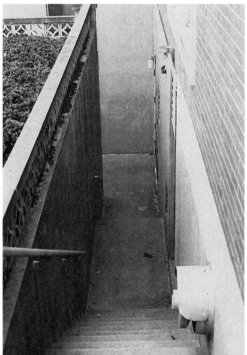

Was Art Jones' death a homicide, accident, or rigged suicide? Reconstruction of the physical evidence and postmortem examination of the victim's body enabled Dr. Wecht to determine the nature of this tremendous blast. (Mark Blohm)

to expel four seniors just two months from graduation and suspend others. What I say will ramble, but it will be the truth—and I have to do something besides shriek with pain.

Let me say first that I will be with you on the 19th of April because it is right that I should be . . . I called Dan [a physician friend who was organizing the banquet] to tell him I wanted to send a contribution to be part of those honoring you and I assured him I would be there. He said, "Lee and I want you at our table." I thanked him and assured him I would be there "even if the slut comes—indeed, I don't care if she pops naked out of a cake with her tits frosted with chocolate."

I haven't played slave for you—I would never have committed adultery for you—but I have added a dimension to your life and given you pleasure and dignity, as you have me. As Jackie says, "Hy was always a marvelous snob. What happened?" I suppose my check to Dan falls into the "signs of masochistic love" department, having just, not four weeks before, received a copy of your will, with my name vigorously scratched out, and Lynne's name in your handwriting written in three places, leaving her a quarter of a million dollars and her children $25,000 apiece—and the boys and me nothing. It is the sort of thing I have grown almost accustomed to from Lynne—that you did not respond to my note when I returned it leaves me wondering if you sent it together. It isn't your style—but then Lynne has changed your style. Is it the culmination of 14 years of broken promises, Hy, I hope not. "I want to buy you a whole new wardrobe, darling." "I want to get your teeth fixed at my expense, darling." "My home is your home, darling." "Welcome home, darling." "The ring is yours forever, darling. If you leave it with me now, I will leave it to you in my will." "You have, of course, been well taken care of in my will, darling." "Let me buy an apartment with you in New York, darling."

I believed that much of this letter, which became known in court as the Scarsdale letter, actually supported Mrs. Harris's position, especially her statements that Dr. Tarnower had controlled her life, both by love and by the mind-altering drugs. From my experience as a lawyer and from testifying in thousands of court cases, I recognized right away that her statements regarding the finances played right into the state's hand. Prosecutors wanted to show the jury a Jean Harris who was bitter toward Dr. Tarnower, and, to me, the letter did that for them.

It didn't matter all that much, really—all I ever asked for was to be with you—and when I left you to know when we would see each other again so there was something in life to look forward to. Now you are taking that away from me too and I am unable to cope—I can hear you saying, "Look Jean, it's your problem—I don't want to hear about it."

I have watched you grow rich in the years we have been together, and I have watched me go through moments when I was almost destitute. I have twice borrowed fifty cents from Henri to make two of the payments on the Garden State Parkway during those five years you casually left me on my hands and knees in Philadelphia, and now, almost ten years later, now that a thieving slut has the run of your home, you accuse me of stealing money and books, and calling your friend to beg for an invitation . . .

Twice I have taken money from your wallet—each time to pay for sick damage done to my property by your psychotic whore. I don't have the money to afford a sick playmate—you do. She took a brand new nightgown that I paid $40 for and covered it with bright orange stains. You paid to replace it—and since you had already made it clear you simply didn't care about the obscene phone calls she made, it was obviously pointless to tell you about the nightgown . . . I desperately needed money all those years. I couldn't have sold that ring. It was tangible proof of your love and it meant more to me than life itself. That you sold it in the summer your adulterous slut finally got her divorce and needed money is a kind of sick, cynical act that left me old and bitter and sick . . .

You have never once suggested that you meet me in Virginia at your expense, so seeing you has been at my expense—and if you lived in California I would borrow money to come there, too, if you would let me. All of our conversations are on my nickels, not yours—and obviously rightly so because it is I, not you, who need to hear your voice. I have indeed grown poor loving you while a self-serving slut has grown very rich—and yet you accuse me of stealing . . .

I refrained from throwing away the cheap little book of epigrams lying on your bed one day so I would be absolutely sure to see it, with a paper clip on the page about how an old man should have a young wife. It made me feel like a piece of old discarded garbage . . .

You have been what you carefully set out to be, Hy—the most important thing in my life, the most important human being in my life, and that will never change. You keep me in control by threatening me with banishment—an easy threat which you know I couldn't live with—and so I stay at home while you make love to someone who has almost totally destroyed me . . .

In all these years you never spent my birthday with me. There aren't a lot left—it goes so quickly. I give you my word if you just aren't cruel I won't make you wretched. I never did until you were cruel—and then I just wasn't ready for it.

Jean

Many thought the eight-woman, four-man jury would be sympathetic to Mrs. Harris. For eight days they deliberated before reaching a verdict.

Guilty.

Mrs. Harris sat stone-faced as the jury foreman announced the decision. Two of her attorneys, many in the courtroom, and even some of the women in the jury box began crying. But Jean Harris remained expressionless as guards came forward to escort her off to jail, sentenced to fifteen years to life in prison at the Bedford Hills Correctional Facility a few miles north of New York City.

In the years since her conviction, I have kept in touch with Jean Harris by mail and telephone. She is now a friend, no longer merely a client or a defendant in a criminal case. During a trip to New York in June 1991, I was allowed into the Bedford Hills Correctional Facility to see Jean for a few hours. She lived alone in a six-by-eight-foot cell. It held a bed, a sink that offered only cold water, a toilet, a barred window, and a box in which she could keep her personal items. She appeared in great health and has an incredible sense of humor. Lawyer jokes are among her favorites.

HARRIS: A lawyer, a murderer, and a terrorist kidnap an innocent man. The man grabs a gun away from one of them, but it only has two bullets. Whom does he shoot?

WECHT: The murderer and terrorist.

HARRIS: No, the lawyer . . . twice.

Prison was no joke to Jean. Neither are drugs. At 8:30 A.M. every day, she would teach a class on early childhood development and parenting skills to young women in prison. She told mothers as they leave prison to make their families first and to stay away from drugs. She speaks from experience. It took prison doctors more than eight years to wean her from the narcotics to which she had become so addicted.

Jean was eligible for clemency in 1986, 1988, and 1989. Each time, I personally wrote New York governor Mario Cuomo asking that he consider Jean Harris for clemency and parole. A member of Governor Cuomo's staff told me that more than twenty thousand letters had come in supporting Mrs. Harris's bid for freedom, including one note from Barbara Bush. However, politics seem to have consumed Governor Cuomo, great liberal that he is. I told Jean in one conversation we had that because of Governor Cuomo's long-term political aspirations regarding the White House, I believed he would never grant her clemency, though she is probably the one person in prison who deserves to be free.

Thank God that was not the case. In 1992, another opportunity for clemency for Jean arrived. Again, I wrote the governor telling of my support. Finally, on December 28, 1992, just hours before Jean was to undergo heart surgery, the good news came down— clemency had been granted. She had been behind bars for eleven years, ten months, and six days.

A few weeks after Jean was released from prison, she called me at my office and thanked me for all the support I had offered her over the years.

"It feels good to be free," Jean told me on February 15, 1993. "There's so much to do."

While it is easy to sweep many instances where injustice has occurred under the proverbial rug, in Jean Harris's case I know our criminal justice system failed. Maybe it failed because I did not explain to the jury convincingly enough that we had facts, that we had evidence that proved that what Jean Harris was saying was much more likely to be true than what the prosecutor claimed. Perhaps the system permitted an overzealous prosecutor and deputy medical examiner to manipulate the court so that the truth was nothing more than a footnote in the case. A Jean Harris case comes down the pike only once or twice in a prosecutor's career, so you milk it for all it's worth, and that's exactly what I believe happened here. And there should be little doubt that district attorneys are political animals. Those who are elected are responsible to the public, and those who are appointed are answerable to the elected board or executive who appointed them. In any high-profile criminal case, half the people are going to be for a person like Jean Harris and half the people are going to think she's the devil incarnate.

With that in mind, prosecutors frequently travel the politically safe road by not plea bargaining these cases. By taking it to trial, prosecutors can claim victory if she's convicted and blame it on the jury if she's acquitted. That way, the prosecutor can walk away from any high-profile case by stating to the news media that the jury has spoken and it's not for us to second-guess them. This was the major politicolegal pitfall for Jean Harris.

Quite possibly, the jury simply did not like or believe Mrs. Harris. And whatever you think of Dr. Tarnower, he surely did not deserve to die. We may not approve of his sexual escapades, but he was not married and was free to live his private life in any manner he chose. And, as I am sure the jury kept in mind, Mrs. Harris was indeed the direct cause of his death.

As an intellectual, scientist, and physician, perhaps Dr. Tarnower came to realize something the night of his death that the jury never truly understood—the woman who was standing by the edge of his bed throwing towels and nightgowns across the room was a monster and he had created her. It was he who had unethically given her Desoxyn for many years and sent it to her illegally. It was he who ignored her calls and pleas for help. It was he who slapped his lover and told her to get out when a simple hug or a calm conversation over a cup of coffee might have settled the entire affair. But Dr. Tarnower remained Mr. Arrogant to the bitter end. He had taken an independent, strong-willed woman and, with his intellect, his demanding and domineering personality, and his access to mind-altering drugs, made her his slave.

The entire Jean Harris case boils down to the age-old story of the love slave who kills her slave master and is finally free. But for Jean Harris, one prison was replaced by another. Fortunately, her courage, intelligence, and perseverance enabled Jean Harris to be as intellectually productive as possible in a prison environment. She is truly a remarkable person.

8
The Sweetness of Love:
The Trial of Claus von Bulow

Since December 1980, Martha von Bulow has lain in a coma at Columbia Presbyterian Hospital in New York City. The medical attention she receives is of the highest quality, undoubtedly costing her family hundreds of thousands of dollars a year. She has no idea what is happening around her. Her eyes do open occasionally, but no thoughts run through her head. She must be fed intravenously. There is no chance she will ever recover.

Known since childhood as "Sunny" to her friends and family, she is completely unaware that her second husband, Claus von Bulow, was charged, originally convicted, and ultimately exonerated of twice attempting to murder her. She has no knowledge of the lengthy court battle that surrounds the reason she is in her condition. Her children fight among themselves over her multimillion-dollar estate, but she knows nothing of this squabble. Martha von Bulow is nothing more than a breathing corpse with very little brain activity and no independent thinking abilities. At the same time, her physical condition is perfect. She may live for many years.

Although Sunny and I have never met, we have a couple of things in common. We were born the same year, 1931, and only a few miles apart—she in Sulphur Springs, West Virginia, and I just across the Pennsylvania line. Both were coal-mining communities south of Pittsburgh. But my parents were relatively poor; her father, George Crawford, was the founder of Columbia Gas and Electric. He died when Sunny was a small child, leaving behind a massive fortune. Growing up, her every need was met. She went to the best private schools, wore the best clothes, and traveled the world extensively. Money was never a problem for her.

Sunny married Prince Alfred Eduard Friedrich Vincenz Martin Maria von Auersperg of Austria in 1957. He was charming and handsome, but also broke. They had two children, Princess Annie Laurie, born in 1958 and nicknamed "Ala," and Prince Alexander, born a year later. But Sunny divorced the prince after eight years of marriage when she discovered he had not forsaken all others.

In 1966, Sunny married Claus, whom she had met two years earlier at a dinner party. Claus, five years her senior, was a tall, handsome Dane, whose mother was a member of the Danish branch of the von Bulows, a noted family that produced a German chancellor and a conductor who married the daughter of composer Franz Liszt. Within a year, they had their first and only child, Cosima. Together, the family of five shared a mansion in Newport, Rhode Island, during the spring and summer months, and a huge apartment on Fifth Avenue in New York during the cold months. The von Bulows were certainly people of privilege.

But not all the money in the world can help Sunny now. Not long after Sunny became comatose in December 1980, police charged Claus von Bulow, her husband of fourteen years, with trying to kill her. In fact, authorities claimed that on this occasion and a year earlier, Claus had injected his wife with a lethal dose of insulin so he could cash in on her estate and marry a secret lover. If she died, Claus would stand to inherit $14 million from her estate. Despite Claus's insistence that he was innocent, on March 16, 1982, a jury in Rhode Island found him guilty of attempted murder in both instances. He was sentenced to thirty years in prison.

Because Sunny was from the Pittsburgh area, the local newspapers, the *Pittsburgh Press* and the *Post-Gazette,* gave significant play to von Bulow's trial, making me well aware of most of the facts of the case. Even with the overwhelmingly negative press reports against Claus, I never really formed an opinion on his guilt or innocence. I am painfully aware of dozens of cases that I have been personally involved in where it appeared a person was certainly guilty of a crime, only to discover later that the evidence was completely circumstantial and the person charged was undoubtedly innocent.

In the late summer of 1982, Alan Dershowitz, a law professor at Harvard University and a renowned criminal defense attorney who had been retained by Claus von Bulow after his conviction, telephoned me. Did I have any time available in the near future to discuss a case with him? Dershowitz wanted to know. I had no idea he was talking about the von Bulow case. As it happened, I would be speaking at a trial lawyers conference on the Harvard campus a few weeks later, so we scheduled a time for us to get together. Since then, Professor Dershowitz has become one of the nation's premier criminal defense lawyers, handling the appeals in such famous cases as Jeffrey MacDonald, Leona Helmsley, and Mike Tyson. Of course, he was not as famous in 1982, but just as respected in legal circles.

For about two hours, Professor Dershowitz and I discussed the von Bulow case in his office on campus. The prosecutors, he told me, had relied heavily on medical and scientific evidence to convince the jury to convict Claus.

"It is our belief that the medical evidence the prosecutors have is flawed," Dershowitz continued. "If we can knock down their medical case, there is no way the guilty verdict can stand."

He promised to send me all the medical reports available, including the toxicology report, the police investigative reports, and the transcripts from the first trial. He also made it clear he would like for me to meet with and talk to von Bulow about the case.

A few weeks later, I did get to meet von Bulow at a small private dinner party held at his luxurious Fifth Avenue apartment. Alan Dershowitz and criminal defense lawyer Thomas Puccio, a former federal prosecutor who months earlier had sent several government officials to prison in the Abscam trials, were present. So was Dr. Michael Baden, a friend of mine and a prominent forensic pathologist, now codirector of the forensic science laboratory for the New York State Police Department. He is also a former New York City chief medical examiner. Baden was working for Dershowitz and von Bulow on the case. Claus himself had a companion for the evening, Andrea Reynolds, the wife of television producer Sheldon Reynolds.

Von Bulow had called and invited me to attend the meeting, which he described as part dinner party, part strategy session. He had asked me to bring Sigrid, my wife. Because she was out of the country working on her doctorate, I took my oldest son, David, then a student at Yale University and now a lawyer in Washington, D.C.

A very European-type butler met us at the front door. I do not recall his name, but it very well could have been Alfred, of Batman fame. Von Bulow's fourteen-room apartment was larger than most houses, decorated traditionally. The floors were marble, and much of the furniture appeared to be antique.

I found von Bulow to be a warm, gracious host. Claus was born in Copenhagen, Denmark, in 1926. His father was a playwright and theater critic. He received his law degree from Cambridge University and then worked for several years as an assistant to oil magnate John Paul Getty.

Von Bulow was not the least bit hesitant to discuss the case. As far as he was concerned, the allegations against him were absurd. He exuded confidence in himself, in his lawyers, and in Dr. Baden and me as his expert witnesses. He said he knew without a doubt that we would be able to show that the allegations against him were false.

As we sat in his living room prior to dinner, the conversation turned to Sunny. She and Claus had met at a dinner party when she was still married to Prince von Auersperg, and von Bulow immediately became infatuated with her. Since the prince traveled frequently, Claus said it was not difficult for him and Sunny to carry on a torrid love affair. Within months of Sunny's divorce from the prince, they married. A year later, she became pregnant with Cosima. After the delivery, Sunny had a tubal ligation. That is when, Claus said, Sunny lost all interest in sex. They still loved each other, but Sunny informed him she no longer wished to carry on a sexual relationship with him and asked if he minded seeking another means of satisfying himself sexually. The only condition was that he be discreet.

With complete authority and conviction, von Bulow stated he still loved Sunny. My instincts told me he meant it, even though he sat there before us with another woman. He did nothing to hide his relationship with her. They frequently held hands, hugged, and had their arms around each other and kissed.

But who was I to judge? After all, his wife was among the living dead. That may sound cruel, but she was in an irreversible coma, and he was a handsome gentleman, very cultured and affluent and wanting female companionship. By not hiding his relationship with this other woman, Claus showed he felt no embarrassment or guilt. And Andrea Reynolds, his companion, was not the least bit shy, constantly speaking out and defending Claus. She was very much a part of the conversation that evening. And it was obvious her opinion carried great weight with Claus.

Even though the defense attorneys accepted her, it was clear that her presence and role in the case did not thrill them. I mean, here you have a person charged with trying to kill his wife to get her money so that he can run off with another woman, and that person goes out in public or into court with a lady friend on his arm. That certainly does not make it easy on the lawyers.

Over dinner, Claus mentioned that Sunny had an incredible sweet tooth. She would frequently overindulge in sugar-rich egg-nog, ice cream, and candies. He also said that Sunny had grown quite fond of wine and liquor in recent years and had almost become a habitual drunk. Claus also talked about his wife's long-time propensity toward self-medication. He said she would take a large number of pills and medications even when the illness was not that significant. Here was a woman who could have bought the Mayo Clinic and could have afforded any doctor in the world. She simply did not like physicians and wanted to medicate herself. This was and still is a very dangerous thing for anyone to do.

Claus said that during the first weekend of December 1980, he walked into their bedroom and found Sunny on the floor, her head bloodied from an apparent fall. Claus immediately called an ambulance, which rushed Sunny to a nearby hospital. Doctors pumped her stomach and discovered that she had overdosed on aspirin. According to the toxicology report, which I reviewed later, Sunny had swallowed what is equal to sixty-five Extra-Strength Ty-lenol tablets. Even the doctors admitted that had Claus not discovered Sunny when he did or had he waited even a few minutes longer before calling 911, Sunny probably would have died.

"Why would I save my wife's life one day and three weeks later try to kill her?" Claus asked. "If I had wanted her dead, I would have left her in the bedroom to die by her own hand."

After an excellent dinner and over several cups of coffee, we had Claus re-create the events of December 21, 1980, the night Sunny fell forever into her second coma.

The family—Claus, Sunny, Cosima, and Alex—ate an early dinner so they could catch the seven o'clock showing of the movie *9 to 5*, starring Dolly Parton, Jane Fonda, and Lily Tomlin at a local theater in Newport. The family returned home from the movie at about ten. Claus said he went to his study to do some work while Sunny, Alex, and Cosima headed for the library. About thirty minutes later, Claus asked Sunny if she wanted anything from the kitchen. She said she would love some leftover chicken soup. While Claus was getting the soup, Sunny became weak and fell to the floor. Alex picked his mother up and carried her into her bedroom, all the time asking repeatedly if she had taken sleeping pills or barbiturates. She denied it.

Claus told us that when he returned with the soup, Sunny assured him she was okay. He then headed back to his study to take a business telephone call. As Alex was helping his mother into bed, she asked if he would open her bedroom window. Even though it was well below freezing outside, Alex knew his mother liked to sleep under a lot of blankets but in a very cold room.

Claus said when he came to bed that night, he and Sunny had a brief conversation before they both fell asleep. Claus awoke at five-thirty the next morning to walk the dogs for an hour. Then he immediately went to his study to work. About eleven o'clock, as he wandered into the kitchen and found Cosima eating breakfast, he asked if she had seen her mother. Cosima responded that Sunny was still sleeping.

Worried, Claus headed for his bedroom. As he entered the master bedroom, he saw that Sunny was not in bed. He said he found her on the cold marble floor of her bathroom. Sunny's head was directly alongside the toilet seat, Claus said. Her lips were swollen and her mouth was bleeding slightly at the corners. The water was running in the sink. She was still breathing. Her body was cold. Claus ran to the phone and called 911. Sunny would experience heart failure a few minutes later and lapse into the coma that currently consumes her.

No one at the dinner party directly asked Claus if he was guilty of this horrible crime. And he never did anything to try to persuade us that he was innocent. To him, his innocence was a given, a natural assumption, and he assumed that none of us questioned his innocence.

After I arrived back in Pittsburgh, I immediately studied the files that Dershowitz had sent to me. There were several oddities that made this case different from many others I have handled.

The most significant from my investigative standpoint was that there was *no dead body*. Sunny had not died. There was, therefore, no autopsy, no organ samples to examine or test, very little medical evidence. Most of what I had to review were the observations and opinions of the doctors who treated her before and immediately after she lapsed into a coma.

Claus, who was free on a $1 million appeal bond, had hired Alan Dershowitz to handle his appeal and win him a new trial. Alan made it clear to me that I was being retained to prove that the prosecution's medical evidence was flawed and untrustworthy.

Without a body to examine, I told him, it would be difficult. But I pledged my professional willingness to assist him to the best of my ability.

Within a few days, I had received from Dershowitz most of the medical findings, police reports, and transcripts from the trial. For several days, I analyzed the documents. The questions I asked myself were (1) what chemical compounds, if any, might Sunny von Bulow have taken or been forced to take? (2) were drugs ingested or injected? (3) if there was more than one drug, did they have a multiple or exaggerated effect, as had happened with Elvis Presley? and (4) is Sunny von Bulow in a coma because of an accident, a suicide attempt, an atypical but natural disease process, or something very sinister?

The first thing I did was to review the transcripts from the trial, which began February 2, 1982, in Newport, Rhode Island. Newport is the site of many of our country's largest mansions and estates. It is where the elite of New England have their summer homes. Together, Claus and Sunny owned Clarendon Court, a stone mansion modeled after an eighteenth-century British country manor. It sits on ten acres of neatly cut grass and well-kept gardens between Rhode Island Sound and Bellevue Avenue. Bankers estimated that Sunny von Bulow had inherited $35 million.

For his original trial, Claus von Bulow had hired Providence criminal defense attorney John F. Sheehan at the suggestion of U.S. senator Claiborne Pell, a wealthy Democrat from Rhode Island, who also owned a summer home in Newport. Claus's other lawyer, Harold Price Fahringer, was also handling the appeal of Jean Harris, who had been convicted of murdering Dr. Herman Tarnower the year before. In fact, media coverage of the von Bulow trial was comparable to that of the Jean Harris case, with one big difference: the judge in the von Bulow case permitted television cameras in the courtroom to videotape the entire trial, allowing it to be seen by the whole world.

On the surface, the prosecution's case had seemed pretty damning. Alexander von Auersperg, Sunny's twenty-two-year-old son from her first marriage, testified that his mother had spoken to him twice about divorcing Claus—just before she lapsed into her first coma in December 1979, and just before her second coma.

After Sunny's second episode, Alexander and his sister Ala became suspicious of Claus and hired ex-Brooklyn district attorney Richard Kuh to privately investigate Claus and their mother's episode to see if foul play had been involved. Over the next several months, they would pay Kuh one hundred thousand dollars to garner evidence against their stepfather.

The key piece of evidence that Alexander presented to Kuh was a small black bag. Alexander and Sunny's longtime maid, Maria Schrallhammer, said they had seen the black bag on several occasions at the von Bulows' New York apartment and at the Newport mansion. Kuh had Alexander seize the bag. It was in their possession for more than a month before being turned over to medical investigators. According to police records, the black bag, which was once apparently a container for a large calculator, contained an assortment of hypodermic needles, syringes, vials of pills, powders, and liquids, and an empty box of Lidocaine (a painkiller). However, neither Kuh nor Alexander took an inventory of what was in the bag when they first seized it.

Ms. Schrallhammer even told the jury that the word *insulin* was written on one of the vials. The black bag was taken from a closet in Claus von Bulow's study. However, no such bottle was found. The outside of one of the needles in the bag tested positive for insulin. Prosecutors said this was proof that the needle had recently been used to inject someone with insulin.

The maid also denied a major contention made by Claus—that Sunny was an alcoholic or a drug user. Ms. Schrallhammer testified that Sunny had no more than two or three drinks of alcohol a day. She also said von Bulow was lying when he said that Sunny frequently binged on sweets.

The prosecution's first medical witness at von Bulow's original trial was Dr. Janis Gailitis, who had treated Sunny when she suffered her first coma. Dr. Gailitis had visited the von Bulow home several times over the prior two years to treat Sunny for various minor medical illnesses. Claus called him when Sunny began vomiting uncontrollably on December 27, 1979.

Dr. Gailitis said Sunny fell unconscious on her bed, continued to vomit for a minute, and then completely stopped breathing. The physician cleared his patient's throat of debris and revived her through mouth-to-mouth resuscitation. For a brief period, she lapsed into a coma and was hospitalized for more than five weeks. After running several tests, he diagnosed Sunny as having bronchopneumonia. He also reported that her blood sugar level was abnormally low—less than 41 milligrams. Even after some glucose "pushes," as they are called, her sugar level continued to drop until it neared 20. The normal range is anywhere from 80 to 120, but many people get along just fine with a blood sugar level lower than that. When it drops to near zero, it becomes extremely dangerous no matter who you are. But even with the extremely low blood sugar level, Sunny recovered.

For the next year, Sunny's health was on a roller-coaster ride, according to Claus and various medical reports. Some days she felt well enough to engage in a healthy exercise routine. Other days, she complained of dizziness and severe headaches. Claus said the bad days became much more frequent after her first coma. Tests made during a routine visit to her New York City physician, Dr. Richard J. Stock, again showed her blood sugar level to be very low—23 milligrams. Dr. Stock diagnosed his patient as experiencing "reactive hypoglycemia," a condition in which extra insulin is produced in the body. However, the physician told the court that the excess insulin was certainly not enough to induce a permanent coma.

Sunny's second illness came nearly a year to the day after her first coma, and three weeks after her aspirin overdose. After lying unconscious on the cold marble floor of the bathroom for some time, Sunny's body temperature had fallen to 81 degrees, according to the emergency technicians who responded to Claus's 911 call. Body temperatures are somewhat like blood sugar levels—what may be tolerated by one person can be bad news for another. But any time the body temperature falls below 90 degrees, there is danger the system will go into hypothermic shock, causing the heart to beat irregularly and possibly leading to a cardiorespiratory arrest.

It is amazing that Sunny survived this incredibly low body temperature. By finding her when he did, Claus saved her life. If he had waited even a few more minutes, she probably would have died. At the hospital, tests showed Sunny's blood sugar level to be 29 milligrams. The insulin level in her system was a sky-high 216 —the normal being under 15 microunits per milliliter.

"She was the most severe case of coma I have ever seen," Dr. Gerhard Meier, who treated Sunny after the second coma, told the jury at the trial. He said tests showed that the incredibly high insulin levels in Sunny's system and the low blood sugar levels do not naturally occur in a normal person's body.

The jury was told, and correctly so, that the pancreas produces insulin when there is too much sugar in the blood. It is the job of insulin to metabolize or eat excessive sugar in a person's blood. But with Sunny's low glucose level, there was no reason for the body to make additional insulin. By process of elimination, the prosecution's medical witnesses testified, that left only an injection of insulin into the body to explain the cause of Sunny's coma.

As their final medical witness, prosecutors summoned Dr. George Cahill, a Harvard Medical School professor and director of the Howard Hughes Medical Institute, to testify. Dr. Cahill, one of the nation's foremost experts on blood sugar, was there to give his opinion as to what had happened to Sunny von Bulow. It would be extremely damaging to the defense's case.

Both the first and second comas, Dr. Cahill told the jury, were brought on by an injection of insulin and nothing else. He said that while barbiturates and aspirin and alcohol found in Sunny's body may have contributed to the coma, they did not cause it. Dr. Cahill and the other experts for the state testified that there were only three means by which the insulin level in Sunny's body would have risen to such a high amount: (1) cancerous tumors in the pancreas that produce insulin, (2) an alcohol-induced disorder of the liver, and (3) an injection. All the prosecution witnesses said their examination of Sunny showed that the first two could be eliminated, leaving only option number three for the jury to believe.

To prove motive, prosecutors placed Alexandra Isles, a thirty-six-year-old actress, on the witness stand to tell the jury that she and Claus had been lovers for two years. She testified that Claus had talked frequently about divorcing his wife. She also shocked the courtroom when she said she had given Claus an ultimatum to leave Sunny von Bulow and marry her or their sexual affair was over. Ms. Isles said the demand was made just a few months before Sunny's first coma in 1979.

Because there was no body, poking holes in the state's theory would be even more difficult. When a person dies, pathologists have the opportunity to examine and test the body's organs. I certainly would have preferred performing some biological tests, but there was nothing to test. If Sunny had died right away, the answers to this mystery would have been much clearer. Through testing body tissue samples, such as the kidneys or liver, we could have learned exactly when and how the drugs were taken. We would have examined the gastric contents to see if the chemicals in question had been digested. All of the organs would have been studied grossly and microscopically to look for disease.

The question posed to me most often about this case is whether anything new could be learned if she died today. The answer is no. The substances we would look for would no longer be in the body. Because doctors have been feeding her water and liquid food intravenously, the toxic substances that probably caused her coma have been replaced in her system and would no longer be detectable. Even if it was a strong arsenic, such toxic compounds would have disappeared from her body and grown out of her hair or fingernails. If chemicals had caused Sunny's coma, they probably would have been undetectable just a few weeks after she lapsed into the coma.

An attempt to kill someone through insulin poisoning was, until a couple of decades ago, virtually impossible for medical authorities to ascertain. The reason: only with recent advances in forensic technology have pathologists been able to distinguish insulin produced naturally in the system from insulin that is injected. The fact that we had no body tissues to examine in this case took us back to the point of speculating and creating hypotheses.

But even with the lack of medical data, there were specific errors I found in the prosecution's analysis of the medical evidence. Regarding the claim that Claus had secretly injected Sunny with insulin in both instances, I had serious doubts. First, no doctor who examined Sunny either time reported seeing needle marks. And if Claus had indeed injected his wife with insulin in December 1979, don't you think she would have told someone after she made a full recovery? Sunny, by all accounts, was a very strong-minded, independent individual who was not afraid to point out Claus's flaws to her friends.

It would also be easy to dismiss another significant piece of the prosecution's evidence—their claim that a needle found in Claus's black bag was caked with insulin on its surface. At the trial, this seemed to be very damning evidence. After all, didn't it prove that someone had indeed used the needle to inject insulin? The problem with this theory is that it is totally wrong. When a needle is used, the outside, where the insulin was detected in this case, is wiped clean as it is withdrawn from the skin. The skin completely collapses around the needle, removing any particles on the needle itself. When laboratory tests on the inside of the needle came back, the only chemicals detected were Valium (a painkiller) and amobarbital (a sleeping pill). And toxicology results taken from Sunny show no traces of Valium in her body. When the lab technicians said the insulin was "caked" on the tip of the needle, that was more consistent with the needle's having been dipped in a bottle of insulin but never used. This raised a suspicion in my mind of a frame-up.

And there was another question I had about this particular needle that the prosecutors claimed was the alleged murder-attempt weapon. Why did Kuh, a former prosecutor, not take the needle immediately to authorities for a fingerprint check? In an interview after the trial, Kuh told a reporter it was because fingerprints cannot be taken from a needle. The fact is that there is a slim possibility that a print could be taken from the needle and a very good chance that a print could be lifted from the syringe's plastic protective shield.

Sunny's toxicology report itself certainly raised several questions. Her blood alcohol level was at .01 when it was finally taken by the emergency room staff. That is equal to less than one shot of whiskey. However, what the medical witnesses did not tell the jury was that eight hours had expired from the time Sunny had fallen unconscious in her bathroom to when the blood tests were performed.

If you recall the Mary Jo Kopechne case, the body burns up an average of .018 milligrams of alcohol in the blood or the equivalent of more than a one-half shot of whiskey every hour. Dating back eight hours, that meant Sunny would have consumed a minimum of five shots of whiskey just prior to her coma. Using the same time dating that is universally recognized and accepted, the toxicology report also showed that she had about a dozen capsules of amobarbital in her blood system. That in and of itself is enough to send many people into a coma.

This is the point where the prosecution's case truly started falling apart. Not only was there this clear and convincing evidence of multiple chemicals in Sunny's system, but Dershowitz had collected sworn affidavits after Claus's conviction from many of Sunny's friends detailing just how much Sunny enjoyed drinking alcohol.

"Her one failing was that once she took one drink, she would not know how to stop," said one of her closest friends in a sworn statement. "She would get heavily intoxicated, and her speech and movements would become uncoordinated. She would overturn pieces of furniture, bang her head against door frames, and on occasion simply collapse in the powder room."

And there were a dozen similar statements depicting episodes like this one—all refuting the prosecution's claim that Sunny did not abuse alcohol. It was amazing how Sunny's friends came forward after Claus was convicted to paint a different portrait of her.

Joy O'Neill, Sunny's New York exercise instructor, testified that Sunny had told her on several occasions that she injected herself with insulin to help keep her weight down and Valium to help get to sleep at night. "I told Sunny that I was really gaining weight," Ms. O'Neill said. "Sunny said what I probably needed is a shot of insulin or vitamin B. At least you could then eat everything you wanted, including sweets, she said."

Ms. O'Neill's story was corroborated by famed novelist Truman Capote, who had been a friend of Sunny's for more than thirty years. He had never met Claus. In his affidavit, Capote described Sunny as "an expert of self-injection" who frequently would inject herself with some drug while he watched. Capote also testified that he had seen Sunny with a small, zippered black bag in which she carried her needles and drugs. It would be easy, I thought, for prosecutors to dismiss such testimony from one person, but not from two, especially when one of the witnesses is of the stature of Truman Capote.

During the trial, prosecutors and their medical witnesses dismissed Claus's claim that Sunny was suicidal. The state attorneys told jurors they should ignore the episode in which Sunny digested more than sixty-five aspirin tablets. It could not have been a suicide, they said, because there was no suicide note.

National statistics show that 85 percent of people who commit suicide leave no suicide note. And all my experience reviewing death cases backed me up: Sunny's digestion of so much aspirin certainly placed her case within a quite plausible suicide category.

And I came across another interesting note in the toxicology report. The expert medical witnesses who testified for the prosecution at the original von Bulow trial had not been told that on the night she slid into her coma, Sunny had digested eight tablets of Inderal, a drug used to treat migraine headaches and hypertension. Many musicians and actors take an Inderal to calm the butterflies in their stomachs before going on stage. According to medical literature, Inderal interacts very dangerously in people who have insulin-induced hypoglycemia. It also interacts dangerously with aspirin.

The medical picture I developed from Sunny's toxicology and medical records was not very clear. It was obvious that she took drugs—in great variety and quantity—very sporadically. She did not act like a regular addict. She did things in a haphazard, crazy sort of way. While it is very possible that Sunny did not intend to kill herself, the more I read, the more I realized that that was probably what happened. But even worse for Sunny and those who love her, she did not die. While her body breathes, her mind is lifeless.

My conclusions and final report to Professor Dershowitz stated that Sunny von Bulow was a walking pharmacy. Like Elvis, she had ingested several chemicals that probably interacted in such a negative manner that her body, already frail from the low blood sugar levels, did a tailspin into an irreversible coma.

What about the incredible levels of insulin in Sunny's body? The insulin levels were high, but the prosecution's own test, I determined, was completely unreliable. It came out later that there were two blood samples: one taken as Sunny was wheeled into the emergency room and one taken after doctors had given her a glucose push to increase her blood sugar levels. Also, it was later learned that one of the samples had been tossed out prior to testing and that lab technicians were unsure which sample it was. This is important because if it was the sample taken after the glucose pushes, the insulin in the system would be artificially high, as the pancreas excreted the hormone to combat the artificial sugar injected into Sunny's blood.

And there was another significant problem with the insulin test results. When the Boston laboratory reported their findings to the prosecutors, it said that the third test performed on the blood samples showed a level of 216. Fifteen is considered normal. But what of the first two tests? The first reading came back 0.8 and the second came back near 1,000. Those are incredibly huge differences. The fact that none of them was ever replicated invalidates them all. None of the results, including the 216 level the prosecutors relied on, could be deemed scientifically credible.

Because the main goal of the defense lawyers was now to get Claus's conviction overturned, they asked me to file a complete affidavit detailing my findings. I filed this affidavit with the Rhode Island Supreme Court on September 26, 1983:

> Based upon my review and evaluation of all the medical and scientific investigative materials submitted to me in the case of *State of Rhode Island* v. *Claus von Bulow* it is my professional opinion as a forensic pathologist that there is not adequate or sufficient evidence to justify and scientifically buttress an allegation that Mrs. von Bulow's serious illness, manifested by a loss of consciousness and marked hypoglycemia, which necessitated her admission to the Newport Hospital on 27 December 1979, was caused by an improper insulin injection administered by her husband, Mr. Claus von Bulow. There are quite adequate and sufficient opinions and conclusions set forth by the various treating physicians in the hospital record for that period and in subsequent treatment, which would indicate that her unconsciousness and medical problems had been produced by disease processes unrelated to any actions by a third party.
>
> It is interesting and significant to note that Mrs. von Bulow did not make any accusations against her husband following her release from the Newport Hospital on 2 January 1980, and her eventual clinical recovery. The fact that she maintained her domestic relationship with Mr. von Bulow would certainly seem to indicate that she did not entertain any thoughts or suspicions that her husband had injected her with any kind of medication or chemical solution. There is no medical basis set forth in the records that would substantiate a theory to the effect that Mrs. von Bulow suffered retrograde amnesia pertaining to any events that had occurred immediately prior to her illness on 27 December 1979.
>
> Mrs. von Bulow had been hospitalized for acute salicylate poisoning on 1 December 1980. There can be little doubt that this episode was caused by the suicidal ingestion of approximately 65 five-grain aspirin tablets, which would have

been taken at the same time or over a very short time interval. This well-documented event strongly suggests that Mrs. von Bulow suffered from some kind of mental illness, and certainly serves as a logical psychological predicate for a reasonable, subsequent medical conclusion that she continued to harbor suicidal intentions prior to the time of her second episode of coma, which resulted in her admission to the Newport Hospital on 21 December 1980.

On 21 December 1980, at approximately noontime, Mrs. von Bulow's blood alcohol level was 0.009%. Applying well-accepted chemical data, it can be determined that the blood alcohol level would have been approximately 0.12% twelve hours previously, at midnight, December 20.

Following Mrs. von Bulow's admission to Newport Hospital on 21 December 1980, it was ascertained that she had a 1.06 mg% blood level of amobarbital. Insomuch as there were no areas of skin ulceration or soft tissue necrosis, which would have been produced if this much amobarbital had been injected subcutaneously, it is almost certain that Mrs. von Bulow ingested at least one dozen 100 milligram capsules in order to have developed a blood level of 1.06 mg%. Because of the easily detectable, bitter taste and consistency of amobarbital, it is extremely unlikely that such a large quantity of this drug could have been surreptitiously administered in either liquid or solid food.

The levels of amobarbital and ethanol (alcohol) found in Mrs. von Bulow following her admission to the Newport Hospital on 21 December 1980 certainly would have been sufficient, acting in concert, to have produced unconsciousness and coma. Indeed, such levels of these two drugs have been known to produce death.

In light of all the background information and medical findings in this case, it is my professional opinion that Mrs. von Bulow ingested the alcohol and amobarbital voluntarily, and quite probably, in a suicidal attempt.

The development of severe hypothermia in Mrs. von Bulow before and during her hospitalization for treatment of the second episode of coma would have affected the body's metabolism, including the various physiological processes that involve glucose and insulin. It should be kept in mind that Mrs. von Bulow suffered from a serious medical condition known as "reactive hypoglycemia"; hence, it is quite possible that the changes in her glucose and insulin metabolism could have been quite substantial in the face of dramatic lowering of the body temperature. Therefore, the interpretation of the glucose and insulin blood levels obtained at that time would be compromised to the point of scientific inaccuracy and could not be accepted as being scientifically credible.

Among those matters that are universally well-known and accepted by all knowledgeable, experienced forensic pathologists is the fact that the majority of individuals who successfully commit suicide do not leave suicide notes.

It is quite common for individuals who commit suicide to do so by taking two or more different medical compounds or other chemical substances. This is also true in cases of accidental death caused by the toxic effects of two or more drugs, especially those that act synergistically (e.g., alcohol and barbiturates).

On the other hand, it is extremely uncommon for more than one drug or chemical substance to be utilized or administered by an assailant who murders an individual by poisoning. In almost all such cases, only one particular substance is administered.

The chemical tests and physical observations concerning the needle, which was allegedly used by Mr. von Bulow to inject the amobarbital into his wife, actually disprove such a theory. As a matter of fact, the tests and examination conducted by Bio-Sciences Laboratory were performed in such a way as to subject their findings and conclusions to much criticism and render them scientifically inaccurate and unacceptable as medical evidence from the prosecution's standpoint.

In conclusion, following my evaluation and analysis of all the materials, it is my professional opinion as a forensic pathologist and medical-legal investigator, based upon a reasonable degree of medical certainty, that Mrs. von Bulow's unconsciousness and coma, which led to her hospitalization on 21 December 1980, was most probably due to a combined overdose of ethanol and amobarbital. The subsequent development of hypothermia and severe hypoglycemia were complications of her toxic condition and central nervous system damage.

Furthermore, Mrs. von Bulow's hospitalization on 27 December 1979, was most probably due to natural causes, consistent with the findings, conclusions, and opinions expressed by her treating physicians set forth in that hospital record.

There is not sufficient basis to buttress and defend the contention that either or both of her comatose episodes in 1979 and 1980 were caused by the intentional injection of insulin (1979) or insulin and amobarbital (1980).

On October 17, 1983, Alan Dershowitz presented Claus von Bulow's new case to the Rhode Island Supreme Court. He told the justices that the jury's guilty verdict should be reversed on two grounds: (1) the medical evidence presented by the prosecutors was totally flawed, and new medical evidence actually went to prove Claus's innocence, and (2) the seizure of the black bag from Claus's closet by the private investigator violated Claus's Fourth Amendment rights protecting him from illegal searches and seizures. Dershowitz pointed out that no search warrant had ever been obtained to search Claus's study and his closet.

On April 27, 1984, the Rhode Island Supreme Court overturned von Bulow's conviction. In 1985, Claus von Bulow was retried on the attempted murder charges. But this time, defense attorneys were well aware of the flaws in the medical evidence that I and other forensic scientists had discovered. And it was to Claus's benefit. This time, the jury acquitted him of all charges. A couple of days after the verdict, Claus called to thank me.

Based upon the medical and scientific evidence, I do believe with all my heart that Claus is innocent of this crime. His case is very similar to the Jean Harris case, but fortunately it ultimately concluded successfully. Much like Jean, Claus did not come across as your average Joe or Jane. They were both very self-confident. However, the defense attorneys for Claus had learned much from the Harris case and decided not to put Claus on the witness stand to defend himself. Jean had testified and the jury disliked her immensely. The same probably would have been true of Claus. But his lawyers concentrated on the medical evidence, and once they destroyed that, there was nothing left for the prosecution to stand on.

9
The Impossible Dream:
The Case of Karen Diehl

Perhaps no single class of crimes so deeply angers the human heart as does child abuse. The very words evoke horrifying images of helpless innocents being gratuitously beaten by depraved parents. People too sick to treat their own children with basic human dignity do not deserve to live in this society, we say, and mostly we are right. So powerful is this inclination to condemn parents in alleged cases of child abuse, however, that it must be kept in check until all the facts are in.

Having been a forensic pathology consultant in more than two hundred child abuse cases, over 90 percent of which involved deaths, I've had the unpleasant experience of learning the most intricate details of many a child-battering incident firsthand. I've seen kids who have been beaten and kids who have been tortured, kids who have been starved and kids who have been drowned, kids who have been burned on hotplates, even infants who have been held by the ankles and swung against walls. But I've also seen good parents on trial for making tragic mistakes, for falling victim to circumstances beyond their control, and sometimes even for crimes they didn't commit.

It was, therefore, with mixed feelings that I found myself listening to a case summary that a Virginia Beach attorney by the name of Tom Shuttleworth was describing over the phone one evening in April of 1987. I had just gotten home from the hospital, and because it had been a long day, I was looking forward to eating dinner, reading, and relaxing. But as the attorney related the details of the case he had recently taken on, I found my curiosity being stirred.

Shuttleworth's client, a thirty-six-year-old mother by the name of Karen Diehl, faced charges of child neglect, assault, abduction, and murder in the death of an adopted son. Her husband, Michael, who had separate legal representation and was being tried separately, faced identical charges. Although the incident had occurred in October 1986, the usual series of pretrial delays had dragged the whole process out until May, when at least one of the trials was expected to begin.

The facts of the case were these:

On the morning of October 24, 1986, police and paramedics responded to an urgent call from a Virginia Beach campground where the Diehls had been staying since September with their seventeen children. Fundamentalist Christians, they apparently had begun building this clan of four natural and thirteen adopted children some fifteen years earlier in Idaho. At the time these events occurred, however, they had been traveling around the country in a converted schoolbus for nearly two years.

When the authorities arrived, they found thirteen-year-old Andrew Diehl in a state of cardiac arrest. Despite every effort to revive him, the boy slipped into a coma and steadily deteriorated until his demise five days later. The anatomical cause of death, which did not seem to be in dispute, was massive internal head injuries resulting in the termination of the body's vital functions. What was in dispute was the manner in which those injuries were produced.

According to his client, Shuttleworth said, the boy had been walking in the aisle of the bus that morning when he collapsed and struck his head, possibly on the edge of a bunk bed, possibly on a plastic crayon box on the floor. There may also have been a second fall after he was helped up to a standing position.

Unfortunately, Shuttleworth added, the case history was a bit more complicated than that. As fundamentalists, the Diehls had been known to employ corporal punishment in disciplining their children. This, in fact, was something they had freely admitted to when questioned by the authorities about the assortment of bruises, cuts, and scars that covered Andrew's body. They had also invited detectives onto the bus, where a wooden paddle and a variety of restraining devices were found.

Armed with this highly volatile evidence, Shuttleworth told me, the local district attorney was proceeding on the theory that Andrew's fatal wounds had, in fact, been caused by a blow to the head that Mrs. Diehl allegedly administered with the paddle three days before his hospital admission. But while the record would demonstrate ample evidence of some highly unusual and excessive disciplinary techniques, he added, he did not believe she had caused the injuries that killed him.

Based on what little I knew, I hesitated to get involved. After all, what kind of case could be made for a pair of itinerant "born-agains" who had admittedly inflicted bodily harm upon their own child? But then, I reminded myself, it is not for me to turn down a case based upon my gut reaction to it, to deal with moral values or judgments. It's not that I'm insensitive to such considerations —as a matter of fact, I like to believe that I'm more sensitive to the larger dimensions of a case than most. But in my capacity as a medicolegal forensic pathology consultant, it's simply not for me to determine whether or not something that somebody may or may not have done is morally correct. That's just not my job.

What was important was that I had plenty of experience evaluating the precise kinds of medicolegal questions that appeared to be involved here. If anyone could determine whether this child had died as a result of a blow or a fall, it was I. By the end of our conversation, I told Mr. Shuttleworth I'd be willing to review the case.

Over the next few weeks, he sent me all of the materials I needed in order to conduct a competent review—namely, the hospital and autopsy reports, microscopic tissue slides, autopsy photos, and CT scan results. I wasted no time getting into them. As I read through the report from Virginia Beach General Hospital, I was shocked to discover the extent of the alleged "abuse." Following the stabilization of his heartbeat at the campground, Andrew had been rushed to the emergency room, where he was found to be unconscious, unresponsive, and critically hypothermic. His buttocks were bruised and bare, his lower lip was cut, an area above his left eye was bruised and scratched, his ankles, feet, wrists, and hands were blistered and swollen, and "multiple old scars'' covered his torso and limbs. Clearly, this boy had been handled in a way no child ever should. But what was it that killed him?

My answer lay in the CT scan results. They showed, mainly on the upper right side of the head, a large subdural hemorrhage— a pooling of blood between the skull and the brain—and massive swelling of the brain itself. This was typical of severe head trauma patients, but what puzzled me was the absence of any corresponding head cuts, skull fractures, or hemorrhaging within the brain itself. In most cases where enough force has been inflicted to kill a person, you're going to see some, if not all, of these injuries. In a juvenile, whose bones have not yet developed to their full thickness, some kind of brain contusion or bleeding is especially likely.

The subdural hemorrhage alone had apparently done enough damage, however, for within the hour, the attending neurosurgeon, a Dr. James D. Dillon, had determined Andrew to be brain-dead and an operation to drain the hemorrhage unnecessary. The boy was placed in the intensive care unit for further observation, where his condition steadily deteriorated until his death early Wednesday morning.

I turned immediately to the autopsy report, curious as to the precise cause of the boy's quite rapid decline. In his external examination, the pathologist, an assistant chief medical examiner by the name of Gregory P. Wanger, had noted a large red and yellow bruise on the top of the head and smaller red bruises over the left eyebrow and on the back of the head. Like the neurosurgeon, he had found no cuts or fractures, but upon opening the skull, he discovered the "large, bulging" hemorrhage that had shown up in the CT scan. He also discovered the brain to be "markedly softened" and shifted to the left, with "contusions" and "necrosis"—or tissue death—in several areas, including some located very close to the brain stem.

This, I knew, was critical. The brain stem, the portion of the brain that connects it with the spinal cord, is where the body's vital centers are located. If they are compromised by swelling and/ or hemorrhaging, as they were here, there can be a disruption of the nerve pathways that send messages to the lungs and the heart. In addition, the boy's documented severe thrombocytopenia, or low blood platelet count, would explain why the hemorrhage did not clot. Based upon my preliminary review of the medical evidence, this was as much as I could conclude about the head wounds.

I turned to Dr. Wanger's case summary to see what his own conclusions had been and was shocked to find what I considered to be a serious overstepping of a pathologist's professional bounds. Under "Cause of Death," Dr. Wanger had typed: "Head injuries due to blows." In his last paragraph, he had also found it necessary to add that "the location of the head injuries is inconsistent with a typical fall." Among his other supposedly objective findings were that the abrasions on Andrew's wrists were "consistent with binding," that the contusions on his thighs were "consistent with the whip recovered at the scene," and that a scar on his chest was "consistent with blows from a linear object."

Without knowing a thing about how this case was investigated, I could tell right off that I was looking at an example of overzealousness. As far as I'm concerned, an autopsy protocol is not the place to speculate about what kinds of instrumentality caused which wounds. There's nothing wrong with sitting down with detectives and prosecutors later to tell them what one thinks, but one does not go into a postmortem examination with preconceived notions about the cause of death, even if one has a Mirandized confession. In an autopsy protocol, one deals with tangible, physical evidence, identifying and describing such variables as size, shape, consistency, color, weight, volume, and location. A good medicolegal autopsy should be able to stand purely on its own and should really be unassailable. Because of the manner in which this one was conducted, I could see that it was extremely assailable.

Included among the materials Shuttleworth had sent me were all the local press clips on the Diehl case to date. Although by now I had a fairly good idea about the cause and manner of Andrew Diehl's death, I realized that I knew next to nothing about him, his family, and the events leading up to his death. And so I read on. The incredible story that emerged is one I've since been able to flesh out through my review of court transcripts, police reports, and my continuing correspondence with the Diehls, their attorneys, and various other individuals connected to the case.

The story really begins some sixteen years before that tragic October morning, when Karen Louise Schwein, then a twenty-year-old sophomore at a small college outside Detroit, sent a book called *The Family Nobody Wanted* to the brother of a friend. Since first reading it as a teen, Karen had been inspired by this story of a couple who had taken it upon themselves to make a home for otherwise unadoptable children. Her friend suggested that her brother might be just the right person to share the dream with.

The man to whom she sent the book was Michael Joseph Diehl, a college graduate and former navy lieutenant then working as a freelance carpenter and timber sales regulator for the Idaho Forestry Service. Michael had grown up in the same town as Karen, the Detroit suburb of Wayne, and the two had even attended the same high school, but because he was five years older, they had never met. Her letter apparently interested him, however, for soon the two were corresponding regularly, and by the spring of 1971, they were married.

The Diehls settled in the tiny northwestern Idaho town of Coolin, where Michael continued with his work while Karen began contacting the state and private adoption agencies in pursuit of their first child. But while there were plenty of children in need of homes, it wasn't just any children the Diehls were looking for. "Right from the start," Michael told me, "we never tried to find healthy, normal children, because we could have our own, and therefore it wouldn't be right to take 'normal' children out of the market when there were so many childless couples."

Even so, as perfectly fertile newlyweds, the Diehls encountered stiff resistance to their plans. Frustrated, they decided to have their own child, and in September 1972, Karen gave birth to a boy, Brian. Two years later, after being denied again, they ended up having twins, Jeffrey and Nathan. Later, Karen would bear one last natural child—another boy, named Daniel.

Although pleased with this new family, the Diehls apparently were not ready to give up on their dream just yet. They had even gone so far as to buy a five-bedroom house in the nearby town of Post Falls in anticipation of the clan they planned to assemble. They kept making inquiries until finally, in 1975, they convinced the state Health and Welfare Department's chief social worker to inspect their home. The worker liked what she saw and soon afterward approved their adoption of Michael, a six-year-old Yukon Territory boy whose physical and mental growth had been stunted by his mother's ingestion of radioactive iodine during pregnancy.

From that day on, the Diehls never had any trouble adopting children.

In the spring of 1976 there was Matthew Patrick, a Filipino from San Diego who had been born with severe body and facial deformities some ten months earlier. Soon after came Carrie, a mulatto born to a mentally retarded St. Louis woman and initially thought to be retarded herself. Anjela Joy, a two-year-old who had lost her mother in a Chicago tenement fire that left her a severely scarred deaf-mute able to breathe only through a tracheotomy tube, was adopted in 1981. And in October of that year, the Diehls took in Dominick, an eight-year-old product of the Chicago slums and a succession of foster homes and psychiatric institutions who suffered from behavioral disorders that the agent warned put him beyond hope of recovery.

Kevin and Benjamin, black brothers orphaned in New York City, were added to the family in March 1982 after social services officials had all but given up on finding homes for them; and although four-year-old Benjamin was healthy, Kevin, five, suffered from sickle-cell anemia. In August 1983, the Diehls took in their largest batch yet—four more black children born to an unwed and physically abusive mother in Chapel Hill, North Carolina. While seven-year-old Shauna and six-year-old Leanndra had escaped with only slight emotional scars, Laurie, four, was prone to hurting herself, and two-year-old Jarrad, the only boy among the four, was a dwarf—a deformity the emotional repercussions of which doctors said were aggravated by early psychological trauma. Another sister, Christine, who had not yet been born when the first four were adopted, was taken in in March 1984.

Finally, in September of that year, the seventeenth and final addition to the Diehl family was made. Kammie Helen, a cerebral palsy victim, had been found as an infant on a garbage heap in Calcutta, India, and had spent her early childhood in a children's hospital. When the adoption agencies learned of the Diehls' eagerness to take her, they waived the requested shipping fee of fifteen thousand dollars. Wheelchair-bound, she could not talk or move her limbs and was severely emotionally withdrawn.

"My career was being a mother," Karen recently told me. "I was gifted to do what I did. I have the ability to know emotional needs at any given time. We never set a number. It goes back to God's direction: the children the Lord sent us."

"The Lord" had not always been a part of the Diehls' lives, but as their family grew, so too did their faith. Although both Michael and Karen had been raised as Catholics, they had lapsed during their college and early adulthood years into what Michael calls "a state of limbo." But a few years after their marriage, he said, they developed "a real hunger again for God," and in the spring of 1976 they were "born again." They joined the nearby Cornerstone Christian Fellowship Church, an evangelical congregation affiliated with the United Church of Christ. Soon, they were a welcome addition to this community of former Catholics and Protestants.

As the couple's religious convictions grew, so too did their desire for a simple life. In 1982, with eight hundred dollars in special service and maintenance subsidies coming in each month from the state, Michael quit the forestry service and lumberjack work to become a full-time father. Although money was tight, with their mortgages and debts paid off, and subsidies eventually reaching twenty-two hundred dollars a month, they were able to get by. And by making and mending clothes, reading books bought at Goodwill Industries instead of going to the movies, tending their own garden, baking their own bread and granola, and buying staple foods in bulk with stacks of coupons, the Diehls were even able to live comfortably.

Around the same time, the Diehls removed their children from the Christian school they had been attending and, with the blessings of the state, began teaching them at home. Five days a week, the children would assemble before a blackboard to study science, math, English, geography, and history. Like all children, they even had homework. "It was the best thing that ever happened to those kids," said Karen. "They thrived on the same level of discipline day in and day out. In this consistent environment they made much more progress than they ever would in school."

The lack of daily interaction with the community had its drawbacks, however, and during the winter of 1983–84, the children's visits to doctors and therapists all but ceased and Karen dropped out of a parent-support group. But as far as the Diehls were concerned, everything the children needed was right there at home.

In January 1984, in the midst of another long, cold winter, the Diehls decided that they would escape the following one by taking a long drive to visit Michael's parents in southern Florida. But although it was originally planned as just a three-month trip, in the back of their minds was the idea of settling elsewhere. In addition to the inclement weather, the Ku Klux Klan's national headquarters were just thirty miles away, and some of the Diehls' black kids had already been harassed and spat upon.

Michael proceeded to convert a 1956 schoolbus he had bought the previous year into a trailer home, equipping it with a microwave oven, two stoves, seventeen bunk beds, two storage bunks, a combination table/double bed, a five-gallon water jug, a five-gallon toilet, a TV, an icebox, a CB radio, and a sewing machine. As a final touch, he installed a plaque across the door that read, "Our Trust is in the Lord." On November 26, they began what would turn into a thirty-two-thousand-mile, twenty-three-month trek across forty states.

The Diehls made their way west across Washington State, then south through Oregon into California. There they wound up staying in campgrounds for over two months, offering advice on everything from parenting to religion to an ever-growing fan club. As they traveled on, commented the Diehls' pastor, "it became more and more evident to them what they were doing. It became a ministry type thing." Before long, Karen was sending a regular newsletter to friends and supporters. "For us," she wrote of their mission in one such letter, "it is learning to trust in His total ability and desire to completely take care of us every single minute and day of our lives."

So great was this trust, apparently, as well as the conviction that what they were doing was good for both the children and the people they were meeting along the way, that while camping at Death Valley National Monument in January of 1985, the Diehls decided to extend their vacation into a journey of indefinite length. With their minds thus made up, the family proceeded to zigzag its way across the country, wintering in Texas and the Southwest and moving on through the Midwest in the spring. They arrived in Michigan in July, just in time for a double family reunion, then moved east to New England for the autumn. From there, they headed down the coast, arriving at Michael's parents' home in time for Christmas.

In March 1986, the family pulled into Virginia Beach to watch a taping of *The 700 Club*. The next day, they found themselves guests on the show, whose host called them "a great example for us all." It didn't take long before they were a big hit in the area, and in June, the local paper featured them in a front-page spread entitled 17 CHILDREN GET FAMILY-SIZED HELPING OF LOVE. With this popularity came comfort, and it soon became clear to the Diehls that Virginia Beach would not be just another stop.

While staying at a campground in Seashore State Park, they found a ten-bedroom hunting lodge in the city's Back Bay area that seemed to suit their needs exactly. Unfortunately, they didn't suit the needs of its owner, who wanted about six times the ninety-five-thousand-dollar value of their Idaho home. The Diehls, however, were undeterred.

"We sensed with awe the presence of the Lord," Michael wrote in their summer newsletter. "Standing in the yard, I thanked Him for bringing us Home. In the real world there appears to be no way we can ever move into that house. And yet I know that the Lord will move us in. Sixty years ago He had that house built for my family. You couldn't pay us a hundred thousand dollars to leave Virginia Beach, because this is where we have our hearts."

Neither "the Lord" nor anyone else moved them into that house, however, and after a two-and-a-half-month trip around the South, the Diehls found themselves back in Virginia Beach, parked at the Indian Cove Campground with autumn approaching. As Karen told me, "We came back because we were hoping that maybe something would work out. And I can give it to you in Christian terms: both Mike and I felt very strongly that the Lord was leading us to Virginia Beach for whatever reason."

When the Diehls adopted eight-year-old Dominick Joseph Ortley on October 16, 1981, they had no real idea of what they were getting themselves into. The son of a white, drug-addicted prostitute and an abusive father of either black or Hispanic descent, Dominick, together with his younger brother, had been mercifully snatched up by social workers from a Chicago slum at the age of five. But for the next three years of their lives, the brothers were shuttled from one foster home to another, ultimately becoming residents of a series of psychiatric institutions.

Eventually, a Minnesota family adopted the brothers and soon afterward moved to a community about one hundred miles north of Post Falls, where an agent with a private adoption firm got to know them. A few weeks after meeting them, the agent received a frantic call from the family—they could no longer handle Dominick. The agent, who had nineteen children of her own, took the boy home for a couple of weeks while trying to decide what to do to avoid reinstitutionalization. Then it dawned on her. She called Karen Diehl to discuss the case, and soon afterward, Dominick was a Diehl.

Among Dominick's known problems were manipulativeness, hyperactivity, rebelliousness, stealing, and lying. When he wasn't acting out, the skinny, dark-complexioned boy was an emotionally withdrawn loner who liked to read books and draw sketches. The Diehls knew right away that they were not dealing with a normal child, but then few of their adopted children were what one would call "normal."

Immediately, the Diehls set out to show the boy that the nightmare of his first eight years was over. As Karen would say at her trial, "When Andrew came into our home, Mike and I told him on a number of occasions that he was home, that he was our son, that we loved him, and that nothing that had happened before would ever affect our love for him. That he belonged. That he was a Diehl." In a note that he kept in his school desk they had written: "Dear Nick, Yes, we do love you very much—enough to go through this miserable time with you. No, we will never quit. Yes, we are praying for your complete healing."

The Diehls had renamed many of their adopted children in an effort to separate them from their often traumatic histories, and Dominick's, they judged, had certainly been traumatic. Although the agency's official stance was that name changing only meant further disruption, for Andrew, Michael felt, "disruption was the name of the game, so a name change signified a break with the past and also a chance to acquire a name that he himself liked, that influenced him positively." The name that he liked was Andrew, and so Andrew he became.

Despite this outpouring of love and support, Andrew began misbehaving within days of his arrival. He acted out sexually with the girls and lied to get his way. In school he was often so disruptive that his teachers found it hard to maintain order. And although all the kids were well fed, the Diehls began to find banana peels and granola bar wrappers hidden in cupboards—deeds it did not take long to trace to Andrew. Eventually, the theft of food became so bad that Michael began sleeping on a cot in the kitchen. When Andrew found a way around him, they installed a burglar alarm under a mat in front of the door. That worked for about a year and a half, until Andrew figured out how to short-circuit it.

"He was extremely intelligent, extremely stubborn, and extremely determined to do things his way whether it was right or wrong," Michael told me. "If he wanted something, he took it. It didn't matter if he had plenty of his own. Stealing was a big thing, and then lies right behind it. He took money out of my wallet. He took food out of the cupboard. He took the kids' things from them. Nothing was sacred to that child, and he could lie so convincingly that you could swear he was telling the truth."

Before, during, and after the Diehls' trials, much would be said and written about their methods of child discipline. The accepted truth came to be that their religious convictions had instilled in them a simple faith in old-fashioned beatings and the biblical philosophy that if you "spare the rod," you'll "spoil the child." As I've learned, however, there was quite a bit more to it than that.

Neither Diehl was raised in a household where corporal punishment was used, and with their own emotionally stable children, traditional methods of discipline worked just fine. With others, however, it wasn't so easy. "Other children need more severe disciplinary measures in order to accommodate their particular personalities," said Michael. "And some of our techniques evolved out of necessity when the more normal methods didn't work." Added Karen, "We used creative discipline, the belief that children need strong love and fair and consistent punishment. To me, discipline is love. It is every aspect of a child's life. It teaches him to be self-disciplined. In a society that condemns corporal punishment I would defend my belief in the usefulness of the spanking in the totality of raising the child."

The Diehls administered spankings with a thin, two-foot wooden paddle that they called a "switch." Specific misdeeds would result in specific numbers of spankings, but always they were followed up with lectures and hugging. For the children, the switch became an accepted part of family life, something that could be counted on in the event of serious misbehavior.

"They had to have order in that house," an Idaho social worker told the local paper. "They had rules, and the kids knew what would happen if they broke the rules." Added a family friend,

"The peace that existed in that house when we would walk in defied all reason with me. Anyone who knew them has had to analyze their own disciplinary techniques because Michael and Karen were effective."

When it came to Andrew, however, that effectiveness seemed to reach its limit. Long before they ever spanked him, they tried long talks, sacrificed dessert, and jumping jacks. "He wrote sentences until we used up reams of paper," Michael told me, "trying to get across to him that it wasn't worth it to mess up the way he was doing, trying to find out where the point was that discipline would be effective." If the chosen punishment was cleaning the bathroom, for instance, it could take as long as a month before he caught on. "He was a child of extremes," said Michael. "No mild techniques worked with him. Even the so-called mild techniques had to be carried to an extreme before they had an effect on him."

Two months into their trek, Andrew began displaying a pattern of behavior more troubling than anything the Diehls had yet seen. In February 1985, the family was in Scottsdale, Arizona, when Karen noticed that her bath towel smelled like urine. She and Michael went to where the towels were stored, in a drawer beneath Andrew's bed, and discovered that everything inside was soaking wet. When Andrew admitted to being the culprit, he was made to pay for doing the laundry out of his own allowance. A few months later, the same thing happened again, and again Andrew paid to clean it. A few months after that, it happened once more, this time at the expense of the bus carpeting. Once more, Andrew's punishment was sacrificed allowance.

After the Diehls' arrival in Virginia Beach, the problem became worse as Andrew began urinating regularly in his sleeping bag. It was on the fifth trip to the laundromat that Karen told Andrew if he did it one more time, they would have to take his sleeping bag away. The next morning, when they saw he had done it again, they made good on their promise. But a similar pattern soon emerged with his blanket. When that was taken away, Andrew moved on to his pillow, then his pajamas, then his underwear. By the time the newspaper did its big feature on the family in June, Andrew had lost the privilege of wearing anything to bed at all.

By now the Diehls knew Andrew well enough to realize his problem wasn't biological, and limiting his intake of fluids and supervising his trips to the toilet did nothing. Always, Andrew found a way to hold his urine until he wanted to let it go. When Karen asked him whether he'd been awake when it happened, he would invariably say yes, and when she asked him why he was doing it, he would say, "I just want to." According to Karen, "Andrew had perfect control over his defecation and urination, absolutely down to a second. It was the worst behavior he could think of."

In addition to all the traditional forms of discipline, the Diehls had tried sit-ups, running laps, and jumping jacks. But for a boy as hyperactive as Andrew, physical activity was no punishment. According to Karen, Andrew could do jumping jacks for eleven hours straight, thus turning it into a kind of "positive reinforcement." So the Diehls tried real positive reinforcement, promising to play games with him or to take him shopping if he stayed dry. Only when that proved equally ineffective did they resort to spankings. Not only did the spankings not work, but Andrew soon began soiling the other children's clothes as well.

Perhaps one of the biggest questions this case would raise in my mind, as well as in the minds of everyone concerned, was why, faced with the very real possibility that their son was beyond hope, the Diehls did not give him back to the authorities or at the very least take him in for a psychological evaluation and counseling. When I consider all the agencies that deal with these kinds of problems, all the special education programs in schools, all the diagnostic and therapeutic services available, I can only criticize their negligence. But while it is easy to say this in retrospect, the Diehls, I've learned, saw the situation a bit differently.

"It goes back to what we were told when we first adopted him," Michael explained—"that there was no help available for him anymore. When we heard the agency say that his only future was in the institution and there was no other hope for him, we truly believed there was no other hope for him except for what we could do ourselves." Added Karen, "Andrew was an extremely bright child. He knew every psychological game in the book. Mike and I talked long and hard about whether he would benefit from seeing a counselor. We came to the decision that he would have concluded he had been given up on. His fear of rejection was extreme. He had a lot of misperceptions about life. We came to the conclusion it would not work."

In mid-July, frustrated but determined to discipline Andrew without outside help, the Diehls took a fateful step: they began restraining him to his bed at night with a pair of handcuffs. Amazingly, they soon found that even restrained, Andrew was able to contort his body in such a way as to enable him to urinate elsewhere and lift the other kids' clothing out of their beds with his feet. Soon, the Diehls began to find feces hidden in the children's clothes, under their mattresses, and in their shoes. Eventually, Andrew's own mattress was ruined, and Michael was beginning to fear that the plywood beneath it would soon be too. In August, the Diehls resorted to placing the boy on the rubber-matted floor at night with both hands cuffed.

Early the next month, the Diehls realized that Andrew was filling up on water from the campground faucets during the day so that he could urinate at night. Their solution was to limit him to the bus with the exception of supervised trips. Around that time, too, the couple began noticing a weight loss in Andrew. Concerned that he wasn't eating well enough, they began giving him a food supplement with his meals. But soon, Andrew began refusing to use the toilet at all, and by the beginning of October, he was being restrained to the floor of the bus day and night.

On October 2, Karen went to lift Kammie out of bed and discovered feces smeared on her feet and legs. She knew immediately, of course, that Kammie hadn't done it, and it was then that she made another rash and fateful decision. Impulsively, she told Andrew that if he "pooped" one more time, he would have to eat it. She asked him if he understood her and he said that he did. As Michael recalled, he and Karen "looked at each other and said, 'Please God, not tonight. Don't let it happen again.' Because we knew that we had to follow through on what we told him."

The next morning, however, they woke up to find feces between his legs. "I actually felt sick to my stomach," Michael said, "but both of us felt it would do more harm to him if we didn't follow through on our threat, because our track record up to that point had been total compliance with everything we said to him. You see, if we didn't follow through with it, then that would undermine the validity of our telling him we loved him. If you lie to a child once, that destroys years of trust."

At any rate, added Michael, it worked: after six such incidents, Andrew stopped defecating in his bed. One morning, while Andrew was sitting on Karen's lap, the couple asked him why he had stopped. As Michael remembered, "He looked us straight in the eyes with those big, brown, soft eyes of his, and he said, 'Because you beat me at my own game and I got tired of it.' After five years of calling his bluff, there was nothing left for him to try that was any worse than the worst things he had tried to that point." Echoed Karen, "At the end, Mike and I saw real changes, that he was beginning to accept he had done the absolute worst and that Mom and Dad still love me. He was setting goals for himself. He had never done that."

During the third week of October, the nighttime temperatures had begun to drop into the high forties, giving the Diehls cause for concern about Andrew's sleeping arrangements. On the night of the seventeenth, they sat down with him and had a long talk; when they were finished, he had his pajamas, his blanket, and his sleeping bag back again. For the next three nights, Andrew was dry, and on the fourth day, just before dinner, Karen was sitting with him when he asked her how many nights he had been good. Karen said she didn't know exactly, but that she was very proud of him. That night, he wet his sleeping bag. The next day, when Karen asked him why he had done it again, she said, "He looked me in the eye and he said, 'Because you didn't remember, Mama.' " Andrew was back to square one.

That night, as Michael put the children to bed, Karen was cleaning up the bus when she noticed the switch lying on the floor. She picked it up and continued her way up the aisle. At the front of the bus, she saw Andrew was sitting on the potty, and she asked him if he was all done. Andrew answered yes, but when Karen looked in the bowl, it was empty. Frustrated, she said, she "tapped" him on the top of his head with the switch. This was the incident that the prosecution would seize upon as the blow that killed Andrew Diehl. How hard it was, we'll never know, but as Karen would say under oath, Andrew "did not say ouch. He did not cry out. He did not lose consciousness. He got up, gave me a kiss. I hugged him and said good-night, and he walked to the back of the bus."

On Thursday, October 23, Karen recalled, she was sitting on the bus with Andrew, Christi, and Kammie, waiting for Michael and the rest of the kids to return from the library, when Andrew told her that he didn't feel well. "I'm tired and I'm cold," she remembered him saying. As it was already late in the afternoon, Karen wasn't concerned about his being tired, and because the bus engine had been running all day, she was certain the floor would be warm that night. At any rate, she told him, they would be buying diapers for him the next day, so this would be the last night he slept exposed. Although there was no way she could possibly know it, it would be the last night he slept at all without the help of advanced life support systems.

Virginia Beach police reports of October 24, 1986, offer a sketchy picture of what happened at the Indian Cove Campground that morning. In an initial interview, Karen told Detective Joseph Schuler that while Michael was fixing the kids' breakfast outside, she woke up Andrew and bathed him in the large pan of water they had been using during his confinement. Noticing that his feet were swollen and that he was having trouble walking, she said, she helped him get dressed, then held him by his belt loops as he walked up and down the aisle. She had turned her back on him for a moment to talk to Michael, she said, when he fell. Upon examination, she saw that his lip was bleeding, but after cleaning it up she left him alone because, the report has her saying, "He appeared to be lying there comfortably."

Asked about the marks on his body, Karen freely admitted that the buttock sores had resulted from spankings he'd received for urinating and defecating on the floor, and guessed that the bruise over his left eye had come from the fall. As for some small, circular scars the paramedics had noted on his arms, Karen explained that they were from mosquito bites he had repeatedly scratched. After signing a consent form, Karen accompanied Detective Schuler onto the bus, where she opened a cabinet above the microwave and took out the handcuff, hose clamp, and paddle.

Around six o'clock that evening, after brief interviews with Brian, Mike, and Matthew, Detective T. A. Baum read Karen her legal rights and asked her to sign another form before they went any further. Karen and her children were transported to the nearby police headquarters. Shortly afterward, Michael was brought in from the hospital, and at around eight o'clock, detectives began interviewing him on videotape.

At the time of the fall, Michael said, Andrew was walking up and down the aisle of the bus to alleviate the puffiness in his feet.

It was while he was doing these exercises that he fell. After he and Karen helped Andrew up to a standing position, Michael added, Andrew fell again. But this time they left him alone, believing him to be faking it. When Andrew didn't get up after a few minutes, however, Karen went back to talk to him and discovered blood. She then pulled him up to a sitting position to have a better look at his mouth, but when she saw it was just a cut lip, she propped him up against the refrigerator and left him there. A few minutes later, when he still hadn't come to, the couple realized "that it wasn't a game this time."

They laid him down flat and covered him up, but it soon became apparent that his breathing was irregular. Michael then began administering mouth-to-mouth resuscitation and praying, and when he realized Andrew wasn't coming to, he said, "That's when we really started to pray." Tragically, they waited another forty-five minutes before deciding to call for help.

By the time the interview ended, it was already ten o'clock, and Michael, who had left the hospital with the understanding that he would be reunited with his wife and kids, asked the detectives where they were. He would not be able to see them tonight, they told him, for he was being arrested on charges of felony child neglect and malicious assault. The detectives cuffed him and led him off to the magistrate's office. By midnight, Karen too had been arrested and brought down for booking.

Although it was by now past midnight, Karen had yet to be interviewed on videotape, and so, at 1:00 A.M. Saturday, more than half a day since Andrew's collapse, two detectives sat down with her in front of the camera. Karen repeated what she had told the detectives earlier, adding that when she saw the bruise above Andrew's eye, she assumed that was where he hit himself. But it was during this interview that the accounts of their feeding Andrew his own waste came out, as well as the fact that Karen had "bonked" him on the head with the paddle once, three to four days earlier.

With this, the detectives had all they needed. Michael and Karen Diehl were locked up in the city jail and their bail set, respectively, at twenty-five thousand dollars and ten thousand dollars. By this time, their bus had been towed to the city garage for examination, and by later that day, their children had been placed in foster homes throughout the city.

By Sunday morning, the news was out: "COUPLE CHARGED WITH CHILD NEGLECT OF THEIR FOSTER SON." Following a child-custody hearing Monday morning, the Diehls did their best to explain themselves, but when Andrew died on Wednesday, things took a turn for the worse. That day, the papers were somehow able to report details from the Diehls' videotaped statements. And on Thursday, Dr. Wanger ruled Andrew's death a homicide and the cause of death "head injuries due to blows."

"It was caused by blows to the head sufficient to kill you," a police lieutenant who apparently fancied himself something of a clinician announced at a press conference later that day. "They are of a violent nature. They are not due to someone bumping into something. It was violent enough that it was not inflicted by hands, but the weapon cannot be determined at this point."

The Diehls, who had left the city jail late Wednesday night after Michael's brother put up his home in Minnesota to post their bail, were rearrested that morning on charges of murder and abduction and brought back to court, where a judge imposed an additional two-thousand-dollar bond. While the abduction charges were based on the idea that Andrew had been restrained against his will, the murder charges hinged solely on a "felony murder" theory: put simply, since the fatal wounds had been incurred during the commission of the felony of abduction, the couple could be tried for murder.

Initially, Paul E. Sutton II, a Norfolk attorney who had represented members of the Open Door Chapel in a 1982 abortion clinic bombing, took the case. But shortly afterward, deciding that he had a potential conflict of interest on his hands if he represented both Diehls, he contacted Shuttleworth, a highly respected personal injury attorney whom he knew by reputation, and asked him to represent Karen.

When Shuttleworth first met his client, he told me, he was surprised "to find that she was and is as nice as she is. I read in the paper what she had been accused of and I thought, my God, this woman must have horns. Well, she really doesn't, and far from it; she probably has a halo."

In mid-November, a Juvenile and Domestic Relations Court judge ruled that the Diehls could not visit their children until they underwent psychiatric evaluations. But any information gathered in those evaluations, their lawyers warned them, could be used against them in court. And so, while they ultimately did undergo the evaluations, they decided to withhold the results, and it would not be until May that they saw their children again. This, I thought, was absolutely reprehensible. Was there some fear that the Diehls would now kill off the rest of these kids one by one?

At any rate, in the course of those evaluations, the Diehls learned something else of profound significance. According to the psychiatrist, Dr. Igor Magier, Illinois medical records on Andrew showed that he was most likely a sociopath, someone who could never function within society or differentiate between good and bad. Furthermore, Magier said, prior to their adoption of him, Andrew had been on two types of medication prescribed to control his behavior. Dr. Magier then gave some examples of sociopathic behavior, including the compulsion to lie, the inability to form social bonds, and the total concern for one's own needs above all else. As Karen has told me, "Everything Dr. Magier said fit our son to a tee."

While knowledge of Andrew's history certainly doesn't justify or lessen the impact of his death, it does cast a new perspective on who he was and why he behaved the way he did. It also got the Diehls and their attorneys digging deeper. What else hadn't they been told? Just how hopeless was their effort to raise him? In the months leading up to trial, Shuttleworth and Sutton subpoenaed more records, the bulk of which, I'm told, confirmed Dr. Magier's posthumous diagnosis. As a sociopath, they learned, Andrew had a negative prognosis. And yet no one had bothered to tell them.

At any rate, it was by then far too late to stop and try to figure out Andrew's life. On December 17, the Diehls' preliminary hearing began with Brian Diehl's testimony that Andrew had been hit on the head several times, beaten "about every other day," and had even once tried to escape. The next day, Dr. Dillon testified that Andrew had died from blows inflicted with a blunt object between twelve and ninety-six hours prior to his hospital admission, and that he could not have been conscious and walking that morning. And Dr. John Thomas, a pediatrician on duty at the hospital that day, called Andrew among the five most severely abused children he had seen in his career.

With probable cause thus established, the judge certified the case to a grand jury. Less than three weeks later, on January 5,

1987, the jury handed down indictments against both Diehls on charges of murder, abduction, and felony child neglect, and against Michael alone two additional charges of malicious assault.

On June 5, having completed my evaluation with a careful analysis of the tissue slides, I called Mr. Shuttleworth to review my preliminary findings with him. With a reasonable degree of medical certainty, I told him, it was my professional opinion that Andrew Diehl died from complications of a closed head injury that produced subdural hemorrhaging, brain swelling, and the resulting slippage of portions of the brain into the foramen magnum, the hole at its base. There was no evidence to support the contention that a blow to the head had caused any of these injuries, I said, and plenty to support the contention that he had fallen.

Shuttleworth was happy that my conclusions seemed to bolster his case, but indicated that it was going to be one hell of a tough trial. Because of a series of delays and conflicts, he told me, the state had announced just two days ago that it would be conducting simultaneous trials in separate courtrooms in July. Never in my life had I heard of such a thing. Separate trials, perhaps. But simultaneous? This may have been unique in the annals of American legal history. Both he and Sutton had immediately opposed this plan, Shuttleworth said, but because they had previously argued for separate trials, they had no legal grounds on which to oppose it now.

A month later, Shuttleworth called to tell me that I was all set to testify on Tuesday, July 14. He also informed me of yet another surprise. Under a recent State Supreme Court decision allowing cameras and microphones into courtrooms for the first time ever, Virginia Beach had been chosen as one of four systems in which a two-year experiment in broadcast coverage would begin July 1; the Diehl trials would be the season premiere. Needless to say, Shuttleworth and Sutton had objected again, but those objections had been quickly overruled. I knew I was in for a real circus.

On Monday, July 13, I boarded an afternoon flight to Norfolk. Although I'd testified in civil cases in Richmond a couple of times and once lectured at the Medical College of Virginia there, I'd never been to Norfolk on business. The last time I'd been there at all, in fact, was in 1960, when I was in the air force and won a lottery prize at my hospital base in Montgomery, Alabama, to go see a military demonstration aboard an aircraft carrier in Chesapeake Bay. But aside from a vague impression of traditional southern conservatism mixed with the sophistication of any large city, I had no expectations of the community.

When I arrived around six o'clock, I was pleased to find Mr. Shuttleworth every bit as friendly and articulate in person as he had appeared on the phone. The trial had gotten off to a rocky start, he said, with the selection of an all-white jury, all of whom had heard of the Diehls and none of whom attended church regularly. Four of the jurors were people whom he'd wanted to disqualify. But on the positive side, he half-joked, most of them were parents who believed in spanking children within reason.

The prosecuting attorney, a young guy by the name of Kenneth Phillips, had started off by presenting the now infamous wooden paddle and asking five of the Diehl children to describe Andrew's punishment. One by one, they'd proceeded to demonstrate how their mother used the paddle on Andrew. And the very next day, jurors were shown Karen's videotaped statement, in which she admitted to hitting Andrew on the head with that same paddle. At any rate, Shuttleworth said, there was no time to worry about all that now. Our first stop would be the home of some of the Diehls' friends, where Michael Diehl was waiting to meet me.

When we arrived, we found the house filled with friends and family members. Shuttleworth introduced me to Michael, who looked the same as he did in the papers—tall and wiry, with graying brown hair and wire-rimmed glasses. But as we talked, I was a bit surprised; soft-spoken, intelligent, and personable, he was anything but the fanatical evangelist I had half-expected. Neither overanxious nor detached, he struck me as a sincere individual who wanted a chance to explain his actions.

After dinner, Michael took us outside to look at the bus. It was impressive what he'd done with this old schoolbus. Near the front, just behind the driver's seat, was a combined kitchen and bathroom area, complete with all the fixtures and appliances I'd read about. Behind that was a foldout bed that doubled as a dining room table. The rest of the bus consisted of the children's bunks, which were arranged nine to a side, in three stacks of three beds each. It was certainly a tight fit, but if one were going to travel in a single vehicle in a group of nineteen, this was the way to do it.

After looking around a bit, I decided it was time to get down to business. First, I asked Michael to reenact the events of October 24 to the best of his recollection. He did so, showing me exactly where Andrew was standing when he fell, how he then fell a second time after being helped up, and how he could have hit his head on the edge of a nearby bunk bed or a crayon box that had been found on the floor. The scenario certainly seemed credible, especially in such tight quarters with so many firm, hard objects around. And given what I knew about Andrew's physical state at the time of his hospital admission, the falling itself was perfectly understandable.

We were on our way back out of the bus when I recalled the prosecution's theory that Andrew had been hit on the head while sitting on the potty. I paused at that point to consider this theory with respect to the bus's layout. The toilet sat raised two or three feet off the floor. Above it, the roof of the bus curved in, leaving perhaps a foot or two of space above where Andrew's head would have been. Karen, I remembered reading, had admitted to bringing the paddle straight down while Andrew sat on the potty. As I looked at the bus's dimensions now, I tried to picture how anyone could swing a paddle in that manner with enough force to cause the kind of internal bleeding Andrew had suffered. It just did not seem possible.

After bidding the Diehls and their friends good night, Mr. Shuttleworth and I proceeded to his office, where we reviewed my findings together once more. When we finished, he handed me transcripts of Dr. Dillon's testimony from the previous week and Dr. Wanger's testimony from the previous day. By the time I finally checked into my hotel room, I was pretty tired. But I was interested in seeing what the medical authorities had had to say, and so I sat down to review their testimony.

Dr. Dillon began by explaining how Andrew's hemorrhage had resulted in the compression of the spinal fluid within and beneath the brain and the shifting of the brain from right to left. The combined pressure of hemorrhaging and swelling, he continued, cut off the blood supply at the base of the skull. Asked his professional opinion of the cause of the hemorrhage, he answered, "blunt injury to the head," a conclusion he based on the lack of skull fractures or scalp lacerations. As for how long the hemorrhage would have been there, he said, it was between twelve and ninety-six hours old. This was fine; aside from the age of the hemorrhage and an incomplete explanation of the pathological processes, there was nothing here to disagree with.

On cross-examination, Shuttleworth asked the doctor whether evidence that Andrew had been talking, walking, and eating the night before and the morning of his hospital admission would change his opinion at all.

"No, sir," Dillon responded. "Given his overall neurological picture, it is conceivable the night before that he could have been awake and alert, or he could have been drowsy, perhaps a little slower than normal to respond, or he could have been unconscious." But as for that morning, he added, "It would have been much more likely that he would have been stuporous, or drowsy, or frankly unconscious." Asked what he meant by "frankly," Dillon clarified himself by saying, "I mean definitely unconscious."

Could Andrew's body temperature have dropped from normal to seventy degrees between the morning and the afternoon?

No, Dillon responded, it would have to already have been considerably lower than normal.

Shuttleworth then moved on to the injury above Andrew's left eye, which Dillon conceded was consistent with a fall. Asked further whether the hemorrhage could have been caused by a combination of a low platelet count and a fall, the doctor again answered yes. Pressed on that point, he admitted that, given a low platelet count, "It would not require as much force to produce a subdural hematoma in an otherwise normal individual." As for whether blunt injury of the kind that had resulted in this hemorrhage would have caused Andrew to immediately lose consciousness, Dillon responded that the odds were fifty-fifty.

Finding little that seriously contended with my own conclusions, I turned to Dr. Wanger's testimony and began to read. Having obtained his medical degree in 1979, Wanger was a relatively young man. He'd then gone on to complete his anatomic and clinical pathology residency in 1983, and his training in forensic pathology the next year. Although he was not asked how many autopsies he had done, I was able to conclude that he'd been practicing forensic pathology for only three to four years.

The prosecutor, a former FBI agent by the name of Paul Sciortino, began his direct examination by asking the doctor to describe the wounds to Andrew's head and body. The judge allowed him to refer to several autopsy pictures, making for some rather graphic testimony, but when Sciortino produced the paddle, handcuff, and pipe clamp and began asking whether the wounds were "consistent with" those objects, Shuttleworth rightfully objected, setting off a long and tedious semantic debate over the proper questioning of expert witnesses. Finally, when Sciortino asked whether the scars on Andrew's hand were consistent with cigarette burns, Shuttleworth moved for a mistrial.

"There is no evidence at all that she did that," he told the judge. "And it points up the ridiculousness of Mr. Sciortino's questions. He could ask them if they were consistent with burns from a nuclear accident, and the doctor would probably say they were consistent with that." The judge denied the request for a mistrial, instead instructing the jury to disregard the last question.

As many times as I've heard this instruction given to juries, I've always found it a bit ridiculous. Once something has been said in open court, the damage is done. To ask twelve perfectly competent individuals to simply erase something from their minds is to ask the impossible. At any rate, following this last outburst, Mr. Sciortino finally moved on to what I felt were the pertinent issues.

After establishing that Andrew's hemorrhages were not caused by any preexisting blood conditions, a low platelet count, anoxia, cardiac arrest, or diabetes, Sciortino asked the doctor to explain why they could not have been caused by a fall.

First, the doctor testified, fall-associated injuries usually lie in a "hatband distribution," while at least one of the bruises in this case sat on the top of the head. This was certainly true, but why was he conveniently forgetting the other two bruises, which did lie in a "hatband distribution"? And what about the fact that none of the major brain injuries was near the site of alleged impact?

Secondly, Dr. Wanger said, the vertex bruise was over a curved surface, which he felt corresponded with "more than one impact, which is extremely atypical for a fall." This, too, was generally true, but if there had, in fact, been more than one fall, that could very well explain the more diffuse contusion. At any rate, I failed to understand how a single paddle blow could result in that kind of injury.

Lastly, Wanger said, he had never autopsied a child who had fallen from a standing position on an unmoving bus, leading him to conclude that it "is not a particularly unsafe activity." This struck me as not only silly given what was known about Andrew's poor nutritional state, but unnecessarily facetious as well.

Perhaps anticipating a question from the defense about the

lack of surface injuries to the head, Sciortino went on to ask whether this was uncommon.

"No, it is not," Wanger answered, explaining that the hair "acts in some ways as a lubricant" and may allow a blow "to essentially slide off without producing near as much abrasion as the same injury might produce in other locations." This sounded a bit farfetched. Certainly, hair might play a limited role in padding the head, but it is not a "lubricant" that allows blows to "slide off."

Having elicited Wanger's opinion as to the cause of death, Sciortino then asked him to take the paddle and demonstrate the amount of force that would have been necessary to cause the hemorrhaging seen in this case. Wanger's answer, which I've since learned he repeated in Michael Diehl's trial, struck me as inflammatory and gratuitous. "I think I'm going to need something to hit," he said. "I don't want to damage the furniture." How hard he smacked the paddle down I wouldn't know until Mr. Shuttleworth repeated it for me the next day, but following his demonstration, he added that "probably more than one" and "possibly as many as three" such blows had been delivered. As for how long the boy would have been comatose prior to hospital admission, Wanger said that it could have been twenty-four hours or longer.

Starting into the cross-examination, I was surprised to read the following definition of a medical examiner's role: "My basic role is to take a variety of stories, suspicions, allegations, rumors about a death of an individual, look at what I have at the autopsy table, at the scene, and other pieces of evidence and see whether I think there is any truth to these allegations."

It seemed to me that Dr. Wanger had it a bit backward. As I understand the role of a medical examiner, he begins with the body and other hard evidence, then comes back to what the police, witnesses, and others have offered to see if any of it fits. As I now read, in addition to the detectives who visited the scene, Dr. Wanger had relied upon information given to him by all four of the Diehls' prosecutors to arrive at his conclusions. If this wasn't looking for trouble, I don't know what is.

As I read on, I was further surprised to learn that Dr. Wanger had not even visited the bus. While an M.E. is certainly not required to visit the scene of an alleged crime, it is considered standard operating procedure in the investigation of an unexplained death, particularly where there's an indication that the scene may have played a part in that death. To his credit, Shuttleworth harped on that very idea, asking the doctor why he didn't find it important in the case of a head injury "to see if there were any objects in the bus that the young man could have hit if he fell."

Wanger responded that he had seen photographs of the bus as well as the plastic crayon box that Michael felt Andrew might have hit his head against, but also admitted that he had not taken measurements of the bus. Asked whether the bunk beds were "linear objects," a term the doctor had used earlier to describe the paddle, Wanger admitted that "portions of them were."

"And you didn't think it was important to go out there to look at the bus?"

"Well, I didn't see how the bunks could be used to strike anyone," Wanger responded, displaying once more his propensity for facetiousness.

"Well," Shuttleworth fired back, "you didn't think somebody could fall and hit their head against the bunk?"

"Certainly they could," the witness finally conceded. "Other blunt objects could make blunt injuries."

Shuttleworth then asked Dr. Wanger if he knew whether an adult could even raise a stick inside the bus as high as he had lifted it to demonstrate the alleged blow. The witness did not know. Did he have an opinion as to when Andrew was struck? "Perhaps as long as a day." Would he have been able to eat or talk the morning of the twenty-fourth or the previous evening? "I would be very surprised." Would a blow like the one he demonstrated have knocked the boy out? "More likely than not."

Although the earlier testimony regarding cigarette burns had been excluded, Shuttleworth brought it up again now, pointing out that the witness had been prepared to say that the scars on Andrew's hand were consistent with such abuse even though there was absolutely no evidence that it had taken place. Before passing the witness back to the commonwealth, Shuttleworth asked him how many times he had testified on behalf of a defendant. Never, Wanger answered.

Shortly after finishing the transcript, I faded off into sleep, filled with good tidings about the next day's testimony.

Early the next morning, Mr. Shuttleworth picked me up. When we arrived at the courthouse, I discovered the circus atmosphere

I had been expecting. TV and radio trucks were parked outside, and crowds of people milled about everywhere. It was a real community production, bringing to mind the days of courtyard hangings, when villagers would gather around to watch punishment being meted out. There is something in us, I was reminded, that derives pleasure from seeing people who are injured, and this carries over into the realm of punishment. I do not feel this is the way criminal justice should be pursued in America.

We pushed our way through the crowd into the courthouse, and Shuttleworth led me to a conference room where I would wait until he was ready for me. A short time later, the bailiff came in and told me it was time.

The jury, Shuttleworth warned me, had just finished watching Michael Diehl's videotaped statement to the police, and as I took the stand, many of the jurors were visibly distraught. As is the case in almost any child abuse trial, there was a great deal of tension in the air. This, of course, is understandable. For while in other cases one might say, "He deserved it" or "It was self-defense," everyone assumes that a child is innocent. No matter what a child did, we all feel, the parent must have been negligent, incompetent, uncaring. As I took the oath, this tension was palpable.

Following all the usual questions as to my educational background and professional qualifications, Mr. Shuttleworth asked me what materials I had reviewed in preparation for my testimony. I listed them, adding that I had also visited the bus.

"Would you have been able to render an opinion without going to the scene in this particular case to see the bus?"

"Well," I answered, "I would have rendered opinions to a variety of questions, but I feel that I can better understand and appreciate the background and relate to some of the questions that you have discussed with me by virtue of having gone to the schoolbus and having seen the actual physical premise itself."

Mr. Shuttleworth tried to continue with this line of questioning by asking me whether I would expect the pathologist investigating the case to have visited the bus, but Mr. Phillips objected, and his objection was sustained.

Shuttleworth quickly moved on, asking me whether I agreed with Dr. Wanger's findings that there had been three areas of surface contusion and five areas of brain contusion. My only difference with those findings, I said, involved the so-called contusions near the brain stem. These, I explained, were not actual contusions, but rather areas of necrosis, or tissue death, caused by increased pressure to the region. This, I said, was a "classical kind of situation" in a head trauma patient who has been kept alive for a few days.

Shuttleworth then asked me about the circular scars on Andrew's hand that Dr. Wanger had attributed to cigarette burns. These scars, I pointed out, had already turned grayish white, indicating that they were anywhere from several months to several years old. The same was true, I said, of certain scars Dr. Wanger had observed on Andrew's chest.

Asked about Andrew's low platelet count, I explained that while this deficiency did not cause the subdural hematoma, its effect on the clotting mechanism could very well have permitted the hematoma to become larger than it otherwise would have. As for what caused the low platelet count, I said that it could have been anything from a genetic disorder to poor nutrition and dehydration.

Shuttleworth then got down to the heart of the matter, asking me what I thought the cause of the injuries was.

"I feel that the two subdural hematomas were the result of two or more falls with trauma to the head," I testified. "I feel, as I've indicated before, that that very low platelet count probably prevented the blood from clotting."

At that, Shuttleworth picked up the paddle and surprised everyone present by smacking it down so forcefully on the edge of the witness box that a stack of papers sitting on top scattered to the floor. A blow like that, he said, and possibly two or three such blows, was what Dr. Wanger had demonstrated as the cause of Andrew Diehl's injuries. "Now," he asked, "what's your opinion with regards to whether or not a blow like that caused the injury that you saw in the autopsy that you examined?"

"I would stop maybe just short of saying impossible, allowing for miracles and things like that that almost defy the imagination," I answered, "but I'll come right up to that point—99 percent, if you will—and say those kinds of blows did not produce the trauma in this child." I then gave my reasons for this opinion, pointing out that there had been no surface abrasions or lacerations to the head, no bruises or collections of blood beneath the scalp, no skull fractures, and no cerebral contusions.

"If you come down with great force," I explained, "then you get what is called a coup injury, which means an injury at the site of the blow. And the brain would be impacted upon by the bony skull because the skull would be pushed in. Force that is applied to a localized area enters the body at whatever point. And here we're talking about the skull at that site. There is not the opportunity for a diffusion of force. And when you bump against something that has a flat, broad, rounded surface, something that doesn't have a jagged or pointed edge, the force is not applied to a small area. I can't conceive, based upon the demonstration that you just gave, of blows being impacted against this youngster's head in that fashion that would not have produced at least some —maybe not necessarily all, but at least some—of the injuries that I have referred to. It is beyond my comprehension how that could be done in that fashion."

"Dr. Wecht," Shuttleworth then asked, "do you have an opinion as to whether or not the young man would have lost consciousness with a blow to the head such as I demonstrated to you a minute ago?"

"In my opinion," I answered, "with blows such as you demonstrated, this youngster definitely would have lost consciousness."

Shuttleworth then moved on to the issue of Andrew's hypothermia, which I attributed to the pressure of the swollen brain on the body temperature regulatory center in the medulla. Asked whether Andrew's body heat could have dropped to seventy degrees on the morning of the twenty-fourth, I answered yes, that based on what I knew of the case history, I believed the drop had in fact occurred within just a few hours of hospital admission. "I do not believe that he could have been functioning, walking around, talking, moving, that he could have been conscious with a body temperature of seventy degrees," I said. Andrew, I added, "couldn't have been alive like that for any period of time in the absence of medical treatment."

Finally, asked my complete opinion as to the cause of death, I concluded thus:

"Dominick Andrew Diehl died as a result of acute bilateral subdural hematomas with brain swelling, and pressure by that swollen brain on the vital structures of the brain, the pons and medulla in particular. The knocking out of his body functions that led to the markedly lowered body temperature permitted the development of significantly abnormal levels of critical electrolytes, sodium, potassium, and blood sugar. The secondary effects upon the vital centers of the brain then led to his collapse, his unconscious comatose condition, and ultimately his death.''

As for my opinion of how those injuries came about, I repeated that they ''were caused by the two or more falls with injuries to the head and were not consistent with forceful, direct blows against the top of the head in the fashion that has been demonstrated in this courtroom.''

After a brief recess, Mr. Phillips began his cross-examination by reviewing much of my previous testimony. He then asked me a series of questions designed to establish that the subdural hemorrhages were not, in fact, caused by any of the secondary effects—namely, the diabetes, the anoxic insult, the cardiac arrest, or the low platelet count. In each instance, I obliged him.

Finally getting down to the heart of the matter, Mr. Phillips asked me when the two or more falls that I believed led to the boy's injuries occurred. I told him that they could have occurred anywhere from three to forty-eight hours prior to his hospital admission, but that because he didn't die until five days later, it was impossible to say exactly when each of the falls occurred.

And where had I gotten this history of multiple falls? The first and most important source, I responded, was the physical evidence, which is independent of any history. Beyond that, I added, I had been told by both Mr. Shuttleworth and Mr. Diehl that Andrew had fallen at least once.

From there, what I had expected to be a tough cross-examination probing my knowledge of the medicolegal facts in the case slowly petered out into a series of disjointed questions with no discernible direction. Following a brief redirect examination, during which I was shown the crayon box Michael Diehl had described to me the night before, I was excused and left the courtroom.

There was plenty more to come, I knew, but aside from the fact that I had a plane to catch, I have always considered it unprofessional for an expert witness to hang around the courtroom after he has finished testifying. Still, from what I have learned about the rest of the trials, I wish I could have seen more.

About a week later, I received a letter from Mr. Shuttleworth informing me that while Michael Diehl was convicted of first-degree murder, Karen Diehl was found guilty only of involuntary manslaughter. "I credit you in large part for allowing us to present our defense in such a way as to convince the jury of the involuntary manslaughter as opposed to first-degree murder," he wrote.

I was thrilled, of course, but I was also a bit puzzled as to how Michael Diehl, who had not even been accused of delivering any blows, had fared so poorly. I also wanted to get some more details about the rest of Karen Diehl's trial, and so as soon as I had a spare moment, I gave Mr. Shuttleworth a call.

The day after my testimony, he told me, Karen Diehl had taken the stand as the last defense witness and testified for several hours. Her explanation of why Andrew was treated the way he was, as well as the entire story of how the Diehl family was formed, had gone over well with the jury, he said. But an extremely tough cross-examination by Mr. Phillips had succeeded in eliciting some particularly gruesome details about her disciplinary techniques, and that had done considerable damage.

Shuttleworth had then tried to call Dr. Magier to the stand to testify about Andrew's psychological makeup. But the judge ruled that because Magier had never examined Andrew personally, his testimony was irrelevant, and thus inadmissible. It was a real setback for the defense, Shuttleworth said, if only because the witness was prepared to tell the jury that Andrew was sociopathic. Perhaps if they had known this and understood its ramifications, the outcome would have been even better.

Shuttleworth also told me that because I had testified as to issues not previously addressed by the prosecution, the state was permitted to call in a rebuttal witness—Dr. Faruk Presswalla, a deputy chief medical examiner who had been present for part of Andrew's autopsy. But despite some fairly convincing testimony regarding head trauma, Shuttleworth said, the doctor had weakened the state's case by revealing that he had not looked at the record before that morning, that he had never visited the bus, that he had never even seen a picture of the bus, that he had never seen the alleged murder weapon itself, and that because his colleague wanted to preserve Andrew's appearance for the funeral, he had not shaved the head to view his bruises.

Best of all, Shuttleworth told me, when asked his opinion as to whether the hemorrhages could have been caused by a fall, Presswalla admitted that they could have been "potentiated by a fall after the blow." In other words, he went on to explain, if Andrew were groggy from being hit, he might have fallen, thus intensifying the effect of a previous injury. This, I thought, was pretty damning.

During jury instructions, Shuttleworth had decided to take a gamble and allow jurors the choice between only first-degree murder and involuntary manslaughter. To find her guilty of murder, they would have had to conclude that Andrew died as a result of a malicious act. To convict her only of involuntary manslaughter, on the other hand, they had to conclude that Andrew was fatally wounded during the commission of a less serious offense. But even with the lesser verdict, I was told, the additional guilty verdicts on charges of abduction, neglect, and simple assault and battery made it likely she would receive more than thirty years in prison.

Phillips, he told me, had been quick to attribute Karen's verdict to the fact that he had neglected to tell the jurors that they could infer malice from the charge of abduction. But as Shuttleworth saw it, this was nonsense. "I think we were trying a reasonable doubt case," he said, "and your testimony gave the jury a reasonable doubt as to whether or not a blow to the head caused the child to die. If that in itself didn't create a reasonable doubt, it certainly was one more brick in the wall."

I then asked Shuttleworth why Michael Diehl's trial turned out so differently. The legal situation, he explained, was very complicated. Even though none of the state's eleven witnesses in that case had linked the defendant with the alleged fatal blow, the prosecution had contended that as an "aide and abettor" to his wife's crimes, Michael was guilty of felony murder. Also, Sutton had decided not to present any medical witnesses. Complicating matters further, the judge had instructed the jurors that if they agreed Michael Diehl had abducted his child, they would have to find him guilty of first-degree murder. Apparently, they had done just that, also convicting him on charges of abduction, child neglect, and simple assault.

In September, Michael Diehl was sentenced to forty-one years in prison and Karen Diehl to thirty-one years. Fortunately, enough valid objections had been raised during their trials to ensure that legal efforts on their behalf would not die quite so quickly. Within just a few months of sentencing, both Shuttleworth and Sutton petitioned the Virginia Court of Appeals to overturn the homicide convictions, primarily on the grounds that the abduction statute on which they felt those convictions relied was never meant to apply to parents.

In their brief, Shuttleworth and a partner, Robert Morecock, argued that, historically, Virginia Code said parents could not be found guilty of "kidnapping" their own children, and that to date, no parent had ever been convicted of such a crime in Virginia. Although constant revisions to the code had left the statute's wording somewhat ambiguous, they said, at least two elements of it were quite clear: that parental abduction is only a felony if the child is taken out of the state, and that even abducting one's child in contempt of a court order is just a misdemeanor.

With the battleground thus set, Morecock argued the appeal before a three-judge panel in January 1989, calling the statute vague, confusing, and subject to "nonsensical" interpretations. The court disagreed. In its opinion, the panel rejected the argument largely on the grounds of a 1947 ruling that a parent may be held criminally liable "if he exceeds or abuses his authority to correct a child and inflicts corporal punishment which exceeds the bounds of due moderation." The panel also ruled that because the element of abduction was unique to the felony murder charge, the argument that the manslaughter conviction was tainted held no water.

Fortunately, Morecock had more to work with. Following closing arguments in Karen's trial, a juror had come forward to say that he'd seen a newspaper headline announcing Michael's guilty verdict. Although the judge had let the matter go after the juror promised he would not let it affect his judgment, the appellate panel felt differently. Ruling unanimously that the juror should have been excluded from the jury, the court granted Karen a retrial and released her on bail.

Before the new trial could be held, however, the commonwealth appealed the new ruling to an *en banc* panel of the court, a legal term meaning the full court sitting together. In April 1990, yet another precedent was set as the panel ruled, on a 5–5 tie, to send Karen back to prison. After seven and a half months of freedom and regular visits with her husband and kids, Karen suddenly found herself incarcerated again.

Morecock immediately petitioned the Virginia Supreme Court, but in September 1990, a janitor somehow lost the entire case file. Although it took him six months to reconstruct it, Morecock finally resubmitted the petition. Three months later, it was denied. He re-petitioned the court in July 1991, and in September was denied once more, thus exhausting Karen's state appellate options.

As for Michael Diehl, Sutton, too, did his best to clear his client but ran into similar difficulties. When his argument was finally heard in March 1989, Sutton did not have a tainted jury to work with, and a year later, the appeal was denied. Sutton then appealed the verdict to the Virginia Supreme Court, but was denied again.

In the meantime, both Diehls have been making the best of their prison time, although both have had their share of troubles to contend with. Initially classified as a "suicide risk"—a situation she vehemently denies ever having been in—Karen spent her first five weeks in solitary confinement at the city jail before being moved to the Women's Correctional Center in Goochland, thirty miles west of Richmond. There, she spent four and a half months in maximum security before being transferred to a minimum security hall where she had her own room, TV, radio, and books. But after returning from being out on bail, she was placed in a trailer with twenty-three other women that afforded her almost no privacy. She is now back on another minimum security hall, albeit one that she describes as being "very rough, almost like in prison movies."

With Karen's first chance at parole approaching last July, I wrote a letter to the chairman of the Virginia Parole Board on March 5. In it, I strongly reiterated my contention that she did not intend to kill her son, stating that "while there can be reasonable and understandable criticism of the disciplinary measures that Karen Diehl and her husband exercised in attempting to control Andrew's highly disruptive behavior, such criticism is a long way from constituting plausible forensic pathology evidence of an intentional homicide."

I also discussed her excellent record as a prisoner. To date, I pointed out, she had earned 198 credits toward a Bachelor of Arts degree in social work through a correspondence course at a local college, maintaining an outstanding grade point average of 3.94. More importantly, I added, she had been spending much of her time offering nonprofessional counseling services to her fellow inmates, many of whom are themselves young victims of abuse.

Should she be granted parole, I wrote, "It is her intention to engage herself in activities that would provide assistance to women and children who need psychological counseling and social support.

"Karen Diehl has paid a heavy price for whatever poor judgment she may have demonstrated in her attempts to discipline Andrew," I concluded. "I urge you and your distinguished colleagues to grant her parole request, so that she can be released from prison and be permitted to pursue her life in a productive and meaningful fashion. It would not appear to be in the best interests of anyone if Karen Diehl were to continue to be incarcerated. She has paid her debt to society and is now prepared to participate as a free citizen in a manner that would be constructive and beneficial to the community."

In late May, Karen informed me that while her hearing before the state parole board had gone well, its response to her application was an "incomplete." In other words, no decision had been made. Karen must now wait indefinitely while the board continues to deliberate. By the end of this year, she probably will have received a more definitive response. If it is negative, she will have to wait until the spring of 1994 to reapply. If it is positive, she could be a free woman by now.

As for Michael, he too did some time in the city jail before being moved to a facility located just across the James River from Karen. Shortly afterwards, however, he was moved to the Augusta Correctional Center in the Appalachian Mountains. There, he had just gotten into a daily routine of rising early, working in the kitchen, exercising, and attending a Bible study group when a population redistribution plan led to another transfer, this time to the Keen Mountain facility in the state's panhandle. Within thirty-six hours of his arrival, he was attacked in a stairwell by two men who remembered seeing him on the news, and his leg was badly broken. He was then moved back to Augusta, where he is expected to do the rest of his time. Michael will not be eligible for parole until July 1994.

The fate of most of the Diehls' children has been no happier. Although Michael, Brian, Matthew, and Daniel were initially released into the custody of Karen's relatives in Minnesota and Michigan, the two younger boys were later placed in foster homes in Virginia and North Carolina when Karen's brother and his wife decided Matthew was too much for them to handle. And by the time the Diehls found friends to take the twins, Nathan and Jeffrey had become so acclimated to their new foster home in Virginia Beach that they no longer wanted to go.

As for the remaining ten children, the Department of Social Services began lobbying for the termination of the Diehls' parental rights soon after their convictions. In June 1988, Sciortino even offered the Diehls immunity from prosecution if the couple testified that these kids, too, had been neglected. The Diehls refused, but in November of that year, ruling that all the children had been abused by having to witness what an assistant city attorney called "Andrew's torture," a judge terminated the Diehls' parental rights to those ten kids.

The Diehls appealed this ruling as well, a move which should have delayed further action on the kids. Sadly, it has not. In the winter of 1992, Karen was sitting in the prison recreation room when she heard a familiar child's voice. Looking up, she was shocked and horrified to see Kevin, now a teenager, being advertised for adoption on TV. Karen immediately wrote to the judge and a lawyer, but she has not heard back from the judge and the lawyer's fees were more than she could afford.

Not even considering the apparent legal violation involved here, I feel that the decision to terminate the Diehls' parental rights was wrong and probably quite harmful. The emotional trauma of rejection—in many cases a second or third rejection—is irreversible. After all, these kids won't understand what happened. The separation has registered in their minds not as society taking their parents away but as their parents abandoning them. That the death of one child—which was in large part, if not completely, accidental—should have resulted in the great damage done to all those other lives is a terrible injustice.

When I think of the Diehls and what they tried to achieve, I think of an endeavor that deserves both tremendous commendation and serious skepticism. On the one hand, to seek out for adoption children known to be emotionally disturbed, psychologically traumatized, and physically damaged is to undertake something that requires almost superhuman courage. And to be willing then to devote one's lives to these kids, to educating, housing, feeding, and clothing them, this seems almost the work of saints, almost enough to begin the first move toward beatification.

At the same time, to think that one can accomplish this within the confines of a converted schoolbus with little in the way of funds, community interaction, or medical support is simply not realistic. And when I reflect upon this, I am inclined to think that while there's much good that might have come of the effort, that good was perhaps outweighed by the difficulties and outright impossibilities involved. After all, the Diehls were not Superman and Mother Teresa.

But this is not to say that the blame is all theirs. Far from it. For one thing, the state bureaus and private agencies that approved and should have been monitoring the adoptions obviously did not do their jobs. Whether out of negligence or adulation, they simply let it go. As for the religious community of which the Diehls were a dedicated part, could it not have offered more guidance to them in their hour of need? Why, with all the attention they'd received, were the Diehls so utterly alone?

Seven years down the road, the Diehls have long since accepted that their dream of turning Andrew into a normal human being was an impossible one. But they will never say that about the life they made for themselves in Idaho, on the road, and in Virginia Beach. "It worked," Karen recently told me. "It worked and it was wonderful. Everyone wants you to believe that these poor kids lived in squalor, but they didn't. It was wonderful. The people who saw it on the roads and in the campgrounds, they knew."

10

Best Brothers:
The Delbert Ward Case

Like most people, I have a morning routine. After putting the dog out and the coffee on, I gather the papers from the front stoop and sit down at the kitchen table to digest the news. It was on one such morning in mid-July 1990 that an item on the front page of the *New York Times* caught my eye. Beneath a picture of three grizzled old men gazing sheepishly into the camera from beneath the visors of their tattered baseball caps was the headline A DAIRY TOWN DOUBTS BROTHER KILLED BROTHER. Intrigued, I read on.

Adelbert Ward, a fifty-nine-year-old dairy farmer in the tiny upstate New York town of Munnsville, stood charged with the murder of his sixty-four-year-old brother Bill, who had been found dead in his bed on the morning of June 6. According to court papers filed after his arrest late that night, Delbert, as he was commonly known, had admitted to "placing his hand over the mouth and nose of his brother for about five minutes until he felt he was dead." But other than this supposed confession, the only supporting evidence was what the story described as "pinpoint-sized hemorrhages" found in the dead man's mouth and windpipe. No motive had been ascribed as of yet, other than speculation by a local paper that it had been a mercy killing.

The community had quickly rallied behind Delbert, dismissing the confession as the product of intimidation and maintaining that there was no way so simple and gentle a man could have or would have suffocated his closest brother. Described as "illiterate and unsophisticated," Delbert was pictured on the *Times'* jump page with his eyes closed and his head resting on the shoulder of a friend.

I wasn't sure why, but I immediately smelled a rat. For one thing, if the story had stated it correctly, it seemed to me that the basis upon which the pathologist had arrived at his conclusion was scientifically unsound. I knew from my own experience that asphyxial deaths are among the most difficult to diagnose, and that petechiae—the hemorrhages upon which the local pathologist had apparently based his finding—do not necessarily indicate suffocation. If this man had really been suffocated, there should have been a number of other telltale signs.

I was also thinking of the cases that occur by the hundreds every week, if not every day, in which a public defender or court-appointed attorney doesn't win a murder case simply because he doesn't have the time, interest, or money to really explore its medical aspects. By the same token, I knew of a fair number of cases in which competent forensic pathology review had challenged, and in some instances totally refuted, the opinions of the coroner or medical examiner. While I had no reason to be convinced of Mr. Ward's innocence, I didn't want to see another case simply fall through the system's cracks.

I noted in the story that Mr. Ward was being represented by a Syracuse attorney by the name of Ralph A. Cognetti, and so later that day I gave Mr. Cognetti a call. I told him I was interested in reviewing the autopsy and would be willing to do so free of charge if he was seeking a second opinion. Cognetti, who appeared to be familiar with my name, told me that since the story had broken in the local papers over a month earlier, a number of forensic pathologists had called to offer their services, some for a fee. He planned to use one of them, he said, and would get back to me shortly.

About a week later, I received a neatly arranged three-ring binder from William B. Sullivan, a private forensic consultant and former deputy coroner whom Mr. Cognetti had hired to research the case. Inside were the autopsy protocol, police reports, depositions, local news clips, and a chronology of events.

As I began browsing through the clips and photos, I realized that the Ward brothers were truly a strange breed. Four in all, they were lifelong bachelors with grade-school educations who had spent their entire adult lives tending the simple dairy farm their grandfather had built 125 years earlier in the hills overlooking the scenic Stockbridge Valley. Their father had died in 1946, leaving the place in their hands, and their mother had followed him in 1966. A sister, Emma, the only sibling to marry and bear children, had passed away in 1988.

At seventy, half-brother Roscoe was the oldest. Hard of hearing and tough-minded, he apparently hadn't been much help to investigators, whom he'd refused to answer. Together with sixty-two-year-old Lyman, a tiny, big-bearded man known to be so nervous that he avoided all contact with strangers, Roscoe mainly worked on the farm of a neighbor, Ken Elmer.

The deceased, William, had by all accounts been the head of the clan. It was he who conducted all the farm business and cooked for the others. And according to lifelong friend and neighbor Harry Thurston, Bill "had more everyday smarts and was a lot stronger" than his brothers as well. But as those who knew him say, he was also the least healthy. Afflicted with headaches, stomach cramps, and swollen feet, he had been living in perpetual pain for quite some time. An obstinate man, he'd refused to see a doctor.

Delbert, the youngest of the four, had been Bill's right-hand man. Together, they would rise at 5:30 each morning to do the first milking of their thirty-one cows, and often they could be seen riding their old green tractor into town for breakfast. In the cluttered little house, they even shared a bed together. According to a cousin, Harold "Ike" Ward, who some say lived with a family of turkeys in an abandoned schoolbus behind the house, Bill and Delbert "did everything together. They were always together. They were real close."

Throughout the community, all the Wards were known as simple men who kept to themselves and never gave anyone any trouble. Their joys—chewing Beech Nut tobacco all day and watching *Jeopardy* and *Wheel of Fortune* before bed—were simple ones. And aside from their daily forays into town to eat breakfast or pick up supplies, they were known to pretty much stay put. Delbert, for one, had never wandered farther than Oneonta, some fifty-odd miles away.

"Nobody ever paid much attention to them," said Thurston,

perhaps the Wards' only regular visitor. "The best definition of them is little boys in old men's bodies."

Located on a dusty dead-end road in the hills above the village, the Ward home was nothing more than a dilapidated four-room shack that looked as though it had been patched together from assorted scraps. Inside, a small kerosene stove provided their heat in the winter while an exposed toilet served as their bathroom. Across the yard, which was strewn with farm equipment and appliances in various states of disrepair, sat the rickety barn that housed their cows, three bulls, and five calves.

"When I went to his farm," Cognetti told me, "I was shocked that people could live like that in the twentieth century. I mean it is right out of the last century. If you looked up *primitive* in the dictionary, Delbert Ward's farm would be in there."

But despite the apparent backwardness of the place, the Wards were, by all accounts, successful dairy farmers. After the morning milking, Bill and Delbert would put the cattle out to pasture and clean out the stalls. Later in the day, after working their hundred acres of hay and corn and tending to their other animals, they would do a second milking, often producing as much as 750 pounds a day. Every other day, a county cooperative truck would make its way up the hill to purchase the milk. And according to private investigator Joe Spadafore, who would get to know the Wards well in the months leading up to the trial, their operation had been called "one of the cleanest in the county."

Upon hearing of Delbert's arrest, the community was instantly incredulous. Aside from the known closeness between the two brothers, they said, Delbert was neither mentally nor physically capable of committing an act of murder. "Delbert could never even give the cows their penicillin shots," Emilie Stilwell, a waitress at the nearby Sugar Shack restaurant, told the *Times.* Added Pat Frank, the Wards' niece, "If he had any downed cows, he wouldn't kill them; he'd get a neighbor to come and do it." Or, as Cognetti would later put it, "Delbert Ward could no more kill a half-dead tomcat than he could his brother."

All the Wards were so frightened of death, in fact, that, according to Thurston, they'd refused to go inside the house for a year after their mother died. "Is he going to lie in bed with a dead man?" Thurston asked me. "He would have gotten out so fast he would have made a new door. They're terrified of death." To this day, in fact, the room in which Bill died remains padlocked shut; says Thurston, "They'll never use that room again."

And then there's Delbert's mental capacity to consider. By the time he left school at age sixteen, he had only reached the seventh grade. And whatever he had learned there he must have lost, for whenever he was asked to read or sign something, he would conveniently claim he didn't have his glasses on him. The community, of course, had plenty to say the instant they heard about Delbert's confession.

"You give me ten minutes with Delbert and I could convince him that he tore up my sidewalk," Stockbridge town manager Charles Young told the *Times*—"and I don't even have a sidewalk." Or, as Mr. Spadafore put it one snowy winter day, "Delbert is the type of individual if you told him it's got to be at least seventy-five degrees out there today, he'd agree with you."

"When I went to the jail and met him I was taken by his simpleness," Cognetti told me. "He's very childlike, the most nonhostile person I've ever had the pleasure of meeting. And then when I got into the case I became convinced—and I mean *convinced*—that he was innocent, that there was no way, despite anything, despite if they had come in with twenty confessions, that this man could kill his brother. He didn't have the ability to do it. He doesn't understand those words, kill your brother . . . Bill would cough and Delbert would say excuse me. They were almost united by skin. They were as close to being Siamese twins as you can get. And for Delbert to kill Bill would be like killing yourself."

So what exactly had occurred to result in the arrest of this man on a charge of second-degree murder? I turned to a chronology of events that Sullivan had pieced together for me from the state police and medical examiner's reports, and as I read, the picture gradually came into focus.

Around 5:40 on the morning of June 6, Delbert had awakened Roscoe to tell him that something was wrong with Bill. Unable to rouse their brother, the two men then left the house to alert a neighbor with a telephone. Around six o'clock, Delbert returned with neighbor John Teeple, who went inside to see for himself and found Bill's body limp and his head cool. While Roscoe waited for help to arrive, Delbert went into the barn to take care of the morning milking, and Lyman went off to plow Mr. Elmer's field.

The first of the state troopers arrived about twenty minutes later, followed soon thereafter by emergency medical technicians, the county coroner, and more troopers. By 7:45 A.M., State Police Investigator Robert J. Killough arrived at the scene and, accompanied by the coroner, entered the residence. Bill Ward was observed lying fully clothed on his right side with his eyes and mouth partially open. But no signs of foul play were noted, and after brief interviews with Delbert and Roscoe, the troopers went on their way.

The body, meanwhile, had been transported to the Onondaga County Medical Examiner's Office in Syracuse. There, at around eleven o'clock, Assistant Medical Examiner Humphrey D. Germaniuk began his autopsy. Two hours later, suspicious of the petechiae and certain that he had seen no significant signs of natural disease, he signed the cause of death out as "pending further study" and began trying to reach Madison County district attorney Donald F. Cerio, Jr. When he finally got through at around five o'clock that afternoon, he told Cerio that the case was "bothersome," and that while he could "not rule out homicide by asphyxia," he'd need more information to be sure.

It was here, I realized, that the prosecutorial arm had been set in motion. At 5:10, Cerio called senior state police investigator Pasquale D. Lagatta at the nearby Oneida barracks and said "that he had just been advised by Dr. Germaniuk that he attributed the death to asphyxiation by suffocation." Within the hour, an unnamed officer called the doctor back to confirm these findings. No one will ever know what was said in either of those conversations, but as the officer erroneously wrote in his report, the petechiae Germaniuk had noted are "caused by some sort of pressure being applied to the area where the petechiae are found." Already, I could see how the diagnosis had been misinterpreted.

Sullivan would later liken the whole thing to a childhood game of telephone, in which a message is passed, ear to ear, down a long line of people and emerges as something completely different: "I tell you, you tell someone else, they distort it, and pretty soon you have a confession. It's as clear as day . . . Now we go from 'can't rule out' to 'homicide by asphyxiation.' Isn't it absolutely amazing?"

It certainly was, and yet this was only the beginning.

Shortly after seven o'clock that evening, following a briefing with Cerio and his investigator, Michael O. Donegan, Lagatta sent a contingent of officers to the Ward farm. There, they told the brothers that Bill's death was not due to natural causes and asked them to come to the barracks for further questioning. Later, Spadafore would help me picture this scene: "Here's some guys who really never knew police authorities as anything but the good guys, and four unmarked vehicles show up and say, 'Come on down, we've got to ask you some questions.' Being law-abiding citizens, they jump in."

In the meantime, Dr. Germaniuk's curiosity had been piqued enough by the news that the brothers were lifelong bachelors who shared a bed that he'd decided to go to the funeral home in Earlville for further examination. There, he conducted what is known as a rape kit examination, studying and taking swabs of the dead man's penis, anus, and clothing to determine whether he had engaged in sexual activity before his death. The visual examination showed no signs of foul play, and Germaniuk sent the swabs in for further study. Interestingly, the results of those tests would not come up during the trial. Much later, I'd find out why.

When he completed that examination at about 8:30 P.M., Germaniuk continued on to the Ward residence, where he was informed upon his arrival that Delbert had just confessed to killing his brother. Following a brief examination of the scene in which nothing of interest turned up and no notes were taken, Germaniuk joined the others at the barracks. There, around 11:30 P.M., Delbert was arrested and placed without bail in the Madison County jail.

From the moment the news got out the next morning, the community went to work. Mr. Thurston, a former town justice, among other things, called the courthouse to have an attorney appointed for his friend. Shortly afterward, unsatisfied with the attorney's criminal experience, Thurston initiated an effort to hire his friend a private attorney, and coffee cans soliciting donations for the Delbert Ward Defense Fund began popping up on the counters of local businesses. In the meantime, Ms. Stilwell began circulating a petition asking the D.A. to order a new autopsy, and within a week, close to nine hundred signatures had been obtained.

At a preliminary hearing on June 12, Delbert and Lyman's depositions were entered into evidence. According to a typed question-and-answer statement that he'd apparently signed and initialed, Delbert had responded to investigators' questions by saying that he "felt Bill would be better off away from his pains . . . I decided to put my hand over his mouth. I reached behind me with my right hand and put it over his mouth. He struggled a bit but then stopped. I wanted to make sure that Bill wasn't suffering anymore—that he was dead." In a similarly obtained statement, Lyman had allegedly said, "He was smothered." Asked who did it, he'd then said, "Delbert."

On June 25, nearly three weeks after Delbert Ward's arrest, Madison County Court judge William F. O'Brien III finally set bail at ten thousand dollars. In a tremendous show of spontaneous support, Mr. Young secured pledges from the community within ten minutes, and three hours later, Delbert was on his way back to the farm. That same day, under pressure from Mr. Cognetti and the community, Cerio announced that he would not present the case to a grand jury until after he'd reviewed the report of an independent pathologist to whom he'd sent the autopsy findings.

One month later, that report was finally released. Written by Dr. Nicholas T. Forbes, the chief medical examiner for Monroe County, it simply served to confirm Germaniuk's conclusion and to defend his procedures. "The autopsy procedures performed by Dr. Germaniuk were comprehensive and showed no evidence of significant natural diseases or drug intoxication that might account for Mr. Ward's death," Dr. Forbes wrote. "The strong possibility of an asphyxial mechanism of death in this case was appropriately raised." That was all Cerio needed; on August 3, a grand jury handed up an indictment of Delbert Ward on a charge of second-degree murder.

When I finished reading through the notebook, I called Mr. Sullivan to share my thoughts with him. I told him that it was obvious Delbert had been steamrolled and that he had all the proof he needed right there in his notebook. "You don't need me," I joked. "You testify." He thanked me for the compliment but told me that Cognetti would need me to testify. First, however, he wanted my opinion of how Bill Ward died. By this time, the toxicology report, microscopic tissue slides, and autopsy photos had arrived, and so I was able to begin my real assessment of the case.

According to the autopsy protocol, Bill Ward had been normally developed and well-nourished for a man of sixty-four. On external examination, in fact, the only findings that seemed to have aroused Dr. Germaniuk's curiosity at all were the petechiae he observed in both eyes and inside the mouth. I had seen such hemorrhages many times before. And while I knew that on a percentage basis they were found more often in cases of asphyxia than in natural deaths, I also knew they were by no means pathognomonic, or indisputably diagnostic of a particular condition.

The heart is like a pump; its job is to keep the body supplied with the oxygen and other elements it needs to survive. If it is not pumping effectively, the blood backs up in the veins and begins to exert pressure on the capillaries—the smallest of the body's vessels. At the same time, as the body's tissues are deprived of oxygen, the walls of the capillaries frequently become permeable, losing their ability to retain red blood cells. The hemorrhages that result are known as petechiae.

In short, then, the only thing that petechiae do indicate is a state of hypoxia. While their presence should give any competent pathologist cause to probe further, they should never lead to the automatic conclusion that asphyxia has occurred. To his credit, Dr. Germaniuk did not appear to have made that jump right away either.

Of at least equal significance to me in this case was what had not been observed. For starters, when a person is abruptly deprived of air, the brain takes over and causes that person to do whatever he must to obtain the oxygen he needs. That means that unless he is infirm or debilitated by drugs, there's going to be a struggle. And while a well-executed smothering can leave little external evidence of trauma, the forceful closure of the airways more often than not results in some focal hemorrhaging and tearing of the mucosa—the inner linings of the mouth and nose. In this case, a physically unimposing man had allegedly smothered a stronger man with his bare hands. But as the autopsy report indicated, both the nose and mouth of the deceased were free of trauma or blood.

Another sign a pathologist always looks for in a suspected case of asphyxia is evidence of regurgitation, since the combined physical effort and emotional stress of struggling for air is almost certain to cause some food to come up. As I noted here, Bill had eaten a large clam supper before going to bed, and yet none of it had been found in his esophagus, trachea, or mouth. Nor was there a thinning of the blood or a bluish purple appearance to the skin, two other quite common findings in asphyxial deaths. And while all four of these findings don't necessarily have to be present, the absence of any of them strongly suggests a nonasphyxial death.

As I began studying the microscopic findings, I saw how this could have been so. Internal examination had revealed that the heart weighed 420 grams, more than 100 grams over the average weight for a man of Ward's size and age. Oddly, Dr. Germaniuk had not made note of anything being out of the ordinary. Furthermore, atherosclerosis had caused a 20 percent blockage of the coronary arteries. Although not a particularly significant percentage, this was nonetheless well worth noting. But in his list of pertinent findings, this particular finding was not even mentioned.

Inside the trachea and bronchi, the tubes leading into the lungs, the doctor had found the "diffuse spray" of petechiae that apparently first gave rise to his suspicion of asphyxia. But among his other observations of the respiratory system were clear signs of significant natural disease. For one thing, the right lung weighed almost twice as much as the left, while the lower part of the left lung was covered with scar tissue that held it to the chest cavity. Most importantly, both lungs showed "prominent arteriosclerotic plaques" of the pulmonary arteries—another sign of cardiopulmonary disease. Considered with the enlarged liver and spleen, this was clear evidence of congestion due to an inadequately functioning heart.

I turned to the doctor's preliminary hearing testimony, curious as to how, faced with all these degenerative processes, he could have reached a conclusion of asphyxia. On direct examination, Germaniuk—who had done a modest 750 autopsies in his career—testified that while petechiae can be associated with either natural or asphyxial deaths, he had never seen them in the former. As for the natural processes, he did not feel they were "far gone enough in order to kill this individual." But pressed on how he had made his final determination of the cause and manner of death, all he could say was, "The information that I learned from the body I correlated with the information given to me by the outside investigative agencies."

Aside from a procedure I found a bit backward, I was troubled by the doctor's failure to give proper weight to the clearly observable signs of natural disease. Between clogged coronary and pulmonary arteries, an enlarged heart, and fluid-filled lungs, all the signs of significant cardiopulmonary disease were there. I thought of the deceased's medical complaints and realized that all of them could be related to inadequate coronary artery supply. Stomach pain, for one, is a frequent anatomical designation given by individuals actually suffering from chest pains. Headaches, of course, can be related to many things, but combined with the swollen feet, it would appear that Ward had indeed suffered from poor circulation.

If, on top of that, he had developed some kind of cardiac arrhythmia, or an irregular heartbeat, it is not hard to see how he could have died quite naturally: a few missed beats, a massive buildup of blood, and a heart that simply fails quite unpredictably. This, in fact, is a picture pathologists frequently encounter in autopsies performed on individuals in Bill Ward's age group.

In mid-December, shortly before leaving for a family vacation, I sent Mr. Cognetti my clinical summary. At that point, I had no idea whether he would need me to testify, and it would be another two months before I heard from him again.

In October, I had been contacted by a producer for the CBS news show *Face to Face with Connie Chung* about sharing my conclusions for a segment she was doing on the Delbert Ward case. As it happened, my wife and I had been planning a trip to New York City the following month, and so we arranged to have dinner with her. We discussed the case at length, and when my report was finished in December, I sent her a copy. When I returned to Pittsburgh in January, the producer called to tell me that the segment would be airing on February 11. Eager to catch a glimpse of the Wards and their community in action, I tuned in.

The fifteen-minute segment, which featured Ms. Chung visiting the Ward farm and a fund-raiser at a local restaurant, was well done. Although presented with obvious sympathy for the defendant, it was nonetheless quite fair. Unfortunately, it was tainted by an unfair statement.

Responding to questions regarding the events leading up to Bill

Ward's death, Mr. Donegan, the investigator with the D.A.'s office, said: "There's no doubt in my mind. I know what happened that night up on Johnson Road. And I think Delbert knows what happened up on Johnson Road. He has to live with that the rest of his life." I could not believe Donegan's arrogance. Here was a public official assuming the role of omniscient narrator to stave off all challenges as to the cause of death. But unlike a gunshot or stabbing death, where one can reasonably assume he does know something, the situation here was far more subtle and complex.

As a lawyer and a firm believer in the concept of innocence until proven guilty, I was also offended by the fact that someone from a prosecutor's office could make such statements on national TV about a case that had yet to be tried. Any self-respecting attorney, judge, or professor of criminal law will tell you that a prosecutor should say either nothing at all about a case in progress or at the very most something to the effect that he has evidence which, when presented in court, will lead to a conviction. The fact that Donegan went considerably beyond that was reprehensible. It was as if they were dealing not with some poor cow farmer but with another 1957 Apalachin meeting, the largest gathering of Mafia chieftains in American history, which took place in upstate western New York.

Thankfully, a comment by neighbor John Teeple shed some light on what the whole case seemed to really be about. "The differences between the life-styles of the police and the lawyers and the detectives can't help but color how they looked at the brothers," Teeple told Ms. Chung. "If they're dirty, if they don't have a nice clean house, if they don't speak the language well, something must be wrong with them. Maybe they're dangerous. Ya can't really trust these hill people."

Aside from Mr. Donegan's performance, the only thing that bothered me about the show was that it failed to address the botched autopsy and the medical issues in general. At only fifteen minutes, this was understandable, but still it left me more eager than ever to try to help set the record straight. Thus it was with great relief that I learned, in late February, that I would be testifying in Delbert Ward's defense.

The trial opened on Tuesday, March 19, before a jury of six men and six women of mainly middle-class, farming background.

That afternoon, following testimony by neighbors, paramedics, and relatives, the state called Lyman Ward to the stand. Under the influence of five different types of medication prescribed to control his anxiety (another example of polypharmacy!), he grasped the edge of the witness box for support and struggled in a barely audible voice to answer Mr. Cerio's questions. Yes, he had signed and initialed a statement to the effect that Delbert had told him he was going to murder Bill, he said. But in fact, he added, Delbert had never said any such thing and he had no idea of how Bill died.

"To see him on the stand, you are convinced of the impossibility of him saying those words to strangers," Cognetti later told me. "In this entire case, the closest people to Lyman were Joe Spadafore and me, and he rarely spoke to us. He doesn't talk." That much was made doubly clear the next day, when Lyman, under the strain of Cerio's questioning, began shaking violently, went into convulsions, and collapsed. As several people helped him off the stand, Judge O'Brien cleared the courtroom and postponed the trial. Lyman, declared a "hostile witness," was not asked to return.

When the trial resumed later that morning, Investigator Killough offered the first detailed account of what had occurred in the barracks on the evening of June 6. Around 8:00 P.M., he said, the Ward brothers and their cousin were brought in and separated for questioning. Following an hour of unenlightening answers, an investigator by the name of Eugene L. Rifenburg—who apparently knew the Wards personally—was called in to speak with Delbert. Everyone but Rifenburg and Killough then left the room, and ten minutes later, the two men emerged to report that Delbert had confessed. Rifenburg then went home, leaving the job of taking down the statement in the hands of Killough and his peers. At 10:15 P.M., Delbert signed the confession.

Over the course of the next few days, two other investigators testified that the Wards were "calm and relaxed" during the interrogation, and defended their techniques as sound. But under cross-examination, they revealed that no record of the interviews had been made, and that even though the district attorney and his investigator were present, none of the detainees was immediately read his rights.

At the end of the first week of testimony, Rifenburg himself took the stand. Contrary to the other officers' reports, he said that when he arrived at the barracks, Delbert was "visibly nervous." But after the other officers left the room, he added, the suspect began to calm down and relate what had happened. "It was like he wanted to tell somebody," Rifenburg testified. He hadn't stayed around for the subsequent interview, Rifenburg said, because he felt Killough had it under control.

Donegan was next. It was he, it turned out, who had read Ward's statement back to him prior to Ward's signing it. Of particular interest to me was Donegan's testimony that as he was doing so, Ward would often repeat his answer before Donegan had had a chance to finish reading it. This only bolstered my belief that a confused Delbert Ward was simply trying to get out of there as quickly as possible.

As Mr. Spadafore later speculated, the investigators "put the words in Delbert's mouth. After a long game of role-playing, they said, 'Just tell us what happened and we'll let you go.' What does he know? Bill's dead. He doesn't know why . . . They were overreactive. They were ready to really go to town. They didn't sit back long enough to look at the what-ifs. With Cerio behind the scenes, they didn't open enough gates. They just directed their attention at the guy sleeping with him."

After the trial, I would have an opportunity to speak with Mr. Cognetti about this at length. His legal and personal insights, I thought, were rather incisive.

"Delbert may have said what they say he did," Cognetti allowed, "but you've got to understand the entire scenario and the background of county politics. You have an unexplainable death, and the only person who had been with him is Delbert. You have a new D.A. who was barely elected, a Democrat in a Republican county, a man who had told me on an earlier occasion that his real desire in life was to have been a state trooper. You have a group of individuals—the state troopers—who, after a period of time, begin to get jaded or begin to look at a case with some blinders.

"I think that they sat down and said, 'Look, we can solve this case, we'll all look good, we'll get a plus in our file, and Don Cerio will have shown to the people that he made a right decision. Nobody cares about this guy, nobody's gonna be upset. We'll have him plea to something. We'll send him to jail for just a short period of time and everybody will be happy.' And I think with that thinking in mind, they set about conducting this interview in a way that would produce those results. And that's what they did. This guy had more people talking to him than if he had been John Gotti.

"Delbert has a great need to be accepted by people in authority. And of course for him, nobody better represented that than police officers, and that is why he would tell the cops anything they wanted him to say—because that would endear him with them. They spent how many hours with him? Five or six gun-toting, six-foot, 250-pound state troopers, and they couldn't get a thing out of him. He spends two minutes in a closed room with Investigator Rifenburg and Rifenburg comes out and says he confessed, doesn't hang around to take a statement, and just leaves. Then Killough and the other guy sit down and ask him the questions and he gives them the answers. But there never existed a way to verify what they were saying.

"I think it was a case of overzealousness. If they thought Delbert did it, there was a host of things they could have done which would have satisfied the defense attorney and gotten them the same results. All they had to do was videotape, and they didn't. It's not the impossible task it was five or ten years ago. Everybody and their brother has a video camera. Or they could have had a court stenographer in there. They didn't have to do it in a closed room. They didn't have to rush to arrest him. My God, he wasn't going to leave the farm. He never will leave the farm. He wasn't going anywhere. And I just think once they get it in their minds that someone did it they tend to become lax in their investigation."

As for Cerio's presence at the barracks, Cognetti added, it was "a big mistake. If we wanted to we could have called him as a witness and he would have had to have removed himself from the case, because he was intrinsically involved in the first couple hours of this case and it was his directive which told the police, 'Go and arrest that guy; we got ourselves a killer.' And that's a mistake. A D.A. should never become involved in an investigation. He should just review that which is investigated by the police and not shy away from telling them, 'This is a crappy job. You go back and do it right or don't do it at all.' I think that's a requirement and a mandate of the job."

The second week of the trial opened with several hours of testimony by Dr. Germaniuk. As before, he failed to attach much significance to the advanced pathological processes in Ward's heart and lungs. But worse than that, he now misrepresented the meaning of certain other findings.

On the right side of the deceased's neck, Germaniuk had found a golf-ball–sized nodule which he removed and analyzed, as he did the engorged thyroid gland. The nodule, as his own report stated, was a simple, fluid-filled cyst lined by scar tissue. Now, in open court, he responded in the affirmative to the question of whether this cyst and the condition of the thyroid were consistent with trauma to the neck by a hand or arm. This was an outrageous misreading of the evidence, and yet no one objected. It was quite clear that this cyst was an insignificant preexisting condition, and the thyroid simply further evidence of congestion.

Then there was the matter of explaining the lack of trauma to Ward's mouth and nose by pointing to his heavy beard and lack of teeth. Again, Dr. Germaniuk was misrepresenting the significance of these features. For one thing, the injuries one expects to see in a suffocation victim are to the nose, lips, gums, and frenulum—the elastic piece of tissue holding the lips to the gums—not to the chin. In this sense, the presence of a beard means little or nothing. As for Bill's toothlessness, this would only explain the lack of trauma to Delbert's hand. With no teeth to protect his gums and mouth, in fact, Bill would have been even more likely to sustain injuries.

As his testimony wore on, Dr. Germaniuk continued to paint what, in my opinion, was a flawed portrait of a death. Fortunately for the defendant, Mr. Cognetti would find those flaws. To begin with, the doctor admitted on cross-examination that pulmonary edema can be caused by hypertension and that petechiae can be caused by increased venous pressure, often in places where no external pressure has been exerted. But the real break came on the second day of testimony.

Under further cross-examination, the witness stated that at the time he filled out Ward's death certificate and turned his body over to the funeral home, he had no reason to believe a homicide had occurred. The next day, he said, after learning that Delbert would be charged with second-degree murder but before having received the results of either the toxicology or microscopic examinations, he changed his report. Then came the coup de grace.

"Doctor," Cognetti asked, "if you had never learned that Mr. Ward had confessed to the crime of murder in the second degree, would you, on June seventh, have changed that death certificate?"

"No," answered the witness.

This, as far as I'm concerned, was the end of the prosecution's case. And yet, under redirect examination, Dr. Germaniuk would continue to hammer nails into his own coffin. Asked by Mr. Cerio what he would have found if the death had been caused by pulmonary hypertension, the doctor—who had no particular background in cardiology—began a lengthy discourse on the role of arteriosclerosis:

> The right side of the heart, being a muscle like any other muscle, the harder it works, it's like a weight lifter or someone in the construction industry, the more you lift the muscles get bigger to accommodate the increased weight or increased force necessary to move things or to lift heavier weights. In the right side of the heart, you'll find two things. With the heart working harder to pump blood against this increased resistance, like any other muscle it will begin to get bigger or hypertrophy. The other thing that will happen if it's sudden, you will find that at a certain point the right side of the heart will be unable to continually beat against the increased pressure . . .

Whether the doctor realized it or not, he had just described what had very likely happened to Bill Ward. But amazingly, asked a moment later whether he had found any such evidence in the deceased, he answered no. This was not only incorrect, but considering that he was testifying in open court, intellectually dishonest. At any rate, his prior admission had finished him off as a witness.

As Mr. Cognetti later observed, Dr. Germaniuk's fault in this case was that he "became more an agent of the police than a separate entity whose job it is to render an independent opinion." The various governmental entities involved, he added, "really all worked as one, and that's dangerous. When you do that you've forsaken a role that needs to be played. I think he probably got caught up in it also. This was a real quick resolution of the case.

He just didn't do the job that a medical examiner should do. He didn't use any of his medical expertise in the rendering of his autopsy."

I agree with this analysis. A medicolegal investigative office should never be permitted to evolve into an adjunct of the D.A.'s office. The medical examiner must work with them and be fully cooperative, but he may also draw conclusions that are not helpful to them. He must call it as he sees it. In this case, Dr. Germaniuk should have been aware of the educational status, intelligence level, and social background of Delbert Ward, and as a forensic pathologist working in a medicolegal system, he should have realized that the confessions might not have any meaning at all.

The next day was Delbert's day in court. Calm and composed, he described life with his brothers on the farm. Asked about Bill, he related the health problems that had been bothering him. So great was Bill's suffering, said Delbert, that he had had premonitions about his death. "One day he said one of us was going to wake up dead and the other would be arrested," Delbert testified. "I told him I didn't know. He said he'd like to take a gun and kill himself so he wouldn't be in misery. I said I would take the guns and hide them."

On cross-examination, Mr. Cerio asked him outright whether he had killed his brother. "No, I did not," Delbert responded. "Why would I want to kill him? He was my best brother." Then why, Cerio asked, had he confessed to the crime. "They said if I cooperated it would go easier," answered the defendant, "so I said yes. It wasn't true. I was nervous and shook up. I hadn't eaten all day. I was tired. My brother had just passed away . . . I thought if I said yes, they would let me go home." Rifenburg and Killough, he added, told him he had killed his brother and proceeded to show him how it had happened, using each other as models. "I said no," Delbert recalled. "Then they said yes. And then I said yes."

When the third week of the trial opened on April 1, Delbert's testimony was bolstered by that of Dr. Anthony E. Blumetti, a Syracuse clinical psychologist who had conducted six hours of tests and interviews of the defendant in December. Blumetti testified that with an IQ of only 69, Delbert was "educably mentally retarded," meaning that he could do only repetitive tasks within a structured environment. Combined with his limited social skills and a schizoid personality, Blumetti added, Delbert would likely have been so nervous and confused at the time of his interrogation that he would have agreed with anything.

"His ability to reason will be impaired," said Blumetti. "His major focus would be to get out of that setting . . . His focus would not be on the questions he was being asked, but on getting out of that unfamiliar, threatening environment."

Another nail in the coffin, and I had yet to testify.

I caught a Monday evening flight to Syracuse and was met at the airport by both Mr. Cognetti and James Resti, the attorney who would be handling most of my direct examination. After conferences that night and the next morning, we headed into Wampsville, the Madison County seat and site of the eighty-one-year-old Madison County Courthouse. Inside, I was surprised at the huge crowd of people milling about, then realized that all the talk about massive community support had been no exaggeration. I was introduced to a few townspeople and then to the defendant himself.

Short and frail, with a full gray beard and small, elusive eyes, Delbert Ward was even odder in person than he had appeared in news photos and on the Connie Chung segment. As I shook his gnarled and hastily withdrawn hand, I realized how easy it must have been for the police and prosecutors to pin this guy down. He was as defenseless as a lamb, and my desire to do my best for him was renewed.

Under direct examination by Mr. Resti, I testified that congestive failure of the right side of Bill Ward's heart had caused his death. As simply and clearly as possible, I explained how the blockage of the pulmonary and coronary arteries had led to a backup of blood in the heart and lungs, and supported my conclusions by citing the scarring of the heart, the enlargement of the liver and spleen, and the petechiae.

As Mr. Resti proceeded with his examination, I noticed that Mr. Cerio was increasingly voicing objections and that Judge O'Brien was sustaining most of them. Asked whether the fact that Mr. Ward had been lifting heavy materials the day of his death was consistent with my conclusions, I was not permitted to answer. Asked whether Mr. Ward's swollen feet supported my report, I was cut off in midsentence. And asked if the fact that the decedent had been taking fifteen to twenty aspirin a day would affect the formation of petechiae, I was interrupted yet again. As an angry exchange erupted between the two attorneys, the judge moved for a recess.

When we returned, Mr. Resti asked me my opinion of the official cause of death. This was not a case of asphyxia, I answered, and then described the four findings that should have been present if the deceased had been smothered. Finishing up his brief but effective examination, Mr. Resti then asked me whether Delbert's alleged statement to the police had played any part in my determination of the cause of death. "The statement," I answered, "has no bearing on the physical findings, and the forensic pathology scientific conclusions from those findings remain in place . . . It's of no consequence to me what was said by Mr. Ward under the circumstances in which it was said."

As Mr. Cerio began his cross-examination, it quickly became clear that he was less interested in dealing with the medical facts than in tripping me up. He began one question with "When you spoke to Dr. Germaniuk . . . ," then feigned surprise when I told him I had never spoken with Dr. Germaniuk. When I further informed him that I was not present at the autopsy, he asked me whether I would agree that "having a hands-on participation in the actual autopsy itself would be significantly more important than simply reviewing photographs." As I began to explain why there would have been no particular advantage to that, I was interrupted by a lecture from the judge to answer Mr. Cerio's questions with a simple yes or no.

"With due respect," I told the judge after one particularly ambiguous question, "if yes and no mean one hundred percent, then I will not answer, your Honor. I mean, I will say respectfully to the Court that I cannot answer."

After a lunch break, I was grateful to see Mr. Cerio jump right into the medical issues. But it wasn't long before we had become engaged in a ridiculous semantic debate. Asked whether Dr. Germaniuk's use of the term *prominent* in describing the atheromatosis (deposition of cholesterol plaques and fatty acids along the inner lining of an artery) of the pulmonary arteries wasn't somewhat subjective, I said that it was a nontechnical term but that it had a clear meaning in the English language.

"Doctor," Cerio asked me, "did you have occasion to speak with Dr. Germaniuk about what the word *marked* meant?"

No, I reminded him, I had not spoken with the doctor, but I did know what the word *marked* meant as it's used in pathology. "Marked is not minimal or moderate," I said. "Marked is severe, advanced." As for *prominent*, I added, "It's something that catches the eye quite readily."

"And if I told you that Dr. Germaniuk said *prominent* in his testimony meant five to ten percent," he continued, "would you then disagree that your definition is not the same as Dr. Germaniuk's?"

"Well," I said, "that's rather obvious it's not the same . . . The question is what word do you use for the other ninety percent if you use *prominent* for five to ten percent? What word is left in the English language?"

Ignoring my query, Cerio moved on to the heart, attempting to trip me up further by suggesting that its extra weight could be explained by the autopsist having removed some of its connecting arteries with it. I told him that the differences between the manner in which two pathologists could remove the organ would be minimal. "The heart is the heart and it's not the vessels," I said.

What about the possible presence of blood in the heart's chambers? he asked.

"There's a lot of possibilities if incorrect procedures are used," I said, pointing out that every organ should be drained before weighing. "Dr. Germaniuk has done 750 autopsies. I'm sure he knows how to remove a heart and how to weigh it . . ."

"Doctor," said Cerio, "you are speculating at this point, aren't you?"

"I'm speculating in favor of the competence of Dr. Germaniuk," I said, "and I'm not about to accept that he's an incompetent fool."

Having failed on that score, Cerio opted for a new plan of attack; he suggested that in the nine hours between my arrival in Syracuse and the beginning of my testimony I should have gone to the medical examiner's office to examine the heart itself. "It would, would it not," he asked, "have assisted you tremendously had you yourself been able to view this heart as opposed to viewing simply microscopic slides of a portion of that heart and the descriptive aspects of another pathologist's report?"

"No," I honestly answered, "it would not have assisted me at all. Not only not tremendously, it would not have assisted me at all. It would have had no bearing or relevance whatsoever on the opinions that I have expressed today.'' As I began to explain why a heart that's been preserved in formalin for nine months would tell me less than autopsy slides and photos, Cerio again switched subjects, this time to the idea that the weight of the liver could be explained by pooling blood.

"Not in an organ of that size," I said. "You can get some small hemorrhages, but it's not going to make a difference in the weights of the organs . . . You don't separate fluid from live tissue. The liver weighs what it weighs."

"Doctor," Cerio said a moment later, "it's clear that the blood is not going to remain in the uppermost portions of the body . . ."

"No," I said, becoming frustrated at the D.A.'s sophomoric questions, "don't tell me what's medically clear to you. Blood remains in the blood vessels. You think the blood just seeps out of the vessels and goes all over the place?" As Cerio turned to the judge for help, the judge chose to recess again.

When we returned, Cerio moved on to the petechiae, asking me whether their presence didn't give me a "high degree of suspicion that an asphyxial mechanism had been employed."

"I always have a high index of suspicion, or try to in medicolegal autopsies," I said. "It's a question, then, of putting everything together and seeing what other things you find. Certainly it's one of the things that you think of and then have to correlate with everything else."

In the middle of this discussion, Mr. Cerio suddenly asked me whether I was familiar with a Dr. James Luke and an article he had written on the pathology and diagnosis of deaths by homicidal smothering. Although I knew Dr. Luke, I told Mr. Cerio that I didn't recall that particular article. I was promptly informed that it had appeared in the 1971 *Legal Medicine Annual,* a textbook I have edited since 1969. Furthermore, Cerio seemed happy to point out, I had written in an introduction to the article that "homicidal smothering is an extremely difficult act of foul play for the trained forensic pathologist to detect."

"I agree with that," I told him. "I have not changed my mind about that."

Cerio went on to read me sections from both my introduction and the article itself, asking me after each section whether I'd agree with what he'd read. In almost every case, I agreed, and his plan to discredit me was quickly defused. Interestingly, though, I was reminded that among the more than thirty books I've edited or coedited, this particular annual volume is repeatedly introduced by lawyers cross-examining me. And while this presents me with a challenge to remain consistent in my opinions, it is also a supreme compliment to be told that it is an authoritative text.

From there on out, Cerio's cross-examination quickly devolved into a shameless attempt to smear my credibility. He brought up the fact that among the 290 or so articles I had written, one—on the twenty-fifth anniversary of the JFK assassination—had appeared in the *National Inquirer*, while another—on the House Select Committee on Assassinations—had been published by *Gallery*, a men's magazine. "Any time I can write an article that will reach millions of people," I said, "I'll write it."

By the time Mr. Cerio had finished with me, I was more than ready to get out of there. In my thirty years of courtroom testimony, I can honestly say that I had never encountered a more obnoxious, insulting, and condescending attorney. He had every right to challenge my opinions in a tough, probing, and detailed manner, but when a prosecutor becomes rude and insulting to a witness, he is abusing his governmental position. One of the greatest faults of our criminal justice system, I was reminded, is that politically ambitious, opportunistic people like this man can be elected as district attorneys and go on to abuse people like Delbert Ward with relative impunity.

Grant Kroneck, a neighbor of the Wards who worked as a representative for the John Hancock Mutual Life Insurance Company, had offered to drive me to the airport. On the way, we talked about the trial, and Mr. Kroneck told me how happy the community was that I'd stood up for myself. Still, we agreed, with the way Cerio and Judge O'Brien had manipulated things, it was hard to tell what would happen.

My fears were allayed several days later, when Mr. Cognetti called to tell me that on April 5, after almost nine hours of deliberation, Delbert Ward was acquitted. There had been a couple of jurors who were uncertain at first, he said, but in the end, "They realized that this man is not a raving lunatic, Jack the Ripper type."

Cognetti told me that the state had called in two rebuttal witnesses after I left, one to refute Dr. Blumetti's testimony and one to refute mine. Dr. Michael Lynch, a Buffalo psychiatrist, cited a reported IQ of 80 in asserting that Delbert would have understood his interrogators. But as Resti managed to elicit on cross-examination, that score was based on a test Delbert had taken at age thirteen, when he was still in school. As for the testimony of Dr. Germaniuk's boss, chief medical examiner Eric Mitchell, Cognetti added, his only real contribution to the prosecution's case was the fact that, unlike Germaniuk, he was board-certified in forensic pathology.

I asked Cognetti how my own testimony had been received, and was not at all surprised to learn that a couple of the jurors had been too disturbed by the obvious tension between myself and Cerio to give it the weight they otherwise would have. If I'd just suffered through Cerio's sophomoric questions and insolent manner, he told me, those jurors would have been better prepared to accept my testimony.

In retrospect, I realize, this was partly true. Still, I have no regrets about standing up to Cerio. I'd seen overaggressive attorneys walk all over witnesses enough times to know that if I'd simply let him do the same to me, my testimony would have been useless. Furthermore, I know from my own experience that an unconvincing case by the prosecution is not enough to win an acquittal. Without an alternative, more convincing medical theory as to the cause of death, a jury is more likely than not to accept the official line and convict. My testimony, as the jury's verdict clearly indicates, was crucial to the vindication of Delbert Ward.

Since April 1991, I've learned some far more interesting things. For one, the apparent reason that Cerio never called Dr. Nicholas Forbes as a witness was that subsequent to Dr. Forbes's confirmation of Dr. Germaniuk's findings, he was provided with information that contradicted that which Cerio had given him.

I was also initially surprised to learn that Dr. Germaniuk's swabs of Bill Ward's pants and body had tested positive for spermatozoa. Cerio, as I could have guessed, had gotten so fired up about this discovery that he'd ordered DNA tests done on the samples. The only possible reason he hadn't presented the results as evidence during the trial, Cognetti quite logically deduced, was that the tests had proven the sperm to have been Bill's own. Apparently, Ward had ejaculated during his death, not at all an uncommon occurrence in cases of sudden cardiac failure.

Then there are the unconfirmed reports that one of the troopers involved in questioning Delbert was looking to get hold of the Wards' land, which is apparently quite valuable, and that a picture of Bill shown to Delbert during questioning featured an incriminating pillow next to his head, something that was not present at the time Bill was discovered. Whether or not there is any truth to these allegations, I don't know. But according to Cognetti, this case has had its repercussions on the New York State Police. Two days after the trial, he told me, the ever-so-effective Investigator Rifenburg was reprimanded and ended up taking an "early retirement" in Florida. And in the State Police Academy's next term, an instructor was brought in to teach the officers a new procedure for questioning mentally deficient suspects. Commented Cognetti, "They were hurt by this."

Back in Munnsville, I'm told, life for Delbert and his brothers has resumed its former pace. According to a local news story, Delbert awoke the day after his acquittal at the usual 5:30 A.M., milked the cows, cleaned out the stalls, and then joined his brothers for breakfast in town.

There have been a few changes, of course. For one thing, there's all the new friends. And then there's the award-winning documentary film *Brother's Keeper*, which has introduced the Wards to people across the country. Delbert even got to visit the Big Apple—something I'm told didn't impress him much. But perhaps the biggest change of all is the fact that Bill is gone, for while the Wards' nephew has taken over the job of managing the farm, there's simply no replacing a "best brother." Still, as Delbert himself recently remarked, "Things are getting back to normal all the while."

11

Mysteries of Pittsburgh
Part One:
The Jack Davis Case

For every case that takes me to far-off corners of the country and abroad, I am called upon to perform or review dozens of autopsies right here in the Greater Pittsburgh area. In addition to those postmortem examinations I do by contract for the outlying counties of Westmoreland and Fayette, I am frequently contacted by area officials, private attorneys, and families seeking second opinions on causes of death. And while many of these cases end up being quite routine, some have been among the most challenging and intriguing of my career.

Easily topping that list are the mysterious cases of Jack Davis and Art Jones. Both involved sudden disappearances, suspicious deaths, and accusations of foul play. And both, despite the tremendous amount of time, money, and expertise that has been poured into their investigations, remain essentially unsolved.

Jack Allan Davis, Jr., was a twenty-year-old sophomore at Indiana University of Pennsylvania, a medium-sized private college in Indiana, Pennsylvania, about an hour's drive east of Pittsburgh. A solid and well-liked young man with an eye toward a business career, Davis had his whole life ahead of him. But in the early morning hours of Saturday, October 17, 1987, he disappeared, and when his body was found five days later at the bottom of a campus stairwell, he was said to have asphyxiated on his own vomit.

It was actually not until two and a half years later, in March of 1990, that my attention was drawn to this unfortunate event. I had just returned to my office from lunch when I received a call from a man named John Lynch. He was a stepbrother of Jack Davis, and he and other family members had recently come to doubt the official ruling in Davis's death. It didn't take long for me to realize which case he was talking about. I remembered being vaguely troubled by the news accounts at the time, but when the media coverage ended, so did my interest in the case. Now, as Mr. Lynch outlined his concerns, I realized that my initial suspicions might not have been without merit.

The official account of Jack Davis's demise was this: around two o'clock on that October night, having made the rounds of several parties and bars, Davis was stumbling back to his off-campus apartment when he decided to enter the outside stairwell of a campus building to urinate. There he became ill, passed out, and choked on his own vomit, dying almost instantly.

But Mr. Lynch, together with other family members and an investigative reporter by the name of Marlene Brennan, was not so sure. For starters, he asked, if the death were alcohol-related, why did the toxicology reports show only small amounts of alcohol in Davis's stomach and urine and none at all in his blood? Secondly, given the zero blood alcohol level, how could one explain his having been so incapacitated as to choke on his own vomit? There were other questions pertaining to reports of fighting the night Davis disappeared and the local police department's failure to respond to them promptly. But from my point of view, the most important questions involved the supposed cause and manner of the young man's death. I asked Mr. Lynch to arrange for himself and the parents of Jack Davis to come to my office to discuss the case at greater length.

At the end of the month, I found myself staring into the sad but determined faces of Mr. Lynch and his wife, Marisa; Davis's father and stepmother, Jack and Lisa Davis; and Davis's mother, Elaine Lynch. Once I had all the names and relations straight, I sat back and listened to their story. And what a story it turned out to be.

Jack, the only child of the elder Davis and his ex-wife, Elaine, had grown up with his mother and stepfather, now deceased, in the Pittsburgh suburb of Penn Hills following his parents' divorce. Athletic, studious, and churchgoing, surrounded by loving brothers and sisters for the first time in his life, he was a boy who seemed to be moving in the right direction. In 1986, he headed off to college, where he declared himself a business major, joined the track team, enlisted with the campus Reserve Officers Training Corps, and pledged Sigma Tau Gamma.

Despite his ROTC involvement and membership in a fraternity, Jack was known as a rather independent young man. Thus, when his mother received a call from one of his roommates late one Monday night in the fall of his sophomore year informing her that Jack hadn't been seen since Friday, her first thought was that he had gone away for the weekend, possibly to visit a cousin at Penn State University. She told the roommate that she would check with Jack's father, stepbrothers, and stepsisters to find out where he was.

It didn't take long for Mrs. Lynch to ascertain that something was wrong. No one had heard from Jack since Friday, and for all his independence, he was one to keep in close contact with his family; it was rare, they agreed, for him not to speak with at least one of them every day. Moreover, although he had recently begun to show a renewed interest in his classes, he had now missed all of his Monday classes. Odder still, he had failed to show up for work on Saturday and for a date Saturday night. Early Tuesday morning, Jack's parents and stepmother made the fifty-mile drive to campus to look into the matter themselves.

Upon arriving, the family went straight to the borough police department to file a missing persons report and request a search. But while they were able to fill out the form and even have Jack's description entered into a nationwide computer network, the official search, Detective Sergeant Anthony Antolik told them, would have to wait another twenty-four hours. Jack, he explained, might yet turn up.

The next day, Jack's other stepbrothers, Tom and Mike Lynch, drove to campus with some family friends to join the effort. Also told that it was too soon to begin a search, they decided to print up bulletins bearing Jack's picture and description and to post and distribute them throughout the borough. Shortly after seven o'clock that evening, Davis's car, a black-and-gray 1987 Cougar, was found near a campus pizza parlor. Aside from the fact that Jack was known never to leave his car anywhere, this proved that he had not left campus, at least not on his own. Now certain that something was wrong, the family informed the police that they intended to launch their own search and that the police were welcome to join in if they wished. At that point, the police joined in.

Under the direction of Detective Sergeant Antolik, a fifty-man search party consisting of family members, fraternity brothers, and campus and borough police officers met at the IUP field house, where they were split into four groups and assigned different areas. At about 9:45 P.M., the search began. Half an hour later, Jack's body was found at the bottom of a twelve-foot stairwell outside Weyandt Hall, an IUP science building.

According to police reports and photos, Davis was found lying on his back with his head wedged against the wall of the building. A dark liquid had dried around his mouth and nose, and the button and zipper of his blue jeans were open. When investigators from the State Police Crime Lab in Greensburg arrived, the death was labeled "suspicious." Obviously, the Davis family found it suspicious too.

"When they told me where they had found him," Mr. Davis said, "my first instinct was that he was tossed over the railing. And after finding out that there were some goings-on that evening, I thought that perhaps he got into a scuffle and they grabbed him and threw him over." Mrs. Lynch had similar thoughts: that someone had struck her son, then panicked, and hid his body in the stairwell.

But those initial suspicions were to be short-lived. The next day, following a two-hour autopsy by Dr. Stephen P. Griffin, an Indiana Hospital pathologist under contract with the county, Coroner Thomas Streams held a press conference in the university's administration building to announce the findings. After a night of heavy drinking, Jack Davis had apparently walked down the twenty-one steps to urinate, passed out, regurgitated, and choked on his vomit. The death, he said, had occurred around 2:00 A.M. Saturday, and "there was no indication of foul play." The only sign of trauma, a minor hematoma on Davis's left eyebrow, was attributed to his having bumped his head as he passed out and toppled against the wall.

At that same conference, Detective Sergeant Antolik responded to reports that the underaged Davis had been in two local bars Friday night by stating that Davis had done all his drinking at a sorority party not far from where his car was found. He had not been permitted into Patti's Restaurant, Antolik erroneously reported, and had not consumed any alcohol at Caleco's, a bar located across the street that apparently had admitted him. As for his decision not to search the campus right away, Antolik defended himself by saying that he believed Davis had either left campus or been kidnapped. And as for a reported fight that night between Davis's fraternity and Phi Delta Theta, Indiana vice president of student affairs David DeCoster described it as "just a shouting match."

The coroner's account appeared to be supported by the recollection of another student, Tom Brennan, who had come forward when the missing persons report was published on Wednesday. According to Brennan, he had found Davis standing outside a bar on Philadelphia Street at around 1:30 A.M. Saturday, clearly intoxicated, and had offered to help Davis home. The two got as far as Elkin Hall, an IUP dormitory at the corner of Oakland Avenue and School Street—a block from where Davis's body was later found. There, Brennan said, he went inside the dorm to try to find Davis a place to spend the night; but when he came back out, Davis was gone.

Given this seemingly clear-cut explanation, the family of Jack Davis was forced to accept every parent's nightmare: that Davis had died as a result of alcohol overconsumption. At the funeral, Mr. Davis recalled, the minister decided to use the occasion to preach against the evils of drinking, and at work, Davis found himself in the humiliating position of having to tell people his son died by choking on his own vomit. As for Mrs. Lynch, she told the media that she had chosen to make herself believe that it was an accident. In the days following her son's death, she even gave interviews to the *Pittsburgh Press* and a local TV station in which she warned other youths of the dangers of drinking.

In the ensuing months, however, various aspects of the case began to trouble the family. First, they asked, why would anyone as drunk as Davis reportedly was walk all the way down a flight of stairs to urinate in an area surrounded by trees and shrubs? Secondly, why did it take five days to find him in an uncovered stairwell located in the center of campus? Thirdly, why did the always cleanshaven young man have two to three days' growth of hair on his face in the police photos? And why, in those same photos, did his clothes appear dry when it had rained so hard the night before he was found that the family had had to call off their search?

On top of all this, there was still the unconfirmed report of an interfraternity brawl to contend with. As witnesses to that event told the police, the Phi Delts and Sigma Taus had begun arguing at a bar Friday night and resumed the confrontation at the Phi Delta House on Maple Street around 2:30 A.M. Saturday. At the funeral, family members recalled, several of Jack's fraternity brothers showed up with cuts, bruises, and badly swollen eyes. And as Tom Brennan told the police, Jack himself had been in a rowdy mood during their walk home, making a big deal of wanting to fight the Phi Delts.

This report was now compounded by the news of other campus squabbles that same night. On "fraternity row" in the 200 block of South Seventh Street, a group of people reportedly had been attacked with clubs and several cars damaged with bricks between eleven and eleven-thirty. A troubling coincidence uncovered by the IUP police was that among three students who would have been walking down that block at that time en route from the sorority party to the bars was none other than Jack Davis.

But perhaps the biggest question arose on January 13, 1988, when Coroner Streams called a press conference to release the results of the toxicology studies. The tests, he reported, confirmed his finding of accidental death involving alcohol. But a look at just what those levels were directly contradicted that conclusion: in the gastric content and the urine, the levels were not high enough to render Davis unconscious. More significantly, there was no alcohol at all in the blood.

At this point, I knew something was awry. Jack Davis had either not been as drunk as he was said to have been, or he had lived long enough for his body to metabolize the alcohol that was in his system. Either way, these facts suggested he had not died by choking on his own vomit. I intended to find out how he did die.

At the conclusion of our meeting, Davis's parents signed forms granting me the power of attorney and authorization to review all medical records pertaining to the death of their son. On Monday afternoon, I called Coroner Streams to inform him of these developments and to request that he make and send copies of all autopsy and investigatory reports to me at his earliest convenience. The next day, I sent him the authorization form and went about my other duties.

When more than two weeks passed without a word from Streams, I wrote again, letting him know that the family had been asking me about the case and that I would appreciate a prompt reply. Four days later, Mr. Streams called to tell me that the materials were on their way, and shortly afterward, I received everything I needed to begin my evaluation: the autopsy report, toxicology reports, microscopic tissue slides, and photos of the scene and the autopsy.

At first glance, the autopsy appeared to have been quite thoroughly and competently done. Dr. Griffin began by describing Davis's clothing, the location of what he construed to be vomitus, even such details as how the student's hair was parted and what his pockets contained. Here also, for the first time, I read a description of the injury to the decedent's face: "minimal swelling about the underside of the left brow" and a "0.6 cm. bluish bruise directly overlying the lateral orbital prominence on the left."

I skimmed ahead to the internal examination, curious to see whether there were any corresponding internal injuries of the head. What I found was staggering: the head had never even been opened, and Dr. Griffin had instead satisfied himself by taking a section of skin from the bruised area. From a forensic pathology standpoint, this was inexcusable. In any unexplained death, the head should be opened in order to obtain a complete picture of what happened. Here, a healthy twenty-year-old had been found dead at the bottom of a concrete stairwell with a good-sized bruise over his eye, and yet the pathologist had somehow deemed it unnecessary to execute this part of his job! If the death of Jack Davis were ever to be satisfactorily investigated, I knew right then and there, his body would have to be exhumed and his head opened up.

I turned immediately to the description of the lungs, eager to take a look at the evidence of asphyxiation. Sure enough, what Dr. Griffin described as "grayish tan foamy material with minute particulate matter" had been found in the bronchi, the two tubes leading from the trachea into the lungs. In addition, the doctor had observed patchy areas of collapse at the base of each lung, a common finding in cases of bronchial obstruction. As for the identity of the material, it appeared to be the same as that found on the subject's clothes and in his digestive system.

This was all quite significant, but if Jack Davis had really asphyxiated on regurgitated food, I knew that there should be microscopic evidence of it as well. To find aspirated material in the upper respiratory passages doesn't tell you anything. One doesn't sign out a case as aspiration of vomitus unless one finds food particles deep inside the lung tissue, actually producing an obstructive phenomenon. The reason for looking further is that one doesn't die in a second from aspirating food. The tissues react to the foreign material, and white blood cells, the defenders of our system, rush to the scene, causing inflammation and a buildup of fluid.

To be sure, Dr. Griffin had noted "marked pulmonary congestion" of the alveoli, the tiny air sacs where oxygen is transferred to the circulatory system, as well as "foreign material consistent with gastric content" in the bronchioles, the tiny endings of the bronchi. But as I now looked at what I presumed to be the same slides he had used, I could not find sufficient evidence of any of this. As far as I could tell, Dr. Griffin's microscopic descriptions were considerably overstated.

The slides also raised questions in my mind about the time of death. For one thing, there was no sign of postmortem autolysis, the spontaneous degeneration of tissues that begins shortly after death. Nor was there any bacterial overgrowth, a common finding in people who have been dead more than a day or two. On the other hand, there were signs of acute tracheobronchitis and bronchial pneumonia only twelve to twenty-four hours old, as well as micropulmonary thromboemboli, all evidence of some survival time. When I considered all this together with the zero blood alcohol level and the eyewitness accounts of Davis's having been visibly intoxicated the night of his disappearance, I reached the inescapable conclusion that he had survived for a considerable period of time between his collapse and his death.

On Sunday, April 29, 1990 the *Greensburg Tribune-Review* published the first in a three-part series on the Jack Davis case. Thoroughly researched and well-written, the front-page story raised all the pertinent questions and thrust the case back into the limelight. For part two, the reporters interviewed two other forensic pathologists who had also reviewed the autopsy and toxicology reports and reached conclusions quite similar to my own. It was the arguments Dr. Griffin came up with to defend his findings that surprised me.

Asked how he could stick by his ruling that the death was al-cohol-related even after the toxicology tests showed no alcohol in the blood, Dr. Griffin had said that because red blood cells break down during decomposition, the alcohol could have dissipated as well. But as any pathologist knows, blood alcohol cannot be low-ered so significantly during decomposition as to disappear. And if Davis had been drunk enough to pass out, even a five-day-old body would still contain some quantity of alcohol in the blood. In fact, some alcohol can be formed by decomposition, giving a false level that only good toxicology labs can detect.

What I couldn't understand is why no one called the toxicol-ogist to confirm these odd results. If the authorities really planned to proceed on the assumption that Davis was drunk enough to pass out and choke on his own vomit, why didn't they ask that those samples be retested? At any rate, this was now an academic question; the specimens, I read, had been "routinely" destroyed only six weeks after their release. And yet there was nothing "rou-tine" about this case.

Having expressed these thoughts to the family, I called Indiana County district attorney William J. Martin in mid-May to share my findings. I told him that given the facts that no head examination had been done and that the final diagnoses were not supported by the anatomical findings, I was recommending the exhumation of the body for the purpose of conducting a second autopsy. Mr. Martin, clearly disturbed that his office had not been asked to investigate in the first place, agreed to look into the matter and get back to me.

Several months passed without my hearing anything further from either the family or officials regarding this case, and I was forced to conclude that Mr. Martin had simply decided not to pursue it. Finally, in early October I received a call from Marisa Lynch inquiring about the case's status. I told her that I had rec-ommended exhumation to Mr. Martin and that I was ready to go to work as soon as I was needed. A few days later, Mrs. Lynch called me back to tell me that her husband had met with Mr. Martin and that he had decided to reopen the case. He would be contacting me shortly to set up a meeting.

On October 14, an article in the *Tribune-Review* confirmed that, on the basis of questions raised by me and the family, Mr. Martin had decided to reopen the case. Having examined the stairwell, Martin also had some questions about the likelihood of Davis's body having been in that location for five days. I was surprised to read that there might even be a witness who had looked into the stairwell between the time of Davis's disappearance and his discovery and not seen anything.

"This is not like a retail theft, where I might say, 'The police investigation is good enough for me,' " Martin told the *Tribune-Review.* "We have a person here who lost his life. If he died under circumstances other than the official ruling, if it was foul play, I want to know about it."

The very next day, I was surprised to read in the Pittsburgh papers that Mr. Martin had suspended the investigation. Apparently the D.A. had asked the family at their meeting the previous week to keep quiet about the new investigation in the interest of catching prospective witnesses off guard. But the family, as the *Tribune-Review* article testified, had gone ahead and leaked the news anyway. "I am disappointed in their actions," Mr. Martin was quoted as saying. "My desire is to clear up any questions as to how this man died and I am afraid that the investigation has been compromised at this time."

At the same news conference, Coroner Streams remarked that there was no new evidence to warrant reopening the case. "My office and the police involved still consider Mr. Davis's death an accident," he said. "In the past three years, there has been no new evidence brought forth. If there is information out there, I'll be the first one to reopen the investigation." In an apparent effort to bolster his findings, Streams now revealed for the first time that Davis also had traces of marijuana and cocaine in his blood. This, I thought, was stooping to a new low. Certainly, if the levels of these drugs were worth reporting, Streams would have done so in his initial report. I, in fact, had noted these levels myself and had concluded that they were too low to have been a factor in Davis's death.

To his credit, Mr. Streams now accepted that Davis could have been alive in the stairwell "for a considerable time," but beyond that he was unwilling to accept other possible causes of death. "Just how Mr. Davis got down the stairwell or why, we don't know and probably never will know," he said. "But I can say he was not thrown down the stairs, was not hit over the head, and was not dragged down the stairs. There was no trauma to indicate that." How he could make comments like these without having so much as shaved the subject's hair was beyond me. Still, Mr. Streams had the gall to continue defending his office's failure to open the skull by saying that the examination had been done "very thoroughly and completely."

That afternoon, the *Tribune-Review* reporter called me for comments on Streams's news conference. First, addressing Streams's comment that the alcohol in Davis's blood could have dissipated during the five days he lay there, I told her that this was "the most absurd thing in the world." As for the official cause of death, I added, "There was not anywhere near sufficient material in the respiratory passages to support such a diagnosis. He didn't choke to death." Lastly, I told her, Davis was not in that stairwell the amount of time he was said to have been. "The condition of this body wasn't that of someone who was exposed to the elements for five days," I said.

Over the course of the next few days, all the papers carried accounts of the Lynches' anger over Martin's decision to suspend the investigation, and for a while there was even talk of the state attorney general's office taking over. But on Saturday, I was happy to see that Martin had had a change of heart and was reopening his probe.

That Sunday, the *Press* ran a big story in which the long-simmering debate over the quality of Pennsylvania's county coroner system was revived. This was an issue I had been involved in since 1958, when, as a resident in pathology at the Veterans Administration Hospital, I joined the Allegheny County Medical Society's Committee for the Medical Examiner System, pushing for the replacement of elected and often unqualified coroners by appointed, qualified forensic pathologists.

Mr. Streams, the article pointed out, was an ambulance service owner who had worked as a paramedic and deputy coroner before being elected to his office in 1973. Like all coroners in the commonwealth's sixty-six counties (except for Philadelphia, which has had an appointive medical examiner system for more than forty years), he had not been required to undergo any specific training to take office. Since 1988, however, all Pennsylvania coroners have been required by state law to take a five-day course and test at the

State Police Academy and to undergo eight hours of continuing education a year after that. This is certainly a step in the right direction, but as the Davis case showed, a lack of medicolegal expertise can seriously hinder a coroner.

On Tuesday morning, I appeared on WTAE-TV's *Pittsburgh's Talking*, a popular live talk show, to discuss the Jack Davis case. There, I reiterated my criticism of the way the death had been investigated thus far and publicly called for a new autopsy. As I'd learned in the past, publicity can often change the course of events.

The next morning, I drove out to Indiana, and by ten o'clock was seated in Mr. Martin's office at the County Courthouse with the D.A., his chief investigator, four or five local police personnel, a representative of IUP, and Coroner Streams. I told the group that there was no question in my mind, based upon the toxicology report, physical circumstances, and microscopic tissue slides, that the cause of death could not be what it was said to be. In my opinion, I said, the body should be exhumed. Even Mr. Streams agreed that an exhumation would be useful, although he continued to insist that Davis had died accidentally. But as I left the building a couple of hours later, I was optimistic that things were now moving forward.

Afterward, Mr. Streams and a local police official brought me to the site where the body had been found. On the basis of the news accounts, I had pictured some hidden stairwell in a remote corner of campus. But much to my surprise, I now saw that it was in the middle of campus and not far from a busy street. Granted, the stairwell was unused and did not lie directly on the beaten track; but neither was it in the middle of nowhere. I remembered from my own school days how students are wont to mill about, and how sometimes someone will go to throw a cigarette butt or spit or urinate in an unused area like this. And of the five days the body was missing, three were school days in the middle of the semester. How a human being could have gone undetected in such a place was beyond me. After all, we aren't talking about a missing watch or a ring. We're talking about the body of an adult human being.

But there was something else that puzzled me as well. The twenty steps didn't simply run down to the spot where the body was found. Rather, a set of fifteen steps ended at a landing that extended a good ten feet before dropping off to another set of five steps. It was at the bottom of that second set of steps that Davis was found. On the surface, this seemed to support the conclusion that he had to have walked down there. I simply could not see someone tumbling past that first landing, unless he had somehow gotten up, stumbled, and fallen again. But what was far more likely, I now realized, was that he had fallen from atop the wall at the far end of the stairwell or had been placed at the bottom. If he had fallen, of course, a thorough autopsy would reveal considerable trauma that had somehow been missed the first time around.

The next day, I was pleased to learn that, on the basis of our meeting, Mr. Martin had organized a task force to reinvestigate the death of Jack Davis and was strongly recommending exhumation of the body. A day later, it was reported that Martin and Streams had agreed to go ahead with the exhumation request from the Court of Common Pleas in Allegheny County, where the body was buried.

My elation upon hearing this news, however, was tempered by remarks I learned Mr. Streams had made after I left Indiana. Whether out of malice or plain old political posturing, the coroner had told a reporter for the *Tribune-Review* that I now believed the death was due to alcohol and drug abuse and that I did not expect to find anything significant in a second autopsy. This was ridiculous, not to mention highly disturbing. I had said nothing of the sort about the presence of drugs. As for my not expecting to find anything, what I had said was that I did not yet have any hard evidence and couldn't jump to any conclusions before examining the body.

Over the next couple of weeks, as the exhumation became more and more of a likelihood, rumors regarding the death swirled. One was that the FBI was actively involved in the investigation of murder and drug deals on campus. Another was that Davis had sustained his injuries at a fraternity party that night and that those involved, fearing prosecution and expulsion, decided to cover his death up. But while much of this sounded quite possible, my principal concern was to examine the body.

Finally, on Thursday, November 8, Mr. Martin called to tell me that the exhumation request had been granted without a hearing, and that the autopsy was scheduled for the following Tuesday. Streams, of course, was continuing to look for a way out, arguing that I shouldn't be doing the autopsy since I previously had been retained by the family. But by this time, Streams really had no more official say in the matter.

Shortly before 4:00 P.M. on Tuesday, November 13, a steel casket containing the body of Jack Davis, Jr., was wheeled into the basement lab of St. Francis Central Hospital. Besides myself, in attendance were Mr. Streams, two representatives of Mr. Martin's office, a state police trooper, an IUP police sergeant, and Joe Mancuso, a pathology assistant, autopsy technician, and embalmer who had worked for me at the coroner's office and who continues to work with me on most of my autopsies to this day.

The casket was opened to reveal the remarkably well preserved body of Jack Davis, dressed in a long-sleeved knit shirt, denim trousers, and brown moccasins. A heavy layer of cosmetic material covered his face, neck, and hands. We removed the clothes, revealing considerable blackish gray mold covering the entire body. Straight, fairly long, dark brown hair still covered the head, and the thin brown mustache I had seen in pictures was also present. The face appeared intact, other than a wax-filled area just below the left eyebrow where Dr. Griffin had noted some bruising and had made an incision to study its extent. When we removed the filler, however, I noted that the defect in the skin was too large and its edges too rough to be attributed purely to an autopsy section. Clearly, there had been a laceration.

Following a full external examination in which I found nothing else of particular significance, we proceeded to reopen the body along the original, Y-shaped incision. Everything in the thorax and abdomen appeared to be normal, with no evidence of hemorrhaging, fractures, or dislocations. I was puzzled, however, by the fact that none of the internal organs had been replaced in the body cavity, as is customary following a medicolegal autopsy. A quick check of the casket revealed that they weren't in there either. At any rate, my main concerns were what the neck and head could reveal, and so I moved on to that stage of my examination.

First, I removed the neck organs and tongue. All of the cartilage and bones inside appeared to be intact and free of hemorrhage, and neither the esophagus nor the trachea revealed any trace of food residue or other foreign objects. Indeed, it was not until we dissected and reflected back the scalp from the underlying bony skull that I noticed anything out of the ordinary.

Extending from the left frontal area of the head toward the

midline was a good-sized subgaleal hemorrhage—a collection of blood beneath the scalp but overlying the calvarium, or skullcap. After I opened the calvarium with an electric saw, my suspicions were confirmed: running down the occipital protuberance, the outward-jutting back of the skull, was a three-inch fracture. At the base of this fracture, just above the site where the spine joins the skull, there was a splintering of bone.

I dissected further in an attempt to determine just how great the damage to the head had been. Although no blood had pooled just beneath the skull, I could make out some dark reddish brown discoloration through the dura mater, the toughest and outermost of the three membranes that cover the brain. When the dura mater was stripped back, there was no mistaking it: a large, subdural hemorrhage overlay the left frontal lobe and extended both backward and downward to cover parts of the left parietal and temporal lobes as well. Still moist and glistening, this hemorrhage covered a good three-by-four-inch area.

We next removed the brain itself in an attempt to discover whether there had been any intracerebral hemorrhaging in the areas covered by the outlying hemorrhages. But because of extensive decomposition, it was impossible to tell. Having removed the brain, however, I was now able to study the base of the skull as well. There, I discovered a second fracture, about an inch long and zigzag in shape.

At this point, we turned the body over to continue our study of the head. After stripping the galeal and periosteal tissues from the back of the head, I was able to further study the first fracture I had seen, running from just above the occipital protuberance to the area where the spine joins the skull. Just to the left of this, at the rounded base of the skull, lay a third fracture, measuring 1¾ by ¼ inches. The prominence of the suture lines and vascular tributaries in this area indicated to me a distribution of force that had caused a further pulling away of the bone.

Having concluded with the head, I made an incision down the middle of the decedent's back to expose the spine. There, I found further hemorrhaging within the spinal canal, measuring about five inches in length and running from the midcervical vertebrae down to the eighth thoracic vertebra. Like the subdural in the head, it was moist and dark reddish brown.

At this point, the cause of the young man's death was all too clear. The manner of death, however, was still very much up in the air. What the fractures and hemorrhages seemed to demonstrate were the infliction of both coup and contracoup injuries, indicating the likelihood of a fall that impacted the back of the head. The absence of lacerations or other surface wounds all but eliminated the possibility of a direct blow to that location. Clearly antemortem injuries rather than postmortem artifacts, the hemorrhages also indicated that Davis was alive at the time he sustained them. In other words, they did not result from his body having been thrown down the stairs. In fact, given the total absence of bruises, cuts, or fractures elsewhere on his body, as well as the physical layout of the stairwell, the chances of his having tumbled or been thrown down those stairs even while alive were minimal.

On the other hand, I could not rule out the possibility of foul play. For one thing, there are other flat, broad surfaces besides floors. And considering the injury above the left eye, I had to accept the possibility that he was struck in the face with some blunt object, throwing him backward against either a floor or a wall.

After setting aside the brain, dura mater, spinal cord, and portions of the ribs and vertebrae for further study, Joe closed the body back up for its return to the funeral home. It was by then about 6:30 P.M., and after washing up, I called it a day.

Over the next few days, I received several calls from the news media. But having been instructed by Mr. Martin's staff not to divulge my findings until a news conference we had scheduled for Saturday, I kept my mouth shut. When Saturday came, I drove to the Hyatt Hotel, located just around the corner from the hospital. There, at a very well attended conference, we broke the big story.

Jack Davis died of skull fractures and hemorrhaging, I announced under the glare of the TV lights. "These findings are much more consistent with a fall, rather than a blow," I added. "How the fall occurred is another matter." I went on to describe the three fractures and the hemorrhages, noting that the three-inch fracture at the base of the skull was serious enough to have caused the death alone.

Citing the growth of a beard and the presence of pneumonia, I also expressed my opinion that Jack Davis had remained alive for two to three days after sustaining his injuries. "We now understand why it would not have been possible for him to seek help on his own," I said. "This young man did not aspirate on regurgitated food, and there is no question in my mind that he could not have been dead five days . . . It's possible he was down there all that time, but unlikely. I understand the stairwell was rarely used, but I'm troubled by the fact that you had students milling around, maybe tossing a cigarette down there, and nobody saw anything. It just seems unlikely."

For his part, Mr. Martin announced that the death was now being termed "suspicious" and that phase two of the investigation was beginning. Although there were still more questions than answers, things were looking much better.

Soon after that press conference, I lost all track of the case. The last news item I'd seen on it was a one-inch blurb in the *Press* in January 1991 reporting that the family had little confidence in the new investigation. Later, I heard rumors that both the state attorney general's office and the FBI were taking over the case and looking into a possible drug connection, but nothing ever came of them. Then, in March 1991, John Lynch sent me a copy of a five-page letter he had written to Mr. Martin that exhaustively reviewed the issues and mentioned others I hadn't been aware of.

Two weeks prior to Jack Davis's death, the State Bureau of Liquor Control Enforcement had begun an investigation into Patti's Restaurant, a popular student drinking spot on Philadelphia Street, just a few blocks from campus. Following the death, based on witnesses' affidavits that Davis had been drinking at that bar the night he disappeared, Detective Sergeant Antolik wrote a letter to the bureau requesting a full investigation into the bar. Three days later, an officer began contacting dozens of prospective witnesses, including many of those to whom the borough police had already spoken. But by the following February, when the investigation was closed, he had gotten only fourteen students to speak with him, and of those, only two were willing to repeat their earlier statements that they had seen Davis drinking there that night.

Proceeding with what evidence it did have, the bureau announced on February 16 that the bar and one of its bartenders were being cited for violating state liquor laws by serving Davis, and that the citations "probably will result in a fine or suspension or both." A hearing was set for March 30 before a district magistrate. But for some unexplained reason, it was not until November 17 of that year—over a year after the investigation opened—that the citations were actually issued. Finally, on March 20, 1989, an evidentiary hearing was held before an administrative law judge for the State Liquor Control Board in Altoona; two months later, ruling the investigators had waited too long, the judge dismissed the citations. And in June, the state police announced that they would not be appealing that decision.

Whether it was the local police, the state police, or the LCB judge who dropped the ball on this, I don't know. But if this bureaucratic foot-dragging wasn't adding insult to injury, I don't know what is. Whether or not alcohol played a part in Davis's death, there were ample affidavits testifying to the fact that he was drunk the night he disappeared. Also, under the so-called "Dram Shop Act," Jack's legal next of kin could have sued the bar for serving someone whom they had reason to believe was becoming inebriated. But by the time the family came to me, the two-year statute of limitations had run out. This was unfortunate, for although it would not have brought Jack back, it certainly could have eased the family's suffering a bit.

As this letter also informed me, there were a number of other questions and concerns about the death that remained unanswered. For instance, there was the report that the fraternity jacket Davis had on at the time of his death belonged to a brother known to be one of the biggest cocaine dealers on campus. Then there were the anonymous callers stating that Jack "just had the wrong jacket on at the wrong time" and "was made an example by drug dealers." There was also the report that on the night Jack disappeared, a sorority girl and her boyfriend were jumped and beaten on the way home from Patti's. And there was the report that borough police had dispersed a group of people arguing outside Caleco's earlier that night, as well as an anonymous caller stating that Jack himself had been arrested.

The list of strange circumstances goes on: handwritten statements from two students who had seen Jack in Caleco's that night, each containing a reference to his having thanked them for saving his life; further statements from the student who had identified himself as the last person to see Jack, relating that Jack wasn't really that drunk at the time, that he had urinated on a lawn just prior to his disappearance, and that he had last been seen hiding in the bushes near the stairwell. There was even an anonymous report that he had not entered the stairwell alone.

Recently, I decided to get back in touch with Mr. Martin to see where his investigation stood. The first thing I learned was that he was now Judge Martin of the Indiana County Court of Common Pleas, having been elected to that position in May of 1991. Judge Martin explained that soon after our press conference, his task force reinterviewed everyone whose names appeared in the original reports, but "really didn't uncover anything new or different from what was established." The witness who supposedly had seen an empty stairwell during the time Davis was said to have been lying there never materialized, and the allegations of drug-related violence proved similarly elusive.

"It was just a very curious case that a man could be in the middle of campus and not be found, and that the autopsy was not completely done," Judge Martin concluded. "There's always going to be a question mark over the case. We followed up every lead we got. I had my detectives all over the place." Upon leaving office, he said, he left it termed a suspicious death and put it in the hands of the new D.A.

I checked in next with Antolik to see if his people had come up with anything new. He, too, I learned, had since gotten a promotion, moving up to the position of Indiana police chief. Obviously not well-acquainted with the medical facts of the case, he still stood behind the theory that Davis had gone down into the stairwell to urinate and then fallen. Strangely, however, he now admitted to the additional possibilities that Davis had fallen off the wall or from the top of the stairs. The only scenario he would not admit to was one in which the death occurred elsewhere.

"I consider it one of those cases that are solved but unsolved," Antolik rather cryptically remarked. "We can't come up with a hard, concrete answer, and so I can't really close it. It's like a jigsaw puzzle—we can get an idea of the answer, but all the pieces aren't there yet."

In the interest of thoroughness, I made one last call—this one to the new D.A., a man named Mike Handler. Unable to get Mr. Handler on the phone, I was told by one of his assistants that the case had been officially closed.

For the family, I know, the case is anything but closed. With Ms. Brennan and John Lynch spearheading the effort, unsettling pieces of information continue to be uncovered every day—some of them quite clear-cut, others merely rumors. Whether all these pieces will ever assume enough form to force a reopening of the case, or else splinter—like the ongoing research into JFK's death—into a million different shards of conflicting accounts and implications, remains to be seen.

As I review all of the available evidence, I am left with an awfully bad taste in the mouth. Clearly, Jack Davis did not die in the manner he was said to have died. Just as clear to me is that, while he most likely did fall somewhere at some time, he did not fall down those stairs. As for the possibility of his having fallen off the wall, the fact that his skull was not completely shattered forces me to reject that scenario.

Sadly, without additional hard evidence, I cannot conclude anything more about the manner of Davis's death, although it does stand to reason that if he sustained his injuries in the stairwell, foul play of some kind was involved. Given some of the other circumstances, I cannot dismiss the possibility that he sustained his injuries elsewhere and was then carried to the bottom of the stairwell. When that would have been, and whether or not he would have been alive at that time, is open to dispute. What is not open to dispute is that he lived for at least a couple of days after sustaining his injuries. And while this alone does not prove homicide, it certainly would prove a coverup and, at the very least, negligence. People not necessarily responsible for his death could have felt guilty and worried about the legal repercussions of not seeking medical help sooner. Of course, the truth could be even more sinister.

Even so, I'm forced to wonder whether anyone would have been clever enough in such a moment of panic and fear to take him back to the vicinity in which he was last seen. For that matter, how would anyone even have known where he was last seen? The problem I have with such scenarios is that despite extensive investigation and inquiries, nobody has yet come up with anything of a definitive nature. And it is my experience that when dealing with nonprofessional criminals, more than one of whom knows of a crime, it is almost impossible to keep the deed a secret.

Still, I sincerely hope that for the sake of their own peace of mind, the family of Jack Davis can one day determine the precise manner of his death. But I also doubt that this will ever happen. Short of someone coming forward and either confessing to having placed him at the bottom of that stairwell or admitting to having seen him fall or placed there, I see no way of ever resolving this case. The tragedy of all this is not only that a young man in the prime of life should die such a messy and senseless death, but that because of the incompetence, insensitivity, and apathy of those charged with its investigation, the truth of how it happened should be forever obscured.

12

Mysteries of Pittsburgh
Part Two:
The Art Jones Case

Sometimes, it seems, bad things come in pairs. Less than a year after my autopsy of Jack Davis, a new split-level home in a rural township twenty-eight miles south of Pittsburgh violently exploded, throwing debris hundreds of feet and transforming the structure into rubble. Strangely, the house's sole occupant, a fifty-six-year-old divorced car dealer by the name of Arthur J. Jones, Jr., was nowhere to be found.

Like the Jack Davis case, this one would come to occupy that unsteady ground between science and speculation. But in an almost mirror image of the previous case, this one would pit a family content to accept that which could be scientifically deduced against authorities bent on the notion of foul play. As a forensic pathologist trained to draw my conclusions from the known facts, I would fall squarely into the former camp. And as strange as the ultimate solution to this case might seem, I've been able to justify it by citing something that the great Sherlock Holmes once said: "Once you have eliminated the impossible, whatever remains, however improbable, must be the answer."

I first learned of this case the day after the explosion, when a medical colleague of mine called to refer one of his employees to me. Her name was Lisa Blohm, and she was the only daughter of the man known to his family and friends as Art Jones. Already unsatisfied with the local police investigation of the explosion and her father's disappearance, she and her husband, Mark, were seeking an independent investigator. I lent an ear, and as I spoke with the Blohms over the next few days, I found myself entering yet another mystery.

Art Jones had last been seen returning home in his new Buick Park Avenue at about 7:30 on the evening of September 17, 1991. Seven hours later—at 2:34 A.M., to be exact—an explosion rocked the sedate, middle-class housing development, tossing pieces of insulation, window frames, and curtains into the trees and down the wooded hillside behind the house. A fire that raged for hours had done the rest of the job, and by the time the Blohms arrived at about six o'clock that morning, all that remained was a smoldering pile of rubble and the lamppost at the end of the driveway.

"It was devastating to first come upon it and realize what kind of force had to have taken place," Mark Blohm told me. "It was chilling, because you can look at something like that on the news and say, 'Well, it happened to someone else'—you know, the old 'That's the other guy' routine. But when I looked at that house, the first thought that came to my mind was, had he been there, there was no way he could have survived."

Still, Jones was expected at his Buick dealership in the nearby town of Charleroi for a nine o'clock meeting, and so the local authorities decided to wait until then before launching a search. But because both the Buick and Jones's Jeep were sitting where the garage had once been, it was, admits Blohm, "a thin string to hold on to." And when nine o'clock came and went with no word from Jones, the volunteer fire department went to work, digging through the rubble with a backhoe. In the afternoon, the state police fire marshal and private investigators from Petrolane Gas Service, the manufacturer of Jones's propane tank, joined in. But after a nineteen-hour search of the ruins and the surrounding woods, Jones had not been found.

The Blohms' primary complaint seemed to be the manner in which the authorities had searched the scene, apparently piling up the rubble with little regard for the scene's preservation. "There were questions in my mind," said Mark, "but it seemed to me there was some organization to what they were doing. In hindsight, you can look back and say, 'Wow, what a total screwup this was.' But at the time I think shock was probably the only thing that had really taken hold." At any rate, added Lisa, "We assumed he was home, he was dead, and they were going to find his body. So we didn't question anything until that afternoon, when Woncheck came out and said we had to file a missing persons report."

Samuel S. Woncheck was and is the chief of the Fallowfield Township Police Department, a force of three full-time and six part-time officers whose job it is to protect and serve the community of fifty-five hundred. If it was his determination that Jones was missing, then that's how the police would proceed. But the Blohms, together with at least two of Jones's sons, were quite certain that Jones had been home at the time.

I was baffled. The fact that a nearly daylong search by local and state authorities had failed to turn up any human remains indicated to me that Jones might not have been at home. On the other hand, if the blast had been forceful enough, there's no telling how far he could have been thrown, or how badly obliterated his remains could be. As a forensic pathologist trained to recognize such things, I thought I should have a look myself. I told the Blohms that I'd be glad to assist them in another search of the site if they would obtain the proper clearances.

On the morning of September 25, I donned jeans and rubber boots instead of a suit and tie and headed out of Pittsburgh toward Washington County. Situated about forty-five minutes south of the city, Fallowfield lies in the heart of the Monongahela River valley, the cradle of the region's once-booming steel manufacturing industry. By contract, I knew, the local coroner referred complex cases to a pathologist at the Allegheny County coroner's office. But because no body had been found, there was nothing yet to refer. I was hoping that perhaps I could change that scenario.

Shortly after nine o'clock, I arrived at the Rodgers Manor housing development, which sits atop a wooded ridge overlooking Old Route 71. At the sight of several anxious people huddled next to what looked like a vacant lot, I knew where to park. As I got out of the car, I was amazed: where a house had once stood, only portions of walls and several man-high piles of rubble and assorted debris remained. The Blohms greeted me and introduced me to Jones's sons—Frank, David, and Jim—as well as several other family members and friends who had volunteered to pitch in with the search. Then they took me over to the ruins.

As I walked through the rubble, I realized why the Blohms were

284 Cyril Wecht, M.D., J.D.

so unhappy with the previous week's search: instead of conducting it in an orderly, systematic fashion that would permit them to later reconstruct the scene and look for objects in correlation with specific portions of the house, the authorities had simply pushed things aside into huge conglomerates of debris. It did not seem possible to differentiate that damage which might have been caused by the explosion from that which might have been caused by the heavy equipment. The police, I knew, had been concerned with finding Jones. But now that I saw the damage with my own eyes, I wondered how anyone could have thought that he might be saved.

With the group gathered around, I explained my thoughts on the situation and how I felt we should proceed. First, I told them, I did not expect to find anything more than a few charred bones in the rubble. After all, representatives of the Federal Bureau of Alcohol, Tobacco and Firearms (the ATF) had come down two days earlier at Chief Woncheck's request and conducted a second fruitless search in which they also concluded that the fire had not raged long enough and at high enough a temperature to vaporize the body. And whatever the flaws in the first search, I pointed out, the federal authorities are not blind or incompetent. If they had seen a substantial part of a human body—whether a hand or a foot or even a couple of fingers—they would have recognized it.

I was shown where large portions of the house had flown two to three hundred feet through the air, and I realized that if large objects could be thrown that far, so could a human body. And since no body parts had been found across the street or on the property to the right of Jones's house, it stood to reason that there was going to be something off to the left or to the rear, which is to say on the wooded hillside.

I walked down the hillside and followed a stream a couple of hundred feet, as far as I could proceed in the absence of special equipment and other people. Then I systematically worked my way back up and down the hill, slowly eyeballing the terrain for anything out of the ordinary. After about two hours, I came upon some items that caught my eye. Hard, irregularly shaped, and brown, they clearly suggested charred bones. I placed them into a bag and continued my search, but nothing else of interest turned up. When I'd satisfied myself that I'd covered as much of the terrain as I could, I returned to the site and showed the family what I'd found. Uncertain of their nature, however, I understated their significance, saying only that they required further study.

Slipping on a pair of heavy work gloves, I and the family and friends then began our own search of the several piles of rubble, although by this time I was really not very optimistic. We spent the whole day rummaging, sorting, and piling. We went through a couple of piles completely and others in part, finding clothing, jewelry, and even some cigars in a box, but nothing more that even remotely suggested human remains. Around five o'clock, when it started to get dark, I told the group to continue searching the next day and, if they found anything suspicious, to bring it to me. But most importantly, I told them, they should make certain that the authorities thoroughly searched the woods, because I had a strong gut feeling that that's where the answer lay.

As I made my way to the car, I was approached by various members of the news media who had been waiting all afternoon at the edge of the site. Asked why the family was so sure that Jones was home at the time of the explosion, I said it was simply "because they have no reason to believe that he wasn't." Like the Jones clan, I also took the opportunity to criticize the sloppiness of the initial search attempt. What I did not tell the media was that I had found something that might be important.

The next morning, I brought my collected items to the hospital lab for examination. There we attempted to decalcify the hard pieces for microscopic study, conducted immunological, serological, and chemical tests to see if any human tissue or blood was present, and processed some of the softer material for microscopic study to see if it was human tissue. Although a few of the objects, as I say, looked like human skeletal remains, I could not be sure until the results of those tests came back the next week.

In that evening's paper, I was glad to see myself and a couple of family members quoted in our criticism of the initial search, but I was surprised at Chief Woncheck's defense. "It's a very difficult situation," he was quoted as saying. "You have to be more concerned with someone's life than preserving the scene." While I did not doubt his sincerity for a moment, I did doubt his judgment. Anyone who could think that someone situated inside that house had survived a blast of that magnitude was not using his head. But apparently, Woncheck had thought just that. He had even gone so far as to announce that Washington County Crime

Stoppers was offering a thousand-dollar reward for information leading to Jones's whereabouts.

Over the next several days, speculation was rampant. Chief Woncheck, referring to a 1956 crash landing of a plane that was never found, was quoted in the papers calling Jones's disappearance "one of the biggest mysteries to hit the Pittsburgh area since that B-25 bomber went down in the Monongahela River. I'm sure everybody's speculating. Everybody's wondering, 'Where's Art Jones?' God, I wish I knew." Even John Markulike, general manager of the dealership and a close friend of Jones for over eleven years, had questions. "My theory changes every day," he was quoted as saying. "If Art is still out there running around somewhere, he will eventually have to get in touch with someone in his circle of friends."

The mystery was elevated to a new level a few days later, when the *Press* reported that an employee of a South Side tobacco company where Jones regularly bought cigars had received a check for four boxes from the missing man postmarked "Sept. 18 P.M." This, according to the employee, was strange for two reasons. First, the explosion had occurred on the morning of September 18, prior to the postmarked time. Second, he said, Jones always waited until after he had received an invoice to send in his check. But as anyone who uses the U.S. mail knows, the check could very well have gotten tied up in the system. As for the unusually prompt payment, perhaps Jones had simply grown a little more diligent in his late middle age.

The fact of the matter was that to take a good, hard look at what was then known in this case was to realize that there wasn't much information or physical evidence of a definitive nature. There was no indication of homicide or any kind of foul play. All of the vehicles and dealer plates at the business were accounted for. A review of court records in both Allegheny and Washington counties by law enforcement authorities and investigative reporters had revealed no outstanding judgments, suits, or other legal action involving Jones. And monitoring of Jones's credit cards and automatic banking card had shown no evidence of recent activity.

For these reasons, I chose to adopt a more conservative public stance on the matter, even though I had yet to determine the composition of the items I had retrieved from the scene. "There's nothing in Mr. Jones's background and nothing I'm told from a financial standpoint that would seem to fit in with a scenario that this explosion and Mr. Jones's disappearance were orchestrated as some kind of great ruse," I told the Pittsburgh *Press*. "If he is somewhere else, what did he get out of it? Obviously he didn't benefit. His house is destroyed, his car is destroyed, he's walked away from his dealership, and he can't collect any life insurance." And I might have added, Where does one hide out in such a situation anyway? Where do you go in America when everybody knows your identity?

On October 1, it was reported that the ATF had determined that propane caused the explosion. As for what had ignited it, they were unable to say, and Petrolane had yet to complete its own investigation.

That same day, the lab results came back, indicating that the materials I had found were not human remains. As best as the lab could ascertain, they were a certain kind of hard plastic that had melted and fused together in such a way as to suggest human bones. Now I, too, was puzzled. Having searched the rubble fairly extensively, I was almost 100 percent certain that Jones's remains were not there. And based on the assumption that investigators had done a better job of searching the surrounding woods than I was able to, I was now forced to accept the possibility of foul play. Still, there was no reason to believe that it would have been something of Jones's own doing. If anything, the explosion had been rigged to cover up something that went on in that house.

At any rate, any suspicions of foul play that I may have entertained were overshadowed by my sympathy for the family. To wake up every day not knowing what had become of one's father, father-in-law, or son must have been devastating. As Mark was quoted saying, trying to figure this out was "like going into a tunnel with no light at the end of it. I daydream and all I see is a big question mark."

Inspired by this awful situation to see that some answers were found, I told a reporter from the *Pittsburgh Post-Gazette* that the FBI should be called in to investigate. "I don't mean this in a negative way," I said, "but this is not a job for the Fallowfield Township police." Three days later, an FBI spokesman answered this plea with an announcement that the bureau had no plans to enter the investigation. The FBI, he explained, would only get involved if there were evidence of kidnapping or if the missing person were wanted and believed to have crossed state lines.

Instead, the Fallowfield police and the ATF continued to investigate the case in their own manner, seeking and winning a subpoena in federal court granting them access to Jones's bank records. This was certainly standard procedure in a missing persons investigation, and earlier in the month just such a search had even helped investigators locate a missing West Virginia bank president in a Nevada casino. But for Chief Woncheck to now say publicly that this case mirrored that one and that Jones was in hiding somewhere outside the state was, I thought, overshooting the mark. "What you have is a guy who's taken off for some reason," he told the *Post-Gazette.* "We want to know why and where he went."

At the same time that all this was going on, various parties interested in Jones's estate were busy scavenging what they could from it. On October 5, less than three weeks after the disappearance, Mellon Bank took possession of the dealership's cars and auto parts with the intention of liquidating the company's assets, and most of the business's employees were forced to resign. The day before, Mellon had filed a complaint against Jones for a judgment of over $821,000, including more than $106,000 in attorney's fees, arguing that the dealership had failed to make a $5,000 interest payment on a loan. But to my mind, the reason was, quite simply, panic.

A week later, a Washington County judge appointed a temporary trustee at the request of Jones's attorney and family to oversee Jones's estate, including the car dealership. The trustee, a Washington, Pennsylvania, attorney, was also granted authority to receive reports and various communications from the law enforcement agencies. Two months later, when Jones had still not showed up, the lawyer was appointed permanent trustee. Although state law requires the court to wait a year before granting such status, the judge waived that rule when the attorney testified that because Jones's debts exceeded his assets, the appointment had to be made promptly.

Over the winter, the Blohms told me, Art Jones's assets were liquidated. First, Buick bought back all of the 1992 cars. Next, Mellon Bank auctioned off the other new inventory and used cars. Then the franchise itself was sold in closed bidding, and finally, the trustee publicly auctioned off the office furniture and equipment.

"There still are some outstanding debts," Mark said, "but nothing substantial. Had everything been sold at what it could have been without the time frame they placed on us, everything would have been paid off. The problem was that there were these vultures out there who recognized what was going on and took advantage of it." Mellon Bank, he claims, "grabbed about $100,000 on top of what the note was."

Far more devastating to the family of Art Jones than this financial wrangling, however, was the ongoing speculation by the media, the police, and the public. Lisa remembers Chief Woncheck appearing on a local news show saying that he expected to find Jones on a beach somewhere. And both Blohms remember another news crew making a big deal of a next-door neighbor's comment that Jones had recently asked him to stop mowing his lawn, the implication being that Jones was in such a state of financial ruin that he could no longer even afford to spare ten dollars a week.

"They were very quick to form conclusions," Mark said of the local media. "They actually were just as contributory to the rumors as anyone on the street would be. It was very callous, very unprofessional, and it was that kind of reporting that sent everyone down the street to every barroom and every lunch hall, scuttle-butting about, asking, 'What do you think really happened?' There wasn't a day that went by within the first few months that someone didn't ask, 'C'mon, what happened? You got to know. Where's he at?' And it was extremely trying to bite your tongue, because you couldn't answer. You didn't want to answer too defiantly and say, 'Are you questioning my father-in-law's integrity?' Because you just didn't know."

What was even more frustrating, said the Blohms, was that because they didn't know all the answers, they started to succumb to the rumors themselves. "You're a product of what you hear," explained Mark, "and you eventually hear so much that you start thinking. And it became a force of habit that every brand-new Buick I saw driving down the road I'd be looking for the cigar at the wheel and Art and his sunglasses behind it."

The problem with all this speculation, other than the fact that it seemed to be leading nowhere, was that it flew in the face of everything that was known about Mr. Arthur J. Jones, Jr.

A native of Pittsburgh and an army veteran, Jones had been involved with the automobile industry—and Buick—since 1973, when he became a co-owner of a dealership in the Pittsburgh suburb of McKeesport. From there, he moved on to businesses in nearby Carrick and Pleasant Hills, abandoning the latter in 1990 to buy into the Charleroi dealership. He was tired of being near the city, and according to Mark, "He always wanted to go to a rural dealership."

Divorced from Joan, his wife of twenty-five years, in 1984, Jones had been living alone for close to eight years, eating microwave lunches and dining out. Only his sons David, a freelance photographer, and Jim, then a sophomore at the California University of Pennsylvania, spent much time with him. Jim, in fact, had been living in his father's home off and on for the past few years, and had stayed there most recently from late August until September 8, when he turned twenty-one. He had left, he told the *Press*, because his father was trying to control his comings and goings. "We had your basic father-son relationship," James was quoted as saying. "My father set down rules and I didn't pay attention to them."

A creature of habit, Jones was known to do everything at about the same time every day. After arriving at the dealership between nine and nine-thirty, he would go home for a microwaved lunch and to pick up his personal mail at midday, then return home for the evening between five and five-thirty. Other than belonging to a Presbyterian church, the Pittsburgh Athletic Association, the American Legion, and a handful of professional organizations, he didn't do much else. Perhaps his greatest thrill in life, according to family members and friends, was taking a drive in the country with a new cigar in his mouth. And even then, said John Markulike, "He would always tell someone where he was going."

According to Lisa Blohm, this description was one of the few things the papers got right. "They pretty much described him to a tee," she told me. "He was very predictable. He didn't alter his routine very much at all. He went to work, but I didn't know him to go out too much other than for dinner." Mark Blohm even went so far as to describe him as "a boring guy." "Being a bachelor," he said, "he ate out quite a bit, but he wasn't one to go out. He used to call anyone who went out to the bars a 'honky-tonker.' He'd sit down, turn on the TV, read the newspaper, smoke a cigar. That was about it." Reruns of *Hogan's Heroes* were apparently a big favorite.

And yet despite this character profile, all these people who had never even met the man were speculating that he had staged his own getaway. I was eager for there to be a break in the case to put these rumors to rest, but instead the thing died, and as the months passed by, the case slipped from my mind. I was busy, of course, doing autopsies, consulting, teaching, and writing. But when, on occasion, I did think about Jones, I would always arrive at the same conclusion: that the authorities had simply not searched the area well enough and that he was out there, waiting to be discovered.

I cannot say I was terribly surprised, then, when it was reported on the eleven o'clock news on Saturday, April 25, 1992, that a badly decomposed body had been found that evening in a wooded area along Old Route 71 in Fallowfield Township. Although early efforts to identify the corpse at the Allegheny county coroner's office using an old set of Jones's dental records had proven inconclusive, I knew it had to be Jones. At any rate, the remains were to be compared with a more recent set of dental records the next day.

Over the next few days, I followed the developing news intently. An avid hunter, it seems, had been driving slowly along Old Route 71, scouring the woods for turkey and deer, when a white form about one hundred feet up the brown hillside caught his eye. When he got out to investigate, he quickly realized that it was no turkey and went to call the police. According to the papers, the location of this find was the bottom of a forty-foot cliff about four hundred yards southeast of Jones's property. According to Chief Woncheck, the authorities had stopped their search at the top of that cliff.

As I read this, I found myself getting a bit angry at not having made a greater effort to push the need for a wider search. But in retrospect, I'm not really sure whom I could have pushed. After all, I was not part of the official investigation. And besides, if anyone is trained to locate a body at a crime scene, it is the law enforcement officials, not I. The more I thought about it, the more amazed I was that trained investigators had failed to search the bottom of that cliff. And in light of the fact that neighbors from the bottom of the hillside had reported debris landing on their properties after the explosion, this failure was even less excusable.

By Monday afternoon, authorities had still not identified the remains, which reportedly were so badly decomposed that the age and sex of the decedent could not even be determined. But on Tuesday morning, it was reported that Jones's dentist and Dr. Michael N. Sobel—a forensic odontologist whom I had gotten involved in medicolegal investigative work while I was coroner—had finally made a positive match between the skeletal remains and a set of Jones's dental records. The mystery of Art Jones's disappearance had been solved. But how, exactly, had he died?

The news reports were sketchy, but according to Washington County coroner S. Timothy Warco, the immediate cause of death was a fractured skull. Whether Jones had sustained the injury in the explosion, by falling over the cliff, or from a blow to the head, Warco could not say. Other findings included a fractured rib and areas of singed hair on the left arm and left scalp, the latter indicating that Jones had been exposed to heat or fire.

While the discovery of Jones's body had answered some questions, it had also raised new ones. For one, how could he have survived so powerful an explosion? And assuming that he had, how and why would he have wandered several hundred yards in the dark? Chief Woncheck, apparently realizing now that the case was beyond his department's ken to solve, had handed it over to the state police criminal investigation unit. As for Mr. Warco, he could not yet rule out the possibility of a blow to the head, although he definitely had ruled out the possibility of Jones's having been thrown that distance. And David Calcek, the Fallowfield fire chief, was saying that he found the idea that Jones had survived the blast hard to accept.

Shortly after the body was identified, I received a call from the Blohms. I was amazed to learn that when the remains were found, they hadn't even received a phone call; like me, they had heard about it on the news. But the purpose of their call was to request that I perform an independent autopsy. I hesitated, pointing out that the first one appeared to have been competently done, but the Blohms insisted. And so, with the proper clearance, I arranged to have the remains delivered to my lab.

Shortly before five o'clock on the afternoon of Friday, May 1, the funeral director arrived at the hospital with Art Jones's remains in a black body bag. To make a visual record of the proceedings, I had asked my wife, Sigrid, to come down with her video camera. I could have had anyone do this, of course, but Sigrid had been helping out since our days at Maxwell Air Force Base in Montgomery, Alabama, when she would often accompany me on my weekend moonlighting stints for private pathologists in the area. Now that she was an attorney, I had begun involving her in an official capacity in some of my cases as well.

As Joe removed the body from the bag, we could see just how extensive the decomposition had been. Although some soft tissue remained on the right leg, buttocks, and left arm, Art Jones was mainly a skeletonized and mummified relic, yellowish brown in color. No internal organs or soft tissues were present, and the skull had been detached. Most of the fingers and toes had been lost to anthropophagy, or chewing, presumably by rodents.

I zeroed in on the skull right away, eager to confirm and expand upon the findings of the coroner's office. The skull, one quadrant of which had been removed and which was now held together by black duct tape, showed several irregularly shaped, linear fractures in the right temporal area, or around the right temple. Since there was no concavity or depression to suggest the use of a weapon or any blunt force instrument, these fractures certainly appeared consistent with a fall.

Inside the skull, no brain tissue was present, although dark reddish brown staining extended from the area of the fractures upward and rearward and even downward along the rear portion of the foramen magnum, the opening at the base of the skull where the spinal cord begins. This staining, which the coroner's office had noted but failed to comment upon, appeared to represent an old, dehydrated hemorrhage, further indicating that Jones had suffered severe blunt force trauma. The fact that there was no similar staining on the other side of the skull confirmed that this did not represent dehydrated brain tissue.

I next took a close look at the lacrimal and ethmoidal bones, structures that surround the eye sockets. I wanted to see if there was any merit to the suggestion of a forensic anthropologist from Kentucky whom the ATF had called in after the first autopsy. This individual, who was not qualified to render a cause of death, had felt that an opening between the orbits indicated the possibility of a perforating gunshot wound. As I looked at these structures, I saw that there was no basis whatsoever to this claim. There was nothing to suggest carbon deposits or metallic fragments and no suggestion of circular symmetry to the opening. The defects were quite simply the result of decomposition and possible anthropophagy.

Having satisfied myself as to the cause of death, I moved on to the body itself. As I studied the arms and legs, I saw that portions of the skin did indeed suggest thermal discoloration, or singeing, indicating that Jones had been burned but that he had somehow not been caught in the center of the blast. This, of course, was consistent with my theory that he had survived long enough to walk some distance in the woods. In some way, he had been protected from the epicenter of the blast. Although extensive decomposition made these areas of skin difficult to evaluate, I had Joe take some sections for microscopic analysis. Then I examined the interior.

Aside from a fracture of the left third rib, which had been largely removed for further study, the coroner's office had not found any other bodily injuries. But when we stripped the soft tissues away from the vertebral column, I noticed what looked like a complete fracture of the second lumbar vertebra. And because the vertebrae above and below this one did not show similar separation, I concluded that this was indeed a true fracture and not a postmortem artifact.

After a thorough examination of the rest of the body and a representative sampling of tissues and skin for further study, I concluded my autopsy, satisfied with my conclusions. No one had shot or beaten Art Jones; and given the relatively few fractures, the theory that he had been thrown four hundred yards through the air had to be dismissed. As strange as it seemed, the only solution was that Jones, after surviving the blast, had wandered into the woods, dazed and perhaps blinded, where he stumbled off the small cliff. As for whether he sustained his fractures in the explosion or the fall, there was no way to tell.

The next morning, the second of May, Arthur J. Jones, Jr., was finally put to rest. Sadly, speculation over the manner of his death was not.

Although the story quickly dropped out of the news, I have learned through continuing correspondence with the Blohms and Mr. Warco that federal and state investigators continued to look into possibilities of foul play for months afterward. At one point, Mark told me, the ATF indicated that Jones's death was robbery-related and that they planned to conduct several more interviews to try to get to the bottom of it. Not surprisingly, that aspect of the case never panned out. As for the state police investigator, whom the Blohms say was much more sensitive to them, he soon fell out of touch as well. "I don't know whether the left hand knows what the right hand is doing," Mark told me. "I can't figure it out. They don't divulge much."

Even Mr. Warco was, as late as July, hinting that the ATF might have something more. But because the investigation was still on-going at the time, he was not at liberty to discuss it further than to say that near the body had been found some physical evidence that was still being analyzed. As for his own opinions of what had happened, he was now dismissing the possibility that Jones was inside at the time of the blast and accepting the possibility that Jones "was disposed of."

All of this cloak and dagger secrecy stands in stark contrast to the family's sober acceptance of Jones's death. "Since the funeral," Mark told me, "we haven't done anything, because we consider it a closed subject. We're content to consider it an accident. The theory we have is that they wanted to find something a lot more substantial and the fact that they haven't frustrates them. It's just really frustrating how quick they all were to jump in and create their own little ideas as to what happened."

In early October, Mr. Warco issued a final death certificate stating that the manner of Jones's death "could not be determined." But while this would seem to have finally put the case to rest, it only served to remind me and the Blohms just how flawed the investigation had been. Shortly after the announcement, we were contacted by a number of the small papers that were filling the news hole left by a city paper strike. They wanted our thoughts on the case, and so we let them have them.

Aside from our continuing criticism of the sloppy and incomplete manner in which the site had been searched, we addressed the official besmirching of Art Jones's good name and failure to keep the family apprised of what officials were doing. "The smoke screen that was hitting the papers was very disheartening," Mark told the *Uniontown Herald-Standard*. "How do you defend a family member when you don't even know what's going on? The stories were offensive to the family of a guy who was nothing more than a hard worker. He may not have been Mr. Personality, but he was a hard worker and a decent man."

The whole family seemed to take particular umbrage with the

ATF, which, they claimed, had remained extremely close-mouthed throughout the investigation. "I had a real problem with the lack of information we were getting," David Jones remarked to the *Herald-Standard.* "The feds don't like to give out information, but I think they should have been more up front with the family. The feds kept us in the dark and more or less left the family in the background. They were in no way sympathetic to us." Added Mark, "The ATF from the start did not want the family asking questions. They were just wanting the facts. They more or less had the attitude—'Don't ask us questions, we'll ask the questions.' "

At any rate, all that is now water under the bridge. But the question of what caused the explosion is not. It is, in fact, a question the family is actively pursuing in preparation for a possible products liability lawsuit against the companies involved in the manufacture, installation, and servicing of Jones's propane heating system. Because of the sloppiness of the original search, the answer will be hard to find. But by hiring experts to reconstruct the scene and identify all potentially explosive items in the house, it may eventually be possible to pinpoint what triggered the blast. And while this may still fall short of providing a clear manner of death, it would at least offer another piece to the puzzling death of Art Jones.

Appendix
Where Is JFK's Brain?

1963

Nov. 22. At the conclusion of President John F. Kennedy's autopsy, Captain John H. Stover, Jr., commanding officer of the U.S. Naval Medical School, hands all the film taken by medical photographers during the examination to U.S. Secret Service agent Roy Kellerman. Kellerman is also given the x-ray film by Commander John H. Ebersole, the chief of radiology. Sections of other organs are placed in glass jars in the pathology department safe. The brain is set in formalin and placed in a stainless steel bucket in the closet of Admiral George Galloway, commanding officer of the National Naval Medical Center.

Nov. 23. Kellerman delivers the film and X rays to Robert I. Bouck, special agent in charge of the Protective Research Division of the Secret Service.

Nov. 24. The autopsists meet in Galloway's office to review and sign their report. Sections of organs are reportedly taken for microscopic analysis. That night, U.S. Navy pathologist James J. Humes hand-delivers the report to Vice Admiral George G. Burkley, JFK's personal physician, at the White House.

Nov. 27. On the orders of Bouck, Agent James K. Fox and Robert L. Knudsen, Mrs. Kennedy's personal photographer, take the autopsy film to the Naval Processing Center in Anacostia, MD, for processing by Lieutenant V. Madonia. Fox later returns the prints and negatives to Bouck.

A few days later. Under instructions from Bouck, Fox has additional black-and-white prints made in the Secret Service lab at the Executive Office Building.

Dec. 2. The three autopsists, observed only by a U.S. Navy photographer, meet at the hospital to examine the formalin-fixed brain, which is described, in part, as follows: weighs 1500 grams (upper limit for a normal intact brain); has a "parasagittal laceration of right cerebral hemisphere, extending from the frontal to the occipital lobes and exposing the thalamus"; the "corpus callosum is lacerated"; the "convolutions of the brain are flat and the sulci are narrow, but this is interpreted as a fixation artifact because the change was not observed at the time of autopsy."

They note "no metallic fragments" but do find "numerous small bone fragments . . . in the container where the brain was fixed." Humes makes sections of the hemorrhage on the left side of the brain and of the laceration on the right side, but decides not to make "coronal," or cross-sections, "in order to preserve the specimen."

Color and black-and-white photos are taken of the specimen at this time.

Dec. 6. Burkley picks up and signs a receipt for all the autopsy materials, including the brain, which he says the family wants to inter with the body. Burkley then personally transfers everything to a locked Secret Service file cabinet at the White House. This material supposedly remains in this location, under Burkley's authority, until its transfer to the National Archives in 1965.

Dec. 9. Under instructions from Bouck, Fox has enlargements of the color photos made and returns the enlargements and positives to Bouck, who places them in a locked safe in the Executive Office Building, the combination for which only Bouck and his administrative assistant, Edith Duncan, know.

The autopsy photos and X rays are not included among the materials given to the Warren Commission on this day.

1965

Apr. 22. Senator Robert F. Kennedy writes to Burkley, authorizing him to release all autopsy materials to JFK's former personal secretary, Evelyn Lincoln, who is now working with his effects at the National Archives.

Apr. 26. After meeting to take an inventory of all the material, Burkley, Bouck, Secret Service inspector Thomas J. Kelley, and two other agents hand-deliver a locked chest and a two-page inventory to Lincoln, "for purposes of secure storage and pursuant to an arrangement with RFK under which material may not be opened without his consent." No key is included. Listed under #9 on the inventory are the following items:

- One 9-by-6½-inch plastic box containing paraffin blocks of tissue sections
- Another such box, also containing 35 slides
- A third box containing 84 slides
- A 7-by-8-inch stainless steel container containing "gross material"
- Three wooden boxes containing 58 slides of blood smears taken at various times during JFK's life
- The complete autopsy protocol, signed by Humes, plus seven copies
- A letter of transmittal of autopsy report, plus one copy
- A Nov. 29 office memo from Fox to Bouck concerning the processing of film in the presence of Madonia, plus two copies
- A Nov. 29 memo from Madonia to Fox concerning the receipt of films and prints, plus one copy
- A "certificate of destruction of preliminary draft notes" on the autopsy protocol signed by Humes, plus one copy
- A Nov. 22 memo from Ebersole to Kellerman concerning X rays, plus two copies
- A copy of a Nov. 22 memo from FBI agents Francis X. O'Neill, Jr., and James W. Sibert to Stover concerning "receipt of missile"
- A copy of a Dec. 5 letter from Bouck to Stover concerning "graphic film holders"
- A Nov. 22 memo from Stover to Kellerman concerning the "receipt of photographic material"

A few days later. RFK calls Lincoln to tell her that his secretary, Angela Novello, will be coming to move the footlocker that day. Novello arrives with Herman Kahn, assistant archivist for presidential libraries. Lincoln gives them the trunk and two keys. Lincoln later tells investigators that it was her belief that Novello and Kahn were simply moving the materials to another part of the archives where RFK was storing other materials. She adds that she is certain Novello signed a receipt for them, but is uncertain where it would be today.

1966

October. Attorney General Ramsey Clark contacts RFK about acquiring the autopsy photos and X rays, but RFK is unsympathetic. An argument between Clark and Burke Marshall, the representative of the executors of JFK's estate, ensues, the end result of which is an agreement on a "deed of gift" to the General Services Administration. Reportedly, no other autopsy materials are discussed.

Oct. 29. Marshall outlines the agreement formally transferring JFK's personal clothing and autopsy X rays and photographs to the GSA in a letter to GSA administrator Lawson B. Knott, Jr. No mention of any other autopsy materials is made. In his letter, Marshall notes that "the family desires to prevent the undignified or sensational use of these materials . . . or any other use which would tend in any way to dishonor the memory of the late President or cause unnecessary grief or suffering to the members of his family and those closely associated with him." The following restrictions are attached:

1. that none of the clothing shall be placed on public display and that access shall be permitted only to government officials or "any serious scholar or investigator of matters relating to the death of the late President . . ."

2. that none of the X rays and photos shall be placed on public display, and that access shall be permitted only to government officials until five years from the date of the memo, at which time "any recognized expert in the field of pathology or related areas of science or technology" may examine them "for serious purposes relevant to the investigation."

Oct. 31. Marshall formally transfers the locked footlocker to the GSA. Just prior to this transfer, Assistant to the Deputy Archivist Trudy H. Peterson later tells investigators, the footlocker was brought to the archives, suggesting that Novello may have previously removed it from the building rather than just moving it to another part of the building. Peterson adds that Assistant Archivist Kahn, now dead, may have been the only employee present for the transfer and that no record of delivery is available.

Novello provides the key to open the footlocker. After it is opened, she and Marshall leave. Various officials of the GSA and the Department of Justice then inspect the contents, which they discover include only inventory items 1 through 8, plus three manila envelopes containing copies of JFK's military service records.

Nov. 1. Humes and U.S. Navy pathologist J. Thornton Boswell are summoned to the archives to help categorize the autopsy materials and are shown the photos for the first time.

1967

Mar. 14. JFK's coffin is secretly reinterred at Arlington National Cemetery under tight security. Later asked by investigators whether someone could have slipped additional material into the grave at this time, John Metzler, the cemetery superintendent from 1951 to 1972, says that at the time of original burial, the coffin was placed in a tar-sealed vault, and that during reinterment there was no way anyone could have gotten anything inside.

Oct. 3. The Secret Service forwards the original autopsy protocol to the archives, raising the question of what the inventory was referring to.

1968

Jan. 26. Boswell writes to Attorney General Clark, asking that "an impartial board of experts" be appointed to "examine the available material."

Feb. 26–27. Clark fends off New Orleans D.A. Jim Garrison's lawsuit forcing the disclosure of these materials by naming a panel of four private physicians led by Maryland medical examiner Russell Fisher to examine them.

Summer. After the assassination of RFK, Lincoln later tells investigators, she calls former JFK aide Kenneth O'Donnell to make sure the family is aware of the autopsy materials. According to Lincoln, O'Donnell then calls Senator Edward Kennedy, later calling her back to tell her everything is under control.

1969

January. Clark releases the panel's report. Although raising questions about the location and size of the back wound, it essentially corroborates the autopsy findings and neglects to mention the missing autopsy materials.

Feb. 7. After hearing my testimony as to the need to examine the autopsy materials, federal judge Charles Halleck rules that the government must make them available for my review. The government promptly appeals this decision, effectively tying the materials up long enough to outlast the trial.

Feb. 12. GSA general counsel Harry Van Cleve calls a meeting of Secret Service agents and archivists to address the matter of the missing items. In a report filed the next day, Secret Service assistant director Kelley writes:

"Mr. Van Cleve is concerned that writers like Weisberg or Mark Lane, when they learned that such an inventory existed, would demand to see the inventory and items covered by it. He indicated that he saw no legal reason how the existence of this inventory could be kept from writers of this kind, and that when they learned of the inventory and then learned that some of the items . . . were not in the possession of the Archives, that this would lead to all sorts of speculation and accusation that the government was not being perfectly frank and open in handling this matter, and that it was further proof of the various conspiracy theories which these writers are alleging . . ."

Feb. 13. Kelley visits Burkley at home in Chevy Chase. Burkley says he is surprised to learn that all the materials are not there and calls Lincoln in Kelley's presence. She tells him that she never opened or disturbed the trunk, but that "sometime after its receipt" everything was turned over to Novello, now secretary to the ambassador to Denmark. Burkley also mentions a "Henry Giordano," whom he identifies as a "former White House driver" and "employee of the Kennedy family" who now works as a doorkeeper at the U.S. Senate.

Kelley calls Van Cleve later and advises him that "we should not contact Giordano." In his report, he writes that Van Cleve "agreed with this and stated he felt that the inquiry would have to remain as it now stands; that perhaps we were borrowing trouble in exploring it any further . . ."

1971

Summer. I begin trying to gain access to the autopsy materials.
Oct. 29. The Kennedy family's restrictions on access to the autopsy materials end.

1972

Jan. 8. Dr. John K. Lattimer, head of the urology department at Columbia University College of Physicians and Surgeons, becomes the first person not under government auspices to examine the available autopsy materials. He tells the *New York Times* that they "eliminate any doubt completely" about the validity of the Warren Commission's conclusions but neglects to mention the missing autopsy materials.
March. I am finally granted access to the materials at the archives.
Aug. 23–24. I review every piece of physical evidence available at the National Archives and discover that the brain and microscopic tissue slides are not there. Afterward, I give an interview to Fred Graham of the *New York Times.*
Aug. 27. All of the above information pertaining to the missing autopsy materials is made public for the first time in a front-page *New York Times* story. In it, I am quoted as asking, "Who would have taken the responsibility to destroy the brain?" National Archivist Marion Johnson relates the above history, adding that the inventory of the missing items is being kept secret at the behest of the Kennedy family on the ground that mention of some of them would be "objectionable." Marshall is quoted as saying it is "offensive for there to be all this probing—it is a terrible thing to do to that family."

1975

January. President Gerald Ford appoints the Commission on CIA Activities Within the U.S. (the Rockefeller Commission). Amid the ensuing public criticism of the commission's choice of medical panelists, I and a group of other doctors present a petition calling for full disclosure of all the scientific evidence.

June. In its report, the Rockefeller Commission neglects to mention the missing autopsy materials.

1978

July. I testify before the House Select Committee on Assassinations (HSCA) as a member of its nine-person forensic pathology panel. Asked by Staff Counsel Andrew Purdy to what extent access to the brain would enable a determination of whether JFK was hit by a shot from the front, I testify that "the brain would be extremely important to help us determine whether more than one missile had penetrated" it.

Later, asked by Pennsylvania representative Robert Edgar what I would do to locate the brain, I testify: "I would get the best trained investigators . . . and with an attorney for proper legal guidance . . . I would go back to day one . . . I would get the people who were in charge of the archives. I would depose them under oath." Further asked what I would do if these efforts did not produce the brain, I point out that, if nothing else, "at that point it would be a matter of record. We would know what had happened to that . . . evidence, and we would know who is responsible for it and that would be the end of it." I add that if and when an examination is done, it "would be performed in the most private, discreet circumstances by a competent neuropathologist or forensic pathologist."

1979

Mar. 29. The HSCA releases its final report. In the section dealing with the missing autopsy materials, the committee recounts its efforts to locate them by contacting all of the above-mentioned individuals, as well as several others. According to the report, Novello "had no recollection of handling a footlocker, of possessing a key or keys to such a footlocker, or of handling any of the autopsy materials." Marshall is reported to have said that while he did not know what became of the items, "it was his speculative opinion that Robert Kennedy obtained and disposed of these materials himself, without informing anyone else" because he was "concerned that these materials would be placed on public display in future years in an institution such as the Smithsonian. . . ." He is also reported to have added that he is "certain that obtaining or locating these materials is no longer possible."

In the report's conclusion, the HSCA writes that, although it had "not been able to uncover any direct evidence of the fate of the missing materials, circumstantial evidence tends to show that Robert Kennedy either destroyed these materials or otherwise rendered them inaccessible."

This opinion has never been officially corroborated by the FBI, the Secret Service, the National Archives, Admiral Burkley, the Kennedy family, or anyone else who would have firsthand knowledge of the items' whereabouts.

(Information contained in this appendix was compiled from the following sources: the reports of the President's Commission on the Assassination of President John F. Kennedy and the House Select Committee on Assassinations; documents obtained under the Freedom of Information Act from the U.S. Secret Service, the National Archives, the General Services Administration, the Armed Forces Institute of Pathology, and the Department of the Army; *The New York Times.*)

Index